DANIEL C. THOMPSON is Professor of Sociology at Howard University. He is a member of the American Sociological Society. He has published numerous scholarly articles and is co-author of *The Eighth Generation* (1960). In addition to his academic activities at Dillard University, he himself became a recognized Negro leader, as a result of this study of leadership in New Orleans.

THE NEGRO LEADERSHIP CLASS

THE NEGRO
LEADERSHIP CLASS

Daniel C. Thompson

Prentice-Hall, Inc. *Englewood Cliffs, N.J.*

A SPECTRUM BOOK

301.155
T37n

46294
Jan. 1964

In Memory
of
Theodore L. Miller
Businessman, Leader

FOREWORD
by Martin Luther King, Jr.

THIS GREAT NATION of ours is in the midst of a social revolution. Few of us realize the gravity of the change which is taking place, because it proceeds so steadily. Only the burning of a bus by Alabama klansmen, or the rioting of students at Ole Miss, and the protest marching of over a thousand Negro citizens in Albany, Georgia, punctuate the tremendous transformation which is under way.

It is a testimony to our democratic institutions that we can accommodate such change without chaos, and a testimony to the minorities in our midst that we do so without wholesale violence. Many a civilization before us has floundered and fallen on its inability to provide equal rights and opportunities for all its citizens. But we are just beginning to come under the judgment. The strivings of a few civil rights organizations have now begun to blossom into the full flower of a mass demand for dignity. The Negro citizens in the plantation country of the Mississippi delta and the share cropper in Tennessee are now saying to the Southern power structure and Negro leadership alike that "we must be free, Now!" Whether we as a nation meet this challenge or go the way of many a culture before us depends on the ability of every person and every institution in this nation to face squarely and justly the problem of racial injustice.

Our ability to understand the dynamics of this quiet revolution may well be a determining factor in our attempting to face it squarely. Dr. Thompson has contributed a great deal to this understanding through his study of Negro leadership in one of the key cities of the South. This is truly a work of painstaking research and sound scholarship. It will contribute far more validly to the understanding of changing patterns of leadership than some of the journalistic accounts which have preceded it. At every point the author reveals the capacity to adhere to objective appraisal and creative analysis.

This study is of further significance in that Dr. Thompson was actively involved in the leadership patterns within the New Orleans Negro community. His work there with the Coordinating Council of Greater New Orleans pioneered with a pattern of leadership which we will find emulated throughout the South for years to come.

The coordination of all the forces of the Negro community into a single cooperating power block is one sure answer to the exclusion of Negroes from the "powerful decision-making" structures of our governments, whether national or local. The continued use of the vote, continued work in the courts, the mass march of protesting citizens, and the withdrawal of economic support from discriminatory businesses are all ways of asserting the fact that we, too, are a part of this society, and while we do not want to disrupt its orderly processes, we cannot in good conscience sit by while we are ignored in all of the basic policies which affect the community's life.

White and Negro leadership alike are fast realizing that the equality of opportunity for more than one-tenth of the population can no longer be ignored. Both groups are attempting to deal with this fact, and though some seek to thwart this surge, even they know that the tide of history is sweeping the world toward the necessity for recognizing the inherent worth of every individual, regardless of color, creed, national or economic background. The decisions made in New Orleans by its leadership will be decisive in determining our role in the community of nations. The new economic alignments of Europe will soon spread to Asia and Africa, where people may find it very difficult to trade with a society that has not worked out an equitable life for persons of color.

Patterns of leadership are changing, and will continue to change in an attempt to keep up with mass demands. Gandhi's oft-quoted statement is so applicable today, "There go my people, I must catch them, for I am their leader." What was once thought of as radical now seems moderate, and many an "appeaser" now finds himself able to bargain from a position of strength and is flabbergasted by his new role.

Dr. Thompson has indeed done us a service by documenting these changes. Let us hope that the coming period will bring further enlightenment from the disciplines of social science. The very life of our nation hangs in the balance and interpretation and analysis of this creative moment of history is certainly one key factor on the scale.

ACKNOWLEDGMENTS

MANY PERSONS contributed to the production of this book. A total of 318 persons were interviewed, including 100 "top" race relations leaders in New Orleans, plus several others throughout the nation. They gave freely of their time, information, and insights. In the truest sense of the word, I have served as a literary focus in the expression of their ideas, philosophies, and aspirations. For this privilege I am deeply grateful.

Special recognition and thanks are due Dr. Paul Ylvisaker of The Ford Foundation and President A. W. Dent of Dillard University: the former for his encouraging faith in the proposed project and recommendation that it should be financed by the Foundation; the latter, for making available whatever University facilities and resources I needed, and for his helpful insights into the phenomenon of leadership. Thanks go also to Professors Giles A. Hulbert of Dillard University and Forrest Laviolette of Tulane University, whom I often consulted during the research phases of the study.

I wish to express my obligations and gratitude to Miss Barbara M. Guillory, Sociologist and Research Assistant at Dillard University, who participated in, and contributed immeasurably to every phase of this project.

D. C. T.

This book grew out of a Research Project on Leadership at Dillard University supported by a grant from The Ford Foundation from September 1958 to August 1962:

Research Assistant
Barbara M. Guillory

Project Participants

Thomas E. Crittenden	Forrest Laviolette
Lois M. Foucher	Erlma M. Lemle
Ben Gorman	John W. Martin
Charles G. Hamilton	Murray Richardson
Bill Harrell	Milton L. Upton
Giles A. Hubert	John Walton
J. Harvey Kerns	

TABLE OF CONTENTS

1

INTRODUCTION

IN RECENT YEARS several social scientists have made studies of leadership in which the leader is regarded as essentially a decision maker. Among the most notable and influential of these studies are R. S. and Helen Lynd, *Middletown in Transition;* C. Wright Mills, *The Power Elite;* and Floyd Hunter, *Community Power Structure.* These studies tend to regard as leaders those who have the power to make decisions involving the lives of a large number of other people. There is at least one point of agreement among them—a very small, well-organized group of "men of power" makes almost all major decisions regarding the life and welfare of their individual communities, and maybe even of the nation.

Perhaps the most fruitful study for our purpose is Floyd Hunter's analysis of "Decision Makers" in "Regional City."[1] One of his most provocative statements is that in Regional City (Atlanta, Georgia) Negroes are constantly reminded to "keep their place" and wherever this place may be it is nowhere near the top power group. He insists that "none of the leaders in the Negro community may operate in the same echelons of power as the top leaders in the total community."[2]

The main problem dealt with here is this: *If New Orleans, like Atlanta, has no Negroes in the power structure, then how do they get things done?* This book, therefore, is in a sense an elaboration and extension of Hunter's thesis regarding the place of Negro leadership in the decision making function of a major southern metropolis. Throughout this study I shall explore the changing status of Negroes in New Orleans and attempt to assess the role of leadership as a factor in these changes.

NEW ORLEANS AS A "TYPICAL" SOUTHERN CITY

New Orleans proved to be a fortunate choice for a study of changing patterns in race relations for at least two important reasons. One, it has the

[1] *Community Power Structure: A Study of Decision Makers* (Chapel Hill: University of North Carolina Press, 1953).
[2] *Op. cit.,* pp. 138-139.

largest concentration of Negroes in the South. In 1960 the total population of New Orleans was 627,525, of whom 37.4 per cent, or 234,931, were Negroes.[3] Two, the system of race relations in New Orleans is experiencing rapid and decisive changes. Since every aspect of social life in this city developed according to the principle of subordinating Negroes to whites, any change in any phase of this biracial pattern affects directly or indirectly every other aspect of the social system. Thus, the changes in race relations now transpiring are extraordinary in scope. They affect not only behavior patterns, but also, and perhaps even more fundamentally, the psychic foundations upon which the segregated social system rests. This is manifested by changes in certain fundamental attitudes toward traditional moral, ethical, religious, legal, and scientific rationales that undergird the biracial system and inevitably determine both the form and content of race relations. As we will see later, there are many interrelated causes for these changes.

When this study of leadership was begun in the fall of 1958 New Orleans, like many other communities throughout the South, was rapidly approaching a climactic stage in race relations. In many important respects, of course, New Orleans is unique in the history and development of its racial patterns. In some instances these patterns are different from those found in any other metropolis. There is one pervasive characteristic, nevertheless, that dominates all southern communities: they are more or less rigidly organized along biracial lines. I do not intend to imply that racial patterns in New Orleans are the same as in all southern communities, nor that they are different from those in every other southern community; rather, for analytical purposes, New Orleans is regarded here as a "typical" southern city. That is, every problem in race relations anywhere in the South exists to some degree in New Orleans. Consequently, an understanding of the nature of these problems in this one city may give us a far better knowledge of the essence of these problems as they exist in our total society than we could get if we attempted to generalize about them on a regional or national level.

LEADERSHIP AND THE AMERICAN CREED

The concept of the leader is ancient. The leader's position has been recognized and respected in every society in history. Yet the leader's actual role, his specific duties and functions, have varied greatly according to time, place, and the magnitude of problems to be solved. Because his role has been so varied, attempts to state what the leader is are often unclear, confusing, and even contradictory.

Perhaps the earliest definition of the leader is as a person who leads in the physical sense of the word. Vivid examples of this meaning are found in romantic accounts of soldiers fighting on horseback—for example, the gen-

[3] Bureau of the Census, *Louisiana: General Social and Economic Population Characteristics*, p. 20, Table 32.

eral who sits elegantly astride a prancing white charger with sword uplifted, ready to lead his men daringly into battle.

The popular concept of the leader defines leadership in terms of success. Thus, a leader is anyone who has achieved distinction in a particular field of endeavor. Consequently, a person might be described as a "leading" educator, physician, businessman, actor, or socialite.

A more restricted concept of the leader equates leadership with authority. Thus, a leader is regarded as synonymous with the top official or executive in a bureaucratic organization. All persons, then, who hold top positions of authority, such as president, director, chairman, or secretary in a civic, business, religious, or political organization, may be classified as leaders.

Still another concept of the leader considers leadership a rare talent possessed by only a few geniuses in any given generation or age. Thus, it is not uncommon for philosophers of history to regard as leaders those giants who have in one way or another decidedly influenced the course of history. This approach was summarized by Jennings: "All great men who shape the character and direction of their organizations and eras have a rare and delicate mixture of the prince, hero, and superman."[4]

Some scientific studies of leadership have emphasized the significance of certain psychological traits in leaders. Among the most frequently cited of these personality traits are initiative, ambition, perseverance, intelligence, originality, integrity, self-confidence, and social effectiveness. There is wide agreement that the successful leader in any given society is likely to exemplify some combination of these personality traits.

All the definitions of leadership cited above agree on at least two interrelated points: one, the leader is one who initiates, stimulates, coordinates, and directs the activities of others, his followers, in the solution of some common problem or the achievement of some specific social (as opposed to individual) goal. And, two, those who achieve high positions, or meet with notable success in any group, are likely to be individuals who can be identified as champions of the group's basic values, and who symbolize norms that the group accepts as essential for its survival at a particular time and location, and in a given situation.

The founders of our federal government were men strongly influenced by their belief in two cardinal principles: *personal freedom* and *equality*. They succeeded in dedicating this nation to a way of life calculated to attain a political democracy, where every citizen might come to enjoy the same degree of freedom, equality, and protection. Inherent in the very fiber of our government is the commitment to change, to make progress. The fact is, the high ideals to which our nation is pledged presuppose, and indeed make inevitable, the formation of social groups and social movements designed to push back the frontiers of democracy, to break down opposition to individual achievement, and to overcome all barriers to equal citizenship for Americans, regardless of race, religion, or national origin.

[4] Eugene E. Jennings, *An Anatomy of Leadership* (New York: Harper & Row, 1960), p. 1.

Since our nation is essentially dedicated to change, the role of leadership in the United States is somewhat more challenging than it would be in less dynamic societies. In order to progress the American people are constantly called upon to change old habits, to surrender traditional privileges, and to accept new and often untried ways. Therefore, unlike leaders in more conservative, tradition-bound societies, who are often pledged to revert to old ways, maintain the status quo, or prevent change, leaders in the United States are expected to offer their people some solution to existing problems. That is, they are expected to suggest means whereby new patterns of behavior, new ways, and new programs can be substituted for the old and the traditional. Thus, an editor of *Fortune* magazine described our national way of life as a "permanent revolution." And it is not surprising that nearly all successful leaders in the United States are pledged to bring about some kind of change in our society. As a rule, successful American leaders are dedicated to the advancement of something. Some even label themselves "Progressives," "New Dealers," "Fair Dealers," "Reformers," and so forth.

In this study, we regard as leaders those individuals who by their efforts are able to initiate, stimulate, coordinate, and direct the activities of others in the solution of common problems or the achievement of specific social goals. The sample of leaders selected is composed of those who have manifested the ability to *get things done* or to achieve goals generally regarded as valuable and beneficial to the Negro community. Included also are some whose efforts are directed to preventing Negroes from attaining these goals. Most studies of leadership have tended to emphasize the *status* of the leader; this study is primarily concerned with the *role* of the leader.

ISSUES OF PRIMARY CONCERN TO INTERRACIAL LEADERS

In order to assess the role of leadership in the changing status of Negroes in New Orleans two interrelated steps had to be taken. First, the study had to assume some definite time-depth. The status of Negroes in American society has been rapidly changing since the first Negroes landed in this country in 1619. Consequently, when we refer to the status of Negroes, we must keep in mind that we are generalizing, and that there are significant exceptions.

Despite the dynamic nature of the status of Negroes in American society generally, and in New Orleans society specifically, in order to trace changes in given areas of society, it is necessary to begin with some point in time and describe *the status* of Negroes as if it were static. For our purposes, the changing status of Negroes in New Orleans will be marked from 1940. This date was chosen as a base year for several reasons: one, 1940 is a logical base year because it marks the end of the Great Depression and the beginning of two decades of unprecedented prosperity, from which Negroes, like other Americans, benefited. Two, it marks the beginning of our technological and psychological preparations for World War II. The results of this war definitely established the United States as the leader of the free world. More and more we find it necessary to prove to other nations that we believe in the democracy we attempt to sell. Three, 1940 was a census year. Census data provided us with certain basic information about areas or aspects of New Orleans society according to which we can measure the changing status of Negroes over a twenty-year period, to 1960.

A second major step necessary in evaluating the changing status of Negroes and the role of leadership in the process of change has been to isolate the main issues or goals delineated by Negro leaders in 1940. This was done to determine to what extent the Negro community has been able to solve what it regarded as its fundamental problems twenty years before. In other words, to what extent has the Negro community achieved its expressed goals since 1940?

In order to answer this question it was deemed essential to isolate the cardinal social issues with which the Negro community was concerned. The progress that the community made toward the resolution of these issues has been plotted. Those men and women who concerned themselves with the solution of these major problems and the achievement of the primary social goals envisioned by members of the Negro race are regarded here as race-relations leaders. Also included are those who have concerned themselves with hindering Negroes from achieving their started goals.

How the issues were selected. A careful examination of scientific studies, "uplift" organizational reports, and constitutions and by-laws of agencies and associations, and a systematic interpretation of the contents of the Negro press[5] reveal at least three major issues with which the Negro community express pointed concern over the twenty-year period. They are citizenship, earning a living, and education. In each of these areas New Orleans Negroes through their organizations or spokesmen, clearly define the inherent problems, propose solutions, and formulate specific goals. They try to see that interested Negro and white leaders are induced, at one time or another, to pledge themselves to solving these major problems of status.

SELECTION OF LEADERS

The functional approach to leadership, therefore, makes it possible for us to identify leaders as opposed to "celebrities." The leader is one who for some period of time identifies overtly with the Negro's effort to achieve stated social goals. This identification may be brief, narrowly focused, and even ineffective; nevertheless, it designates the individual actor as a participant in the Negro's effort to achieve personal freedom and equality—first-class citizenship. On the other hand, the celebrity, as used here, is one who

[5] The Louisiana Weekly, the only local Negro newspaper, has been a strong force toward unity within the Negro leadership class in New Orleans. For the last twenty years, at least, it has led in defining racial issues in the city, and has constantly prodded Negro leaders to work cooperatively for racial advancement.

for some reason other than the above has a decidedly high status in the Negro community. Very often he is an individual who is respected because of his wealth or high social position, or because he holds a high-status occupation. It has been customary for both Negroes and whites familiar with the Negro community to think of these persons as leaders. However, upon examination one finds that Negro celebrities seldom, if ever, concern themselves with the status problems of the Negro masses. By and large, they are content to pursue their own social and economic interests with little or no time or thought given to the Negro's struggle to achieve full equality in American society.

I do not mean to imply that celebrities may not become leaders. The truth of the matter is that some of the most effective race relations leaders are recruited from the ranks of the celebrities. But there are also some very effective race relations leaders, in the sense in which leadership is used here, who never become celebrities, or who are not even recognized widely as leaders. For example, during the critical months of 1957 and 1958, when the National Association for the Advancement of Colored People was driven underground in Louisiana because it refused to submit for inspection its membership lists (for fear that those who belonged to it might be subject to economic and social reprisals) a new, loosely organized group of citizens, the New Orleans Improvement League, essayed to carry on the most essential projects in which the NAACP was interested. During this interim period (as we shall see later) that organization was responsible for effecting certain significant changes in the status of Negroes. Its leader was a local physician, who had hitherto been more or less unidentified with problems affecting the Negro community. For this brief period, he was a successful leader. When the NAACP was reinstated, he retired from this role and went back to the pursuit of his professional interests.

Finally, a functional approach to the study of leadership narrows down the concept of the leader so that it includes only those who are, or have been, actively engaged in the solution of some common problem or the achievement of specific social goals. For our purpose, we may classify all leaders into two categories—*intraracial* and *interracial*.

Intraracial leaders. Those leaders whose social activities are largely directed toward the solution of problems and the achievement of goals that are of primary concern to members of their own racial groups are classified as intraracial leaders. Their leadership role does not impose upon them sustained contact, communication, or negotiation with persons of another race. Accordingly, in a biracial society such as that of New Orleans, most Negro and white leaders may be classified as intraracial leaders.

Interracial leaders. Leaders who spend much of their time avowedly promoting interracial cooperation or the improvement of race relations are classified here as interracial leaders.

Throughout this study we are primarily interested in the role of interracial leaders, because it is they who operate on the frontiers of race relations. Also, it is upon them that the Negro community must rely to get things done in the broader community where white "men of power" must be dealt with. Many of the analyses and interpretations presented here utilize information supplied by intraracial leaders, since it is often from among their ranks that effective interracial leaders are recruited, however they are not included in the basic sample. More pointedly, the sample was selected from among interracial leaders who have identified with some issue of race relations, or engaged in definite social action calculated to bring about solutions to problems stemming from the limited citizenship, economic discrimination, and inequalities of educational opportunities experienced by Negroes.

It must be kept in mind that leadership, as such, is not a recognized occupation in our society. Most leaders identify themselves as full-time employees of some agency, institution, or enterprise. Leadership, therefore, is very often an avocation rather than an occupation. Consequently, the one hundred leaders (seventy-five Negroes and twenty-five whites) selected as the primary subjects for the interviews reported on in this study represent various occupational groups.[6] Among the most highly represented occupational groups are religion, law, labor, politics and government, health and welfare, business, and education. Race relations leaders are usually very busy people who are working toward success in some occupation, and their role as community leader is appended to or, in most cases, detached from their remunerative activities.

There are, of course, a few leaders in New Orleans, as in all large cities with a sizable Negro population, who may be described as "professional" Negro leaders. These are people whose main occupation is to promote Negro welfare or better race relations. But even they are generally recognized members of one of the traditional occupations. In fact, almost all professional race relations leaders have been recruited from the traditional occupations for a more or less temporary period of time.

Negro race relations leaders usually belong to several racial "uplift" organizations, and serve on whatever interracial committees might be active at a given time. White liberals sometimes work toward racial betterment through interracial committees and organizations. Active segregationists generally hold multiple memberships in organizations dedicated to the preservation of white supremacy, and are active participants on various committees and programs designed to preserve segregation.

In order to study the leadership role as it is acted out by the various leaders in New Orleans, it was necessary to examine closely some of the most

[6] In all, 318 persons were interviewed. 218 of these (139 Negroes and 79 whites) are not included in the basic sample, either because the interviewers were not convinced of their interracial leadership status or because the information they gave was too narrowly focused, dealing with only a few questions on the designated schedule. Some, however, gave valuable information regarding the issues discussed in this book.

important organizations, agencies, and committees in which these leaders hold membership or official positions. Therefore we have examined the activities, pronouncements, philosophies, and goals of The National Association for the Advancement of Colored People (NAACP), the white Citizens' Councils, The Urban League, The Ku Klux Klan (KKK), The Interdenominational Ministerial Alliance (IMA), The Consumers' League, The Frontiers Club, The Congress of Racial Equality (CORE), The Southern Christian Leadership Conference, and several other organizations and committees that have sprung up from time to time in response to some specific racial problems. Many of the latter are formed by ambitious individuals who seek to further their own personal interests by "latching on" to some dramatic racial issue.

SOME BASIC ASSUMPTIONS

Throughout the process of gathering, codification, analysis, and interpretation of data, this study has been centered around certain basic assumptions:

(1) Negroes, regardless of station in life, have a common cause—the abolition of racial inequalities.

(2) All successful Negro leaders must identify, directly or indirectly, with the Negro's continuous struggle for full or equal citizenship. They must be actively engaged in the promotion of some issue designed to advance the status of Negroes in some area of life.

(3) Some "liberal" white leaders have joined forces with Negro leaders in their struggle to abolish civil and social inequalities.

(4) Some white segregationists are not white supremacists.

(5) Negro leaders have devised several effective strategies and techniques for dealing with white "men of power."

(6) No one individual, or group, can be identified as *the* leader of the New Orleans Negro community. Instead, from the point of view of influence, we can identify several segments or classes in the Negro community. Each of these segments or classes produces its own leadership.

(7) At the moment there is little effective communication between leaders representing the several segments or classes in the Negro community.

(8) In certain areas of community life Negroes have had notable success in their struggle to gain equal citizenship rights.

(9) As a rule, advancements made by Negroes are due to the foresight, planning, and actions of Negro leaders.

(10) Negro leadership may be divided into two general patterns, intraracial and interracial.

(11) Interracial leaders may be further classified into several distinct types according to their social philosophies. These types often overlap, and at different times and under different circumstances a given leader may be correctly classified as belonging to two or more types.

In any discussion of the role of leadership in the changing status of Negroes certain basic questions arise again and again. Thus, in order that the reader might gain insight into the problems, issues, and actions involved in this study, we have raised certain pertinent questions to which we have sought to provide definitive answers:

(1) Has there been any significant change in the patterns of race relations leadership in New Orleans since 1940?

(2) Who are the Negro leaders in terms of social origin, formal and informal education, career patterns, social status, and philosophies of race relations?

(3) Who are the white race relations leaders in terms of social status and influence?

(4) Are there broad types or patterns into which leaders may be meaningfully grouped according to their philosophies of Negro-white relations?

(5) What are the most successful strategies and techniques used by Negro leaders with Negro people?

(6) What are the most successful strategies and techniques white leaders of Negroes use?

(7) What are the most successful strategies and techniques used by Negro leaders in dealing with white men of power?

(8) What is the nature of communication among Negro leaders in the same areas of community life?

(9) What is the nature of communication among Negro leaders representing different areas of community life?

(10) What is the nature of communication among Negro and white leaders in the same areas of community life?

(11) What is the nature of communication among liberal white and Negro leaders?

(12) To what extent do race relations leaders utilize mass media in their attempts to get things done?

RESEARCH METHODS AND TECHNIQUES

Interpretations and conclusions made throughout this study are based upon data gathered through several interrelated research techniques.

A review of pertinent literature. In the planning stages, efforts were made to review all pertinent published materials pointedly concerned with an analysis and an interpretation of the leadership role. Special effort was made to cover all literature that might directly or indirectly shed some light on the role of leadership in the changing status of Negroes in New Orleans.

In addition to this review of studies of leadership we also made a careful analysis of local white and Negro newspaper articles dealing with some facet of race relations. Furthermore, since race relations in New Orleans evoke national as well as local opinion, it was decided also to review certain national-magazine articles dealing with race relations. These articles have proven to be especially valuable since the debate over civil rights approached a climax in recent years. The public opinion generated and expressed by these national media of communication has been of inestimable importance in the changing status of Negroes.

Another type of literature reviewed consisted of published reports by foundations, organizations, and agencies interested in Negro "uplift." Especially important in this connection are research findings published by segregationist organizations, such as the white Citizens' Councils and the Ku Klux Klan.

Design of schedules. In order to get answers from the selected leaders regarding the questions raised above, it was necessary to design eight different though interrelated schedules:

(1) A schedule of approximately one hundred open-ended questions to be administered to all Negro leaders included in the study.

(2) A revised schedule of approximately seventy-five open-ended questions to be asked known liberal or moderate white leaders.

(3) A schedule including forty or fifty open-ended questions to be asked known white segregationists.

(4) A series of twenty-five special open-ended questions to be asked the twenty Negro lawyers included in the study. (This was in addition to questions designed for all Negro leaders.)

(5) A planned, structured interview of about twenty questions to be asked prominent white lawyers and court officials. These questions were designed to be used in connection with a study of the legal profession.

(6) A schedule of about twenty questions designed to get information on the social role of Negro ministers.

(7) A schedule of twenty open-ended questions designed to discover the racial philosophies and practices of selected white religious leaders.

(8) A schedule of ten open-ended questions designed to ascertain the social role of selected Negro businesses in New Orleans.

In addition to special questions designed for them white liberals, moderates, segregationists—Negro lawyers, white lawyers, court officials, Negro businessmen, and Negro ministers—were generally asked pertinent questions on the main schedule (1).

Selection of research staff. In the selection of interviewers and participant observers, it was necessary to recognize a basic reality—New Orleans is a biracial society. Therefore, psychologically, socially, and legally, a biracial team of researchers was deemed necessary. By and large white members of the research team interviewed white leaders and participated in white organizations or meetings where pertinent racial issues were under discussion. Negro members of the team carried on the same kind of activities in the Negro community.

The biracial team used one very interesting and fruitful interview technique. Certain "top" white leaders were interviewed by both white and Negro interviewers, and certain "top" Negro leaders were interviewed by both Negro and white interviewers. Thus, for example, after a white interviewer had completed a series of interviews with some prominent, powerful white subject, one of the Negro interviewers would re-interview the subject, asking certain of the key questions asked by the white interviewer. The same procedure was followed with selected prominent Negroes. The subjects did not know that the white and Negro interviewers were working on the same project, because the interviewers simply identified themselves in terms of the institution or agency with which they were affiliated. The aim of this technique was to find out if interview subjects would give the same kind of information to both Negro and white interviewers. In other words, we sought to ascertain whether the race of the interviewer made any difference in the answers given. There were several distinctive features brought out by these matched interviews.

(1) Both liberal whites and segregationists alike were much more critical of Negroes in general, and particularly of Negro leaders, when talking with white interviewers than with Negroes. On the whole, they tended to blame the slowness of Negro progress in some areas of community life solely upon Negroes themselves. Some said outright that "Negroes are their own worse enemy." They cited such evidences as "high" crime rate, "immorality," "dishonest and inept leaders." Seldom, if ever, was such frank criticism expressed to Negro interviewers.

(2) White segregationists usually manifested firm belief in the rationales they held regarding the rightness of racial segregation. They expressed these rationales with both Negro and white interviewers. The basic difference, however, was the frame of reference in which these attitudes were expressed. In talking with white interviewers, the segregationists assumed what might be characterized a "missionary" frame of reference. That is, the tone of voice, mannerisms, choice of words, and presentation of materials of these subjects were designed to convert the white interviewer to a philosophy of white supremacy. In talking with a Negro interviewer the same person was likely to assume the role of an apologist. In this role, the white supremacists attempted to give rational, objective, even Christian interpretations of their avowed segregationist beliefs and behavior. One such subject expressed sincere regret that he had had too few opportunities to apprise Negroes of his "true position." He felt that if they understood his position, they would not criticize him as they did, but would realize that he is "the best friend Negroes ever had" in New Orleans.

(3) The main focus of the white liberals' presentations to a white interviewer centered around their attempts to convince him of the rightness of the position they had taken in race relations. Generally, they conceived themselves to be "pioneers," "do-gooders," "mavericks," "queer birds," "troubleshooters," and even "martyrs." Nearly all of them talked at length about

the sacrifices they, their families, and some of their liberal friends had made for "the cause." Some cited family frictions, loss of friends, loss of prestige, harassment from segregationists, and threats of violence resulting from their attempts to provide leadership in race relations.

When interviewed by a Negro researcher, white liberals said little if anything about the sacrifices involved in their interracial activities. Instead, they tended to stress the things they had helped "to get done" for the Negroes. Most of them dwelled at length upon the techniques and strategies they had used with white "men of power" in their efforts to help Negroes attain some definite goals. They usually saw themselves as members of the avant-garde in the Negro's struggle for equal citizenship.

(4) When Negro leaders were interviewed by white researchers there was often detected an attitude of boastfulness. Some emphasized the respect they maintained among both Negro and white leaders to a much greater extent than they did when they were interviewed by Negro interviewers. Most of the information given to white interviewers had to do with specific interracial contacts and participation. When talking with Negro interviewers, on the other hand, Negro leaders complained a great deal more about the lack of respect they had in the Negro community and the difficulties they encountered in attempts to initiate and coordinate the activities of Negroes in the solution of some problem. Furthermore, they tended to be far more critical of other race relations leaders, white and Negro, than they were in interviews with white researchers. In other words, Negro leaders emphasized their interracial leadership role when talking with white researchers. When talking with Negro researchers they tended to emphasize their intraracial leadership role.

(5) On the whole, white leaders seemed to be a great deal more critical of other white leaders when talking to white interviewers than they were when talking to Negro interviewers. Interviews with the former were full of criticism of other white leaders whose position on segregation or desegregation was different from theirs. Thus, white supremacists spent a great deal of time criticizing white liberals and vice versa. When talking with Negro interviewers, however, the liberal's criticism was much milder, and the segregationists attempted to create a picture of solid white unity on the race question, except for a "few misguided whites."

We may conclude, then, that because the sample of leaders included in this study represented both the Negro and the white communities, the biracial team of researchers was able to utilize a dimension that would not have been attained if all members of the team had represented the same race.

Forum interviewing. Certain of the leaders included in the study were important, not only in their own right as leaders, but also as informants. After these key subjects had sat for some hours of personal interviewing they often accepted invitations to talk with three or more selected members of the research team in a type of forum. Usually the leader would meet at some designated place (a university seminar room, in a researcher's home, in the subject's own home, or at a more or less informal luncheon) with the researchers, who encouraged him to deliver what amounted to several short talks on pertinent issues and problems in race relations. After each talk the researchers would ask questions intended to get depth information about the leader's opinions, attitudes, and activities in regard to the topics discussed.

Perhaps the most significant information the forum interview provided was an insight into the "social personality" of the subject. In the forum interview situation all leaders who participated expressed themselves in the way they do characteristically in committees, with groups, and in public meetings. Also, the interviewers felt freer to question, to point out contradictions, and to argue points of view than they could within the more formal interviewer-interviewee relationship. In this way, the leader's wit, intelligence, emotional range, depth of information, and ability to communicate were revealed more clearly than would have been possible in a formal interview, where the researcher is not allowed such wide liberties.

We may say, then, that the forum interview served two significant, interrelated purposes: one, it provided a situation in which the researchers could acquire information about the leader's opinions and activities regarding some major social problems; and two, it provided valuable insight into the personality of the leader, which is always an important factor in getting things done.

Participant observation. Even before formally beginning research for this study, certain members of the research team held membership in a number of civic, social, business, labor, professional, and "uplift" organizations. These social connections provided many opportunities to observe at first hand the strategies and techniques employed by some of New Orleans's most influential race relations leaders. After the study was underway these observations became much more deliberate, systematic, and purposeful. Every effort was made to compare, evaluate, and classify not only the behavior patterns and effectiveness of the leaders, but also the responses of the followers. During the four years' study the author and members of the research staff attended a total of 211 public and private meetings of civic, labor, educational, professional, civil rights, and political organizations. We took special note of the composition of the audiences (in terms of sex, age, race, religion, social status, and occupational connection), audience responses, decision making, and order, as well as the "leaders in action." Before and/or after these meetings we made a point of informally interviewing the leaders and some of the other active participants. Though much of the information so gathered does not lend itself to precise statistical reporting, it did provide valuable insight into the nature and function of leadership.

Perhaps the most definite by-product of our participant observation was the fact that Negro leaders themselves became much more conscious of their leadership functions and status than they had been before. There was a great deal more talk about the leader's responsibility and the follower's role than there had been before the leaders were interviewed and knew that this study was in process. There actually developed a kind of *esprit de corps* among certain of the leaders, which they themselves recognized as a new social element. Several acknowledged that they realized more than ever that they were interested in common issues, and that all Negro leaders labored under pretty much the same handicaps. In fact, many of them began to express a desire for some form of unity and solidarity among themselves.

From a research point of view, then, what can we say has been the value of participant observation as used in this study? It gave the investigators many opportunities to observe the effectiveness of certain leadership techniques and strategies and to evaluate different personalities as they adjust to, expand, or narrow traditional expectations of the leadership role. Participants were able to observe interaction between leaders and followers, the function of definite (as opposed to indefinite) goals, and the formation of plans calculated to accomplish these goals.

Staff meetings. Most of the interviewing for this study was done during the summers of 1959, 1960 and 1961. At the end of each week the researchers came together in a more or less formal discussion of the highlights of their "field" experiences, during which they evaluated the research strategies and techniques used and appraised the findings, hypotheses, and general theories relating to the problem of leadership in the process of social change.

The staff meetings accomplished at least four purposes:

(1) They provided opportunities for each interviewer to interpret his written materials in the light of working hypotheses. In this way, gaps in data could be bridged in the normal course of research. Thus, for example, if significant questions needed to be answered by a particular subject in order to test some relevant hypothesis, the interviewer could simply schedule another session with the interviewee for that purpose.

(2) During the course of staff meetings reports on unusual research experiences were codified, and upon examination a few turned out to constitute relevant sociological and psychological patterns. For example, traits such as punctuality, initiative, the desire to dominate social situations, boastfulness, and identification with the Negro cause, among others, proved to vary significantly according to the social origins of the leaders.

(3) Another important function of the staff meetings was the obvious heightening of researcher morale. This was perhaps due to the fact that each staff member got a feeling of total participation in the study by seeing how valuable his bit of material could be to the success of the project.

(4) By participating in staff meetings, each member of the research team, despite different research abilities, was able to arrive at more or less uniform techniques in handling certain challenging interview situations. Specific problems—such as overcoming hostility and reluctance to answer certain basic questions—were dealt with, and uniform probe questions were settled upon, so that the contents of interviews were easily comparable.

There were also some special staff meetings at which a visiting researcher would discuss pertinent information, research techniques, and social theories with staff members. Through interchange of information and pointed questioning, the research staff was generally able to apply the visitors' insight in the solution of its own problems.

Finally, a complete transcription of each of the staff meetings was made. These records have proved valuable in the preparation of this manuscript.

The leadership conference. At the end of the formal data-gathering stage of the leadership study, Negro leaders included in the study plus some other interested leaders were invited to participate in a two-day leadership conference, a "Summit Conference" of Negro Leaders. The main purpose of this meeting was to provide a group setting in which leaders in the Negro community could, themselves, evaluate the strategies and techniques they had characteristically employed in their leadership role.

Academically, the conference was a success. Each invited leader willingly, even enthusiastically, participated in the discussions and submitted to open criticism of his philosophy of race relations and the strategies and techniques he had traditionally employed.

During the two days of structured discussions the leaders were able to identify the major weaknesses of the Negro leadership class in New Orleans, and to compare the organization and activities of this class with that of the leadership class in some other metropolitan centers. In the process of doing this, researchers were able to get a fairly organized summary of Negro progress in certain important areas of community life according to the way the leaders, themselves, evaluated the achievements Negroes had made toward established goals. Their analyses and interpretations provided important information upon which some conclusions in this study have been based.

2

THE PROBLEM OF SOCIAL CHANGE

SINCE THE VERY beginning of scientific sociology, social change has been a major subject of theorizing and research. Indeed, the earliest and most grandiose sociological theories were those intended to provide a framework for the analysis and interpretation of social change. Thus, Auguste Comte, the "father" of sociology, divided the study of society into two main parts— *statics* and *dynamics*. Statics deals with the established social order. The focus is mainly upon forces that make for stability, solidarity, and immutability of social systems. Dynamics deals with the changes that take place in social systems and attempts to trace the forces that make for flexibility, disorganization and improvement in social relationships. With certain variations in emphasis and interpretation, sociologists since Comte have followed his general approach in efforts to understand the nature of social structure and social interaction.

As indispensable as are analyses of the processes of social change and interpretations of social systems, most knowledge about social change is derived from data collected by people who are not social scientists. This is so because, as a rule, significant social changes transpire slowly, almost imperceptibly. Thus the social scientist is most often caught unaware, so that the conditions in which change takes place are highly developed or passed altogether before he is sufficiently alerted to observe, record, and analyze the more subtle forces making for change. It is not surprising, then, that most analyses of social change are based on previously collected or post-factum data. Quite often such data will have been collected by newspapers, pressure groups, and administrative agencies for nonscientific purposes. And, as may be expected, these data generally suffer from at least two shortcomings. First, they are often incomplete. That is, significant data needed to validate key hypotheses, test existing pertinent theories, or fill gaps in factual material are too frequently left out. Second, post-factum social data usually tend to present only one interpretation of the conditions of social change. Consequently, the social scientist is often led to what data are available to support some preconceived theoretical framework. This has sometimes meant that he has had to ignore possible alternative consequences of particular social forces under analysis.

The social researcher has long felt the need of a laboratory in which he could carry out first-hand experiments designed to test promising hypotheses and to validate accepted laws or principles of social relationships and social change. Since he suffers from the obvious handicap of not being able to set up certain experiments in social action, it becomes eminently important that social systems already in the trauma of change be studied intensely.

Perhaps no other social system has presented a greater challenge for the student of social change than has the system of race relations in the South. Since 1954 social conditions in the South have been so structured that the student of society has had a unique opportunity to make direct, empirical observations of basic, history-making social changes as they have transpired. These changes have occurred in almost every aspect of community and personal life. Fortunately, a number of social scientists were alerted sufficiently to initiate well-planned studies designed to document, analyze, and interpret the forces and counterforces associated with these changes. This is such a study. Throughout this study we have attempted to gain detailed empirical knowledge of changing situations as they unfolded. Each significant stage of the selected changing situation has been documented and interpreted in the light of possible alternative consequences.

THE NEGRO AND THE AMERICAN CREED

The United States is founded upon the principles of political democracy, which guarantee all of its citizens freedom, equality of opportunity, and equal protection of the law. Inherent in the very nature of democracy is the commitment to change—to make progress toward these goals. Consequently, the inveterate inequalities experienced by Negroes in American society have constituted this nation's most abiding and embarrassing failure.

Though this is a national problem of the first magnitude, it is considerably more serious in southern communities than in communities outside the South. This is so because it is in the South that the inequalities experienced by Negroes represent the most glaring contradictions to the principles of freedom and equality that constitute the foundation of our government. Furthermore, it is in the South that the total culture has developed along racial lines, and the most basic traditions and laws are designed to perpetuate a biracial society. In this biracial society, all white people are legally regarded as socially superior to all Negroes. Thus, by and large, Negroes, regardless of achievements, are relegated to an inferior social status and prevented from enjoying many of the rights and privileges accorded other citizens.

The very fact that Negroes as a racial group have never actually enjoyed the political or social equality visualized in the American Creed has presented a constant challenge for every level of our governmental and community life. In order to fulfill the "American dream" each citizen would be expected to progress toward the achievement of a society in which Negroes, like other Americans, would have equal opportunity to exercise the full measure of their citizenship.

It is in this respect that the status of Negroes in the South is essentially different from what it would be in a caste system. A caste system is a static system in which social relationships are not expected to change from one generation to another. What changes do occur in such a system are almost too slow to be perceived in the life span of an individual. In contrast, the pattern of racial segregation as it exists in New Orleans has never presupposed a rigid separation of races, perpetuated by inherited occupations, as would be true in a caste system. There have been times when Negroes in New Orleans were proportionately over-represented in some of the more highly skilled and technical occupations and held important political positions from which they are now barred. The fact is, much of the extreme prejudice and discrimination Negroes experience from whites does not result from norms prescribed by economic, political, and religious dogma (which necessarily buttress a caste system); rather these attitudes result from constant competition sanctioned by these norms. For example, segregationist leaders in New Orleans, representing all socio-economic classes, remind their followers that desegregation should be "resisted at all cost," as one put it, "or hordes of Negroes will swarm in and take over our jobs, our political power, and our homes." Thus,

> not only for status reasons but for economic reasons as well . . . whites are opposed to desegregation. . . . They have long competed with Negroes for jobs. They have been successful in having certain jobs classified as "white jobs" and left a few of the most undesirable jobs to be classified as "Negro jobs."[1]

Open competition with Negroes on a nonsegregated basis would tend to destroy the near-monopoly whites in New Orleans have of economic, political, and social power.

Of course, despite the democratic commitment of our national government and the general acceptance of the principle of equality, the social structure in New Orleans may still be described as biracial. There remain many barriers to be overcome before Negroes can enjoy the full citizenship and equal social status that are intrinsic presuppositions in the equalitarian ideology. Yet significant changes have been made that prove that certain legal and traditional barriers are not nearly so rigid as they once appeared to be. This is due in large measure to the fact that race relations leadership in New Orleans, as elsewhere in the United States, shows at least one outstanding quality: constant resistance to political and social inequalities. At no time have Negroes accepted their subordinate social status as morally, ethically,

[1] Daniel C. Thompson, "Social Class Factors in Public School Education as Related to Desegregation," *The American Journal of Orthopsychiatry*, Vol. XXVI, No. 3, July 1956, pp. 450-451.

or legally just, as would be expected in a caste system. Negro leaders have always defined the restrictions inherent in the low social status ascribed to them as punishment. Thus the ethos of the Negro subculture has never been characterized by resignation and fatalism. Actually, the frustrations and discrimination Negroes experience because they are Negroes, when expressed in their literature, art, music, and social action, is blended with a note of profound hope and faith in a better future. This is the prime reason why Negro-white relationships in New Orleans have been varied and dynamic, never really taking on the basic elements of a caste system as some observers claim. At all times Negro leaders have considered it their most important duty to keep reminding their followers and the nation at large of the basic democratic principles inherent in our American creed. A white liberal has observed that "The new Negro leadership sounds more Jeffersonian than did Jefferson."

SIGNS OF SOCIAL CHANGE

As suggested above, by social change we mean a transition from one system of social relationships to some other system. For our purposes this might mean that Negroes now hold a status or position in the general community that they did not occupy previously, or that at some previous time Negroes held a position or status in the community that they no longer are privileged to occupy. Social change also will have transpired if Negroes alone now possess a status that was once shared with some other group, or if they now share a status that was exclusively occupied by themselves at some previous time.

Further, social change might mean that some rearrangement in patterns of race relations has taken place. Thus, being Negro may result in one's being placed in a higher or lower position in the social system relative to some other group than he had at some other time. For example, Negroes today may have a status higher than that of some other ethnic group whose status was at one time higher or approximately the same. Again, we may say that the status of Negroes has changed when the roles required of Negroes have changed. Accordingly, if being Negro does not now prevent one from participating in certain civic and social rights, duties, responsibilities, and privileges which once were prohibited or when being Negro is a deterrent to such participation that was once permitted, we can say that social change has taken place. Finally, we may evaluate the changing status of Negroes in relation to the status of white people. Consequently, when the social distance (degree of intimacy) between Negroes and whites is appreciably smaller or larger than at some previous time, another dimension of change in the system of race relations is evidenced.

Specifically, any evaluation of the changing status of Negroes in New Orleans must concern itself with the total citizenship role. This role implies the right to equal participation in every aspect of community life. Therefore, when we appraise the changing status of Negroes we must do so with direct reference to the position accorded Negroes in such sensitive and fundamental areas as citizenship, earning a living, and education. And so in this study we try to assess the role of leadership as a major factor in social change within each of these areas.

SOCIAL CHANGE IN A NATIONAL CONTEXT

All geographic and political subdivisions of the United States are intimately and inextricably involved with all other such subdivisions. Together they form a delicately balanced national mechanism. Any significant disturbance or change in any single part of the society will ultimately be felt in all of its parts.

For example, race relations in New Orleans may be affected not only by the size of the Negro electorate in other parts of the state or the percentage of Negroes voting throughout the South but also by the extent of the Negro's political participation on a national level. Likewise, the political strength of Negroes in a few large urban areas outside the South may significantly influence certain key political leaders representing those areas to act on certain civil rights issues that may eventually affect the nationwide status of Negroes. Consequently, despite the fact that the size and organization of the Negro electorate in New Orleans may be relatively insignificant as a force in itself, Negroes in New Orleans do benefit from the fact that anti-civil rights voting blocs in Congress may sometimes be upset because a senator or representative from a large urban community outside the South might need the political support of Negroes in his district to ensure his re-election. In a real sense, then, a study of social changes in New Orleans is a study of changes in American society.

CAUSES OF AND REACTIONS TO SOCIAL CHANGE

In order to make a comprehensive analysis of the causes of the changes in race relations in New Orleans, it may be fruitful to distinguish between those that are predisposing and those that are precipitating.

Predisposing causes. A society is predisposed to change when social lags, problems, and disturbances create strains that make readjustments in the social system imperative. Insofar as the changing status of Negroes is concerned, we may divide predisposing causes into those that are *manifest* and those that are *latent*.

Among the most salient manifest causes of changes in race relations are the following:

(1) Demographic changes. That is, changes in the size, proportion and distribution of the Negro population.

(2) Basic changes in the economy. Among the most important such changes are those due to the introduction of new technology, war, prosperity, depression, labor unionism, new forms of business combinations, and federal

regulations. Any one of these could result in significant changes in the occupational structure of the general society, and, specifically, in the skills and distribution of Negro employed persons.

(3) Malfunctioning social agencies (such as those concerned with health, welfare, protection, and city planning). Malfunctioning on this level might be due basically to antiquated political practices, governmental policies, and outmoded laws.

(4) Changing position of the local, state, and national governments in relation to one another and to other political entities. This has indeed created major crises insofar as the legal status of Negroes is concerned.

It must be remembered that a social system does not necessarily change when predisposing forces impose obvious pressures. The truth is, a social system may continue to order itself according to outmoded laws and "sacred" traditions long after they have become obviously dysfunctional. History is replete with instances of social systems that might have saved themselves from decline and eventual collapse if they had responded positively to the major pressures on them at some given period in their development.

Perhaps the most characteristic technique used by white "men of power" in New Orleans when faced with racial issues and tensions is that they simply tend to ignore or deny the existence of them. Some are notoriously unable to recognize differential or discriminatory conditions from which Negroes suffer. Thus, for instance, after extensive interviews with certain influential white citizens in New Orleans, a researcher concluded that "they are interested in and knowledgeable about projects, not issues." Even when forced to comment on major racial problems they are likely to deny the seriousness of the situations they generate. Like most southern officials and leaders, they are eager to establish the thesis that Negroes are satisfied with existing patterns of racial segregation; that racial problems are more imagined than real; and that all apparent manifestations of dissatisfaction on the part of local Negroes are due to meddling "outsiders," "nigger lovers," the NAACP, Jews, "rabble rousers," the United States Supreme Court, or "Communists."

Among the most persistent *latent* impetuses to changes in race relations in New Orleans we may include the sustained desire for freedom, enfranchisement, recognition, respect, equality, security, and political power on the part of Negroes.

Sometimes this psychic state is referred to as political, economic, social, or spiritual "unrest." It has been obviously characteristic of Negroes throughout the South for decades. The dissatisfaction, rejection, isolation, and hostility expressed by some Negroes often take the form of latent, rather than manifest, social unrest. This latent unrest could prevail indefinitely because of fear of reprisals, loss of prestige, loss of security, vested interests, or lethargy among leaders who are capable of facilitating communication and initiating concerted action on behalf of those who suffer from the strains and tensions of racial discrimination.

Precipitating causes. When social strains are manifest or obvious, and when predisposing causes, or the desire for change, exist in a given social system, the event or incident that triggers ameliorative social action—the straw that breaks the camel's back—may be called a precipitating cause. Among the most significant precipitants of changing race relations in New Orleans since 1940 are World War II and the need for general defense, the organized purchasing power of Negroes, increased political strength and unity of Negroes, organized protests, demonstrations, mob violence by segregationists, picketings, boycotts, the sit-in movement, "freedom riders," and legal action.

These precipitants have forced officials to concern themselves with problems stemming from racial segregation. They ordinarily respond in one of two ways:

(1) Die-hard reactionaries use almost every legal, extra-legal, and even illegal technique to preserve or re-establish the most severe system of white supremacy. They make desperate attempts to reinstate already outmoded, discarded, and illegal patterns of race relations. They may at different times use threats, intimidations, economic reprisals, bribery, "political squeezes," "purges," and bloc voting in their efforts to keep the Negro economically and politically powerless and relegated to the bottom rung of the social ladder. However, the most significant and effective technique is legislation. For instance, since 1954 the Louisiana legislature has passed scores of laws—"black codes"—designed to take away from Negro citizens rights and privileges that they have had traditionally, and to prevent them from exercising those recently granted by federal courts.

(2) Some persons in positions of authority and power attempt to remedy or correct certain manifest racial ills without changing the basic pattern of relationships, or alleviating the latent causes of social strains. This means, in effect, that old methods are applied to new racial problems. Accordingly, some segregationists in New Orleans are now belatedly willing to live up to the "separate but equal" doctrine in education after the doctrine itself has been legally overthrown by the May 17, 1954 decision.

A third possible response to racial strains, and social disorganization resulting from them, might be described as *creative innovation*. There are some officials or leaders on a national level who have proposed such a response. It has been manifested in certain civil rights legislation, executive orders, and judicial decisions affecting the status of Negroes. Nevertheless, the strains and tensions in race relations in Louisiana have not yet reached such an intensity that those in power and authority have indicated a willingness to accept creative innovations in race relations. So far, there have not been any proposals for constitutional reforms aimed at liberalizing the qualifications for suffrage; any effort to include Negroes in decision-making; any legislation against discrimination in employment and education; or any machinery set up to facilitate interracial communication or to guarantee better protection of the civil rights of Negro people. In short, up until now New Orleans' officials—the "men of power"—have made no voluntary effort to bring about positive changes in race relations.

Conclusion

Insofar as the causes of social change are concerned, the crucial question is why a particular society responds in a given way, and not in some other way, to a specific complex of social forces? In other words, why do those who occupy strategic positions of authority and power in one social system systematically ignore pressing social problems, or continue to cling tenaciously to outmoded, ineffective patterns of social relationships, even when these threaten to undermine the general welfare and bring about the ultimate destruction of the society itself, while those who occupy similar strategic positions in some other social systems respond creatively when the same set of social challenges is encountered?

There may, of course, be several reasons for these different responses. Perhaps the most prominent reason is the fact that "men of power" in any given community must operate in a total situational context that is inherently different in some respects from that of any other community. For example, official responses to racial issues and problems in the South may vary in some particulars from one community to another. Upon examination we are likely to find that different official responses are highly correlated with corresponding differences to be found among the communities in question.

Among the most basic differences in the nature and structure of communities we may include the following:

(1) The extent of involvement in the affairs of neighboring communities.

(2) The degree to which the economy is sensitive to national and international markets.

(3) The strength and persistence of social reform movements at a given time.

(4) The level of literacy.

(5) The degree of mental and psychic isolation.

(6) The historical background in solving similar problems.

(7) The extent to which the security of white citizens is influenced by the activities of Negro citizens.

(8) The efficiency and dedication of law-enforcement agencies.

(9) The measure of respect for law and order on the part of the general public.

(10) The extent to which institutions and social agencies have dealt frankly and objectively with racial issues and problems.

(11) The manifest and latent functions of mass communication media.

(12) The moral fiber, tone, or climate that characteristically shows itself when precipitating factors disrupt traditional behavior patterns.

However, it is our contention that when it comes to evaluating the various causes of social change in any social system, the most basic variable to be considered is the catalytic effect of leadership.

Historians have differed in their opinions on this subject. Some scholars, Carlyle for example, have attributed all positive social change to "Great Men." Others have emphasized the importance of contemporary environmental conditions. This idea was philosophically expressed by Leopold von Bismarck, founder of the German Empire, when he said, "The Great Man can do nothing of himself, he can only lie in wait and listen until amid the march of events he can hear the footsteps of God. Then he leaps forward and grasps the hem of His garment."

The most fruitful approach, we believe, is not to say that great men make history, or that history makes great men, but that there is an interaction between the great man and his environment in the sense that the great man uniquely perceives the possibilities of change about him. He seizes the opportunity to relieve the obvious social strains caused by the social system. He does this by organizing and coordinating the unrest—the desire for change—existing in the hearts of men. He initiates some well-thought-out program of change. In the implementation of a program designed to effect social change, this kind of great man might employ three categories of strategies and techniques.

(1) Traditional methods, used to solve new problems or relieve social strains.

(2) Culturally approved, but often unused or untried, strategies and techniques.

(3) Creative innovation.

This last would be used when established strategies fail and new, sometimes radical, measures are needed to solve problems dangerous to the social system. Speaking of such measures a militant Negro leader threatened:

> We are going to remove the cancer, segregation. It is too harmful. We must be firm, courageous, even brutal if need be. This evil requires operation. Consequently in order to achieve our citizenship rights we [Negroes] must deliberately violate every law which is intended to prevent us from becoming first-class citizens.

3

THE NEGRO LEADERSHIP CLASS

Social Characteristics

THE LEADERSHIP CLASS in the Negro community, like social classes in American society generally, is a loosely organized social group. Those who identify with this class represent various ages, social backgrounds, religious affiliations, educational attainments, occupations, incomes, and styles of life. However, unlike social classes, which are of an extremely complex nature, the Negro leadership class is relatively simple in structure, goals, and ideology. Thus, whereas social classes in the broader society are composed of families, the Negro leadership class is composed primarily of individuals. Further, these individuals are participating, have been participating, or are expected to participate actively in some movement, organization, or group whose main purpose is to improve the general status of Negroes or to achieve some more or less specific social goal deemed important in the Negro's struggle for first-class citizenship.

Ideologically, Negro leaders adhere to essentially the same set of principles as did the founders of our Republic. Their writings, speeches, and formal organizational policies express a strong belief in the essential dignity of all men. Further, there is consensus among those who identify with this class that government exists primarily to establish and defend the right of every individual to enjoy equal citizenship regardless of race, creed, color, or social status.

SEX COMPOSITION

The vast majority of Negro leaders in New Orleans are men. This is somewhat surprising in light of the fact that Negro women in New Orleans tend to occupy strong, even dominant, positions in the home and in the economic and cultural life of the society. Indeed, only a few Negro women in New Orleans may be classified as "top" community leaders. As a rule, these few are elected officials in some special-interest organization such as

25

the Parent Teachers Association, a teachers' association, or the Negro Women Voters' League. Occasionally the heads of sororities, prominent women's clubs, or some other women's group may be called upon to perform some more or less temporary community leadership functions. As a rule, however, most female leadership is channeled through guilds or auxiliaries that serve mainly as adjuncts to more powerful organizations dominated by men.

Rarely do Negro women in New Orleans initiate, stimulate, coordinate, or direct the activities of the Negro masses in the solution of major social problems affecting them. None has become a symbol of the Negro's struggle to achieve equality of citizenship. However, as we shall see later, as supporting or "secondary" leaders in the Negro community, certain Negro women have made contributions to changes in the status of Negroes since 1940.

When women leaders were asked to explain why so few of them played a leadership role, they all expressed their deep disappointment that this was true. Most of them related several unsuccessful attempts on their part to recruit other women for much-needed leadership roles in some community or racial project. In summarizing the reasons, or apologies, that other women had offered in refusing to accept leadership positions, women leaders made the following statements:

> The average ambitious woman who holds a job outside the home generally feels that she simply does not have the time or energy to concern herself with wide social issues or problems.
>
> Most women are unalterably resigned to "let men get the headlines." Some feel that their community responsibilities are fulfilled when they encourage their husbands to contribute, in some way, to worthwhile causes.
>
> A surprisingly large number of women still feel that community leadership is a man's job. A few even feel that when women start trying to be leaders, or working to improve the lot of Negro masses, they only make themselves ridiculous, because they are convinced that no "self-respecting" man would follow a woman leader.
>
> Women are just plain lazy. Most of them will not participate in any constructive movement because they don't want to take time out from their social activities long enough to attend meetings.
>
> A large number of women feel inferior. They have no confidence in their ability to contribute to human betterment. They would be frightened out of their wits if they were called upon to plan some important community program or activity.
>
> Women just don't have as much social concern as men. When things are going well with them, most of them will not be interested in other people's problems.
>
> The average woman who is really capable of leadership hates the masses. When one woman tried to persuade another woman to help her plan a rehabilitation program for young unwed mothers the latter confessed that she loathed immoral, vulgar people.

Whether the reasons suggested above are typical, or even valid, cannot be decided here. The only conclusion that can be made definitely is that, even during times of crisis, only a few Negro women have assumed any important leadership role.

AGE COMPOSITION

Any adult who assumes leadership responsibilities, and is accepted as a leader by members of the Negro leadership class, may be considered a part of that class. In New Orleans, Negro leaders range in age from twenty-one to ninety. There are, however, two important characteristics of the age composition of the Negro leadership class in New Orleans.

(1) Few Negro leaders are under forty years of age. The median age of the leaders included in this study is fifty-five. Sixty per cent of the "top" leadership in the Negro community is over fifty years old.

(2) We were unable to discover evidence of a revolt by younger Negroes against the small, established Negro "ruling class" that Louis E. Lomax has discussed.[1] It is true, of course, that there is more liberalism, even radicalism, and a stronger tendency toward revolt against the status quo among the younger leaders than can be found among the older, more established leaders. However, it seems to be not a matter of age, but of "mass" or "class" orientation.

Generally, it is precisely the socially disinherited, intraracial, "mass oriented"[2] Negro leaders who have become outstanding in direct protest against segregation in New Orleans. Those who are "class oriented,"[3] and who have been accorded greater recognition by white leaders and officials, regardless of age, have manifested the "conservatism" Lomax attributed to the NAACP. For example, the Consumers' League, which preceded the student sit-in movement in New Orleans, is led by older Negro leaders; one of its key leaders is fifty-five years old. This organization took direct action through picketing and boycotting, as well as negotiation, in attempts to get white-collar jobs for Negroes in businesses with substantial Negro trade. Several of its leaders were arrested and jailed for protesting job discrimination. On the other hand, some of the younger Negro leaders who are products of middle- and upper-class upbringing have identified with the older, more established and conservative segment of the Negro leadership class.

We may conclude that the basic differences in approach among Negro leaders are not related to age, but to differences in social position. It is

[1] "The Negro Revolt Against the Negro Leaders," *Harper's Magazine*, June 1960, pp. 41ff.

[2] "Mass-oriented" leaders are those who are primarily concerned with issues affecting the masses of Negroes, such as police brutality, unemployment welfare, and voting restrictions. They employ the mass-meeting, public demonstration and boycott as techniques in their efforts to improve the status of Negroes.

[3] "Class-oriented" leaders are those who are primarily interested in raising the cultural level of Negroes. They rely mainly on the technique of diplomatic persuasion to achieve this goal.

typically the group of those who are rising, rather than those whose position is established, who have more vested interest, "which organizes the resentful and the rebellious into a revolutionary group."[4] The older the leader, the more likely he is to have become attached to conservative men of power, or conservative institutional forms. Hence, we would expect to find more conservatism among older leaders than among the young and the "socially disinherited" leaders, since the latter, despite their ambition, have little opportunity to rise in the traditional patterns of a rapidly decaying biracial system. Thus, the "new" segment of the Negro leadership class is composed of young men who are as yet unestablished and older intraracial leaders who are unacceptable as leaders to white men of power.

PLACE OF BIRTH

Most Negro leaders in New Orleans are "native sons," that is, born in New Orleans. Nearly all who were not born in New Orleans migrated there during early childhood from some small town in Louisiana. Some came to the city ten or more years ago from other southern cities. None came from places outside the South.

It is not easy to determine why the Negro leadership class in New Orleans is composed primarily of natives. There are, of course, some plausible explanations:

(1) Leaders in any community are likely to be predominantly drawn from among established individuals and families. This would be particularly true in an old, tradition-oriented city such as New Orleans. We would expect, then, that most of the community leaders, whether white or Negro, would be natives. It takes time for most migrants to acquire the social, economic, and cultural roots necessary for the degree of identification a leader must have in order to become a symbol of a people's goals, successes, failures, and ideology.

(2) Unlike some other cities, New Orleans offers relatively limited attractions for established Negro leaders or successful business and professional men who come from other parts of the United States. In fact, one of the most serious problems the Negro community faces is that of how to hold ambitious native sons who have obvious leadership potential. One leader pointed out that there seems to be a ceiling on the number of capable young men who remain in New Orleans after preparing for business and professional careers. He estimated that the turnover remains rather close to the replacement level. That is, New Orleans generally retains just enough of its young Negro professionals to replace the older ones who retire and those who emigrate from the city.

It seems, therefore, that a primary reason why practically all of those who identify with the Negro leadership class are natives is the fact that successful

[4] Robert K. Merton, *Social Theory and Social Structure* (Glencoe, Ill.: The Free Press, 1949) p. 146.

Negro business and professional men, who are traditionally the sources from which the bulk of Negro leaders are recruited, do not find New Orleans sufficiently attractive economically to migrate there from other states. When capable leaders do come to New Orleans, there is reason to believe that whether they are accepted or rejected by the established Negro leadership class depends to a great extent upon the contributions they are prepared to make to community betterment or, more specifically, to the Negro's efforts to achieve equal citizenship. Those whose pronouncements and activities are adjudged to be sincere and effective in that respect are ascribed the status of Negro leaders.

(3) Some prominent New Orleanians complain that there is a more or less concerted effort on the part of native business and professional Negroes to discourage others from establishing themselves in the city. They cite any number of instances of local leaders refusing to cooperate with, and even actively opposing, younger men who sought to establish themselves in New Orleans. Some even claim that there is an informal organization of native-born Negro leaders who are tacitly pledged not to follow "outsiders" who attempt to promote racial or community betterment. There is some doubt that this is true on an organized level, yet there is ample evidence that some New Orleanians are prejudiced toward "outsiders" to the extent that they cannot be expected to cooperate with them in community leadership efforts.

Whatever might be the reasons for the virtual monopoly of leadership positions in New Orleans by native sons, at least one point is clear: the New Orleans Negro community is to a very large extent isolated from the mainstream of the Negro protest movement. It is seriously deprived of many of the leadership strategies and techniques that other Negro leaders, in other parts of the United States, have developed in getting things done in the realm of racial "uplift."

It is true, of course, that occasionally Negro leaders from other areas come to New Orleans to speak at mass meetings. On such occasions visiting leaders are expected to spell out strategies or techniques that Negroes elsewhere have used in their struggle for first-class citizenship. Most often their suggestions are logical and feasible; yet they would have to be revised in order to achieve an appreciable degree of success in New Orleans. And since the visitors do not remain long enough to acquaint local leaders sufficiently with new approaches, native sons often blunder and fail when they attempt to apply these principles to New Orleans. Therefore, despite the fact that visiting leaders do bring to the Negro community valuable suggestions concerning strategies and techniques of leadership, they are inadequate substitutes for competent, more stable local leaders.

ECONOMIC STATUS

The vast majority of Negro leaders in New Orleans may be characterized as self-made men. As a rule, their fathers were common laborers who never earned more than $3,000 a year. Small wonder, then, that most of them attribute their success in life to hard work, honesty, and perseverance. Some even believe that patience is the most valuable virtue in the struggle for success in any given endeavor.

A small number of the leaders were recruited from middle-class homes in which the fathers were ministers. Only eight, at most, came from upper-income families, where the total annual family income was $7,500 and over.[5] In most instances the mother worked outside the home in order to supplement the father's income.

Because the Negro leadership class, on the whole, was recruited from lower-income families, it is not surprising to note the pride and self-respect members of this class have developed. It can be said that most of the top leaders have succeeded beyond what might normally be expected in their occupations. Only the youngest of them have incomes of less than $5,000 a year, and the large majority of them have incomes of $7,500 and over. A few even acknowledged annual incomes of $20,000 and more. These leaders generally ascribe their success to such virtues as hard work, sacrifice, and perseverance.

Finally, we may say that the majority of Negroes who identify with the leadership class in New Orleans come from lower-middle class homes. This is precisely the segment in Negro society which Rohrer et al. recognized for its industry, high standards of morality, strong family ties, and the willingness to sacrifice for desired goals.[6] Therefore, despite the fact that most of the parents of today's Negro leaders had relatively little to offer them in terms of economic security and social contacts, the structure and atmosphere of their home life as children gave them the solidarity, the values, and the motivations generally associated with the success-conscious middle class in American society.

EDUCATION

One other indication of the rapid, upward social mobility of most Negro leaders in New Orleans is the fact that more than two-thirds of them came from homes where their parents had received less than a high school education. However, several of the parents did graduate from high school and, interestingly enough, 10 per cent held college degrees.

In comparison with their parents, the educational achievements of the Negro leaders reveal a most significant contrast. All of them attended high school, and 65 per cent received college degrees. Significantly, more than half of the leaders included in the sample hold one or more graduate or professional degrees.

Any evaluation or interpretation of the educational achievements of Negro

[5] We refer here to incomes prior to 1940.

[6] John H. Rohrer, et al., The Eighth Generation (New York: Harper & Row, 1960), Chapter 4.

leaders in New Orleans must take into consideration the very significant fact that Americans commonly attach great value to education. College graduates in America generally enjoy greater prestige and respect than do noncollege people. This is especially true among Negroes. The educated Negro leader is likely to serve two important functions: one, it is largely through the better-educated Negro leader that his Negro followers achieve vicarious equality with white people. His achievements tend to "unmask" the inherent fallacies in the doctrine of white supremacy. This is particularly true if he has earned his academic status in competition with whites in an interracial institution, and is regarded as a success in interracial relations. One such leader was cited by a white journalist as "A living contradiction of the many myths about the Negro which haunt the white southerner's consciousness." And two, the well-educated Negro leader is ordinarily better prepared than the less well-trained to deal effectively with white "men of power" because he is more likely to have greater knowledge of the complex problems of race relations and the intricacies of social change.

RELIGIOUS AFFILIATION

Although a third or more of the Negro churchgoers in New Orleans are believed to be members of the Roman Catholic Church, the active Negro leadership is predominantly Protestant. There may be several reasons for this under-representation of Catholics in community leadership capacities. For our purpose we should consider at least two.

(1) There are no Negro Roman Catholic pastors in New Orleans. In fact, there are seldom more than two or three Negro Catholic priests employed in any capacity in the city, and these are teachers. This means that the Catholic Church does not provide this important gateway to the development of leadership among its Negro constituents as do the Protestant Churches, where all pastors of Negro churches are Negroes.[7]

(2) In addition to the leadership role of the pastors themselves, a large number of Negro Protestant Churches, through their various activities, create an atmosphere of race pride and a sense of racial responsibility to a much greater degree than has the more formal, ritualistic Catholic Church. Thus, the atmosphere of the Catholic Church is less conducive to the development of a race-conscious leadership among its members than that of the Protestant Churches, where the pastors are drawn from all segments of Negro society and have a closer identification with the race, its problems, achievements, and goals than white Catholic priests generally do.

Even though the Roman Catholic Church does not lend itself to the creation of a race-conscious leadership as easily as do Protestant Churches, there have always been some outstanding Negro Catholic leaders in New Orleans. They have worked through church auxiliaries, fraternal groups,

---

[7] A recent exception to this statement is a white Lutheran pastor of a Lutheran church for Negroes.

"uplift" organizations, civic committees and leagues, professional associations, and as individuals. In fact, all of the occupational groups to be discussed in the next chapter, except the Protestant ministry, have large representation from among Negro Catholics. Consequently, any discussion of the leadership role of these occupational groups will necessarily include some Negro Catholic leaders.

| On the whole, Negro Catholic leaders seem to be a good deal more class-oriented than the Protestants. This may be due to at least three major historical facts: one, as suggested before, Negro Catholics have not had a race conscious ministry as has been generally true of Negro Protestants. Two, a larger proportion of Negro Catholic leaders in New Orleans were reared in homes where light skin was valued above identification with the Negro masses. And, three, a larger proportion of Negro Catholic leaders belong to old "Creole" business families that have traditionally enjoyed high social status among New Orleans Negroes. Thus, the Negro leadership class in New Orleans is composed of both Catholics and Protestants, yet as a rule, it is the mass-oriented Protestant leaders who have become the chief exponents, or symbols, of the Negro's struggle for equal civil status. |

RACE

It is ironic that in a biracial community such as New Orleans some of the most valuable members of the Negro leadership class are Caucasians, albeit Caucasians who function as Negroes. That is, they are whites who live and work among Negroes and identify with the Negroes' struggle for first-class citizenship.

So far as could be ascertained there are about a dozen such persons in New Orleans who are recognized as race relations leaders. They either teach in "Negro" schools or pastor Negro congregations. Almost all their social, as well as professional contacts, are with Negroes. Unlike other white liberals who identify with the white community and are regarded by Negro leaders and white power figures as liaison persons in the area of race relations, Caucasians who function as Negroes are not so regarded, yet some do play this role effectively. Instead, they identify so completely with Negroes that they are generally regarded as "Negro spokesmen." None of the seven interviewed for this study, or the three included in the primary sample of 100, professed to identify at all with white "men of power."

One influential leader in this category, when asked to name "the three most influential white leaders in New Orleans," confessed that he knew none. This person always refers to himself as a Negro, in the sense that he uses "we" whenever he speaks of Negro people. Another such white is a member of and leader in several Negro organizations and is even an active member in a Negro social fraternity. These leaders manifest the same quality of racial consciousness and sensitivity to injustices as do militant Negro leaders. After listening to a speech made by a functional Negro, a Negro labor union official remarked, "If we had more Negro leaders who feel as [he] does, the solutions to Negro problems would be within our grasp." The Negro making this remark obviously identified racially with the speaker.

The most dominant characteristic that sets functional Negroes apart as a unique group in the Negro leadership class is their uncompromising dedication to the principle that equality of citizenship is an altogether moral issue. They assume the privilege of criticizing, not only liberal whites, but some of the most militant Negro leaders, when they appear to place expediency above the principle of racial equality. Thus, one functional Negro expressed what he called "righteous indignation" at certain officials of the NAACP and heads of Negro political factions. He said,

> Our pride has led us to build a shield of indifference to the past when we were helpless slaves. There is a sense of futility and apathy among us. Our vote is traditionally split and our leaders are bought off. The effect is that every white candidate feels an obligation to speak out against us. We must stop giving permanent allegiance to white political factions. Most of our political leaders are practicing a minor form of Uncle Tomism . . . We must develop a large independent vote if we are going to throw off the burden of second class citizenship.

It may be said not only that functional Negroes identify with the Negro uplift movement, but that Negroes, as we have observed, identify with them. In the truest sense of the word, race ceases to be a significant factor in the interaction pattern in which such Caucasians and Negroes participate. One Negro described a meeting composed of these two racial elements as "the very epitome of what I would call integration at its best."

4

THE NEGRO LEADERSHIP CLASS

Occupational Characteristics

WITH FEW EXCEPTIONS, Negro leadership in New Orleans is an avocation. Those who perform leadership functions in the area of race relations usually do so in addition to their full-time occupational pursuits.

By and large, the Negro leadership class is composed of successful representatives of the following occupational groups: The Protestant ministry, law, labor, business, the intelligentsia (teachers), professional leaders, and medicine.

THE PROTESTANT MINISTRY

Negro ministers constitute the largest segment of the leadership class. A relatively large percentage of them, with the backing of their congregations, have been able to contribute to local and national "uplift" efforts.

There may be several reasons why Negro ministers have become widely recognized symbols of the Negroes' struggle for equal citizenship status. Some of the most tenable explanations are:

(1) The Negro Protestant Church was the first, and in some respects it remains the only, major social institution in which a significant number of Negroes with varying talents and academic preparation have found opportunities for self-expression, the development of self-respect and racial pride, professional employment, and leadership training.

(2) The Negro church is the "parent" of most other organizations and agencies in the Negro community. In some instances the apparentization[1] is widely recognized, as is the case with insurance companies that developed from burial-aid societies. Also, most Negro institutions of higher education still claim affiliation with the various religious bodies that founded them. There is also a kind of indirect apparentization whereby benevolent orders

---

[1] We use here Arnold J. Toynbee's concept. Cf. *A Study of History*, abr. D. C. Somervell (New York: Oxford University Press, 1947).

and certain Negro "uplift" organizations are nurtured by Protestant Churches as an extension of their missionary functions. Important in this connection are lodges and racial-improvement associations, which look to the church for their legitimization or a major portion of their social and financial support.

Finally, the Protestant ministry is a more or less easily accessible profession. Standards for admission are sufficiently flexible on the whole so that Negro ministers are recruited from every academic, economic, and social segment of the community. This means that those with leadership ambitions will find some denomination or particular church that will be willing to accept them in apprenticeship positions which will provide them opportunities to develop and refine their leadership talents.

Ministers, like all other leaders in the Negro community, may be classified as *intraracial* or *interracial*. The activities of the intraracial leaders tend to center around two major approaches.

The other-worldly. As might be expected, the vast majority of ministers are primarily interested in their pastoral role. The peculiar characteristic of the other-worldly is their lack of interest in mundane affairs. They have little apparent interest in or even feeling of responsibility for the general citizenship status of their own parishioners, to say nothing about that of the Negro masses. Their sermons are essentially biblical, dealing only tangentially with social issues. The most obvious goal of their church services is to create an atmosphere of "enjoyment." Little time is spent in attempts to motivate members to assume the social responsibilities generally considered to be incumbent upon responsible citizens. Thus, one such minister made it clear that he regarded the church solely as a "place of worship," and that "the church is no place to encourage people to register and vote or to discuss controversial issues."

Some few ministers in this category do, however, contribute indirectly to racial uplift, in the sense that their church programs provide opportunities for the development of talents, such as in music, public speaking, and leadership.

The denomination-centered. A second large segment of intraracial leaders is composed of ministers who are imprisoned in their own denominational worlds. Some of these ministers are so interested in their personal advancement within the denominational hierarchy that they are often mistaken for genuine community leaders. That is, in order to insure their own promotion they express real or feigned interest in a wide number of social issues. We find that these various social issues are almost always championed in meetings with members representing cross sections of their own particular denominations. It would appear that their avowed concern with social issues seldom extends beyond a more or less nominal, or verbal, or at best financial, support of the limited social programs adopted by their national church bodies.

Yet, again, these intraracial leaders often contribute to racial uplift. Members of their congregations get some limited opportunity, at least, to become acquainted with a few vital social issues. Some even get opportunities to develop leadership potentials, as chairman of various boards or committees for which certain social problems are of major concern.

One other contribution denomination-centered leaders often make to the advancement of Negroes in American society is their effort to provide church scholarships for a small number of young persons who have manifested leadership ability. In this way, some give tangible sanction to the value of education, which is the most estimable avenue of social mobility for Negroes in American society.

Of primary concern to this study of the Negro leadership class are the *interracial* leaders among Protestant ministers. There are two major functional groups constituting this category.

The virtuoso. There is a small number of ordained Protestant ministers who are not primarily engaged in pastoring. They are employed in such secular fields as business, teaching, and labor unions. Very often they are college graduates, and some hold graduate and professional degrees as well. Generally, they are uncommonly conscious of and sensitive to racial segregation, discrimination, and injustice. They are avowed critics of white supremacy in all forms and champions of civil rights.

Some are highly skilled orators and lecturers and are in great demand to deliver keynote speeches and formal addresses and to conduct forums. In these roles, they appear regularly as spokesmen for the Negro's cause before various types of audiences. In this way a few become leaders who are well known and respected by a cross section of the community.

Though they rarely become official representatives of organizations with mass following, practically all of the ministers in this category do hold membership in several organizations whose main purpose it is to improve the lot of Negroes in some area of community life. They often serve on the boards of these organizations, in which capacity they become important in determining what issues the Negro leadership class will champion, and what techniques and strategies will be employed.

The community-centered. In New Orleans, as in most other cities, there are a few prominent Negro ministers who can always be found in the vanguard of the Negro's march toward full participation in community affairs. These ministers are generally well trained, articulate, and courageous. Their churches are made available for mass meetings, forums, and other types of programs designed to acquaint the Negro masses with major social issues affecting them.

These pastors are often heads of secular organizations the major purpose of which is to accomplish social goals sought by Negro people. Some have become outstanding in voter-registration drives and fund-raising for civic organizations, and as organizers of protest movements. Occasionally some have campaigned vigorously for political candidates, and have themselves run for public office.

When Negroes get opportunities to have representation on interracial committees and boards, their representatives are often chosen from among the community-centered pastors. In this capacity these pastors are able to represent the Negro community as common participants with white leaders in the solution of such problems as health and welfare. Some serve as advisors to white groups where certain problems directly affecting Negroes are concerned.

Community-centered Negro pastors have traditionally received recognition from white men of power. White authorities usually respect the influence they have with their Negro followers. Occasionally they are appointed, officially or unofficially, to serve as liaison persons between them and intraracial Negro leaders. In that role they are privileged to negotiate with white authorities for some recognition or right sought by special-interest groups in the Negro community.

As we shall have occasion to point out again and again in the following pages, community-centered pastors continue to make valuable contributions to the Negro's struggle to achieve equal rights in all aspects of the total society. One of the most outstanding of the community-centered ministers in our sample defined the role of the minister as that of "giving responsible leadership." He contended that ministers

cannot ignore violence toward any man, nor injustice toward any people, nor at any time; especially can we least afford it in a free and democratic society whose basic guarantees are toward the enhancement of life and of the person. Therefore, we are dedicated to the winning of freedom.

LAW

It may be said that Negro lawyers in New Orleans are young. Almost all of them graduated from law schools and entered practice during the past ten years. Thus, only a few of the twenty Negro lawyers may be classified as top leaders. Yet all of them, because of their professional positions, do perform significant leadership functions. These functions may be summarized under four general categories. Lawyers who may be classified in the first two categories we designate as intraracial leaders, and those who can best be placed in the last two categories we designate as interracial leaders.[2]

The legal advisors. Negro attorneys falling within this classification feel that their primary role in the achievement of first-class citizenship for Negroes can best be fulfilled by providing legal advice and counsel to organizations and groups in the community the goals of which include racial uplift. They frequently lend direction and guidance to groups in the formulation of such

[2] Materials summarized in this discussion were taken from Barbara M. Guillory, *The Career Patterns of Negro Lawyers in New Orleans*, an unpublished Master's Thesis, Louisiana State University, January, 1960. (This thesis was written under the auspices of the Ford Foundation.)

by-laws and constitutions as are necessary for these organizations to qualify for charters, while at the same time being flexible enough to achieve civil rights goals. They also perform a necessary advisory function when uplift organizations set about to devise programs of legal redress. As we shall see, during the period when powerful legislative forces were attempting to outlaw or seriously handicap certain Negro organizations (particularly the NAACP), Negro lawyers were constant advisors to ad interim organizations designed to carry on their several programs. These lawyers are readily available to advise Negro organizations on what they may or may not legally do in the area of civil rights.

The joiners. A number of the Negro lawyers may be classified as joiners. That is, they join and participate in groups for several reasons. One is that this is a means whereby they become known to potential clients. Another is that they get an opportunity to develop certain leadership potentials that they would not otherwise develop by participating in the activities of various social and uplift groups. This is particularly true because the professional participation of Negro lawyers in New Orleans is largely restricted to the Martinet Society.[3] They have no opportunity to exercise leadership in inter-racial legal associations, or in the many all-white civic organizations in which white attorneys may develop their leadership ability.

Whatever may be the personal reasons why some lawyers are inveterate joiners, one thing is definite: these lawyers are drawn into the membership of some groups because a type of leadership vacuum exists in what would otherwise be effective community organizations. The younger lawyers, therefore, become an active part of these groups, because their training and personalities naturally equip them for the kind of leadership some of these organizations need to be effective.

Some Negro attorneys, then, are affiliated with several intraracial social and uplift organizations. Generally, they immediately become members of the board of directors or are elected to some official position from which they might aspire to become interracial leaders.

Perhaps the most significant contribution this type of lawyer makes to racial uplift is that of educating the Negro masses about the legal techniques and strategies that may be employed in getting things done within the framework of law and government.

The political participants. Some of the New Orleans Negro lawyers have been involved in one way or another with politics. A few of them are heads of political organizations, and become interracial leaders through their con-

---

[3] The Martinet Society was named for Louis A. Martinet, a native of New Orleans and the first graduate of distinction from the Straight University Law School in 1876. Mr. Martinet distinguished himself as a physician, lawyer, publisher, and leader. It was he who initiated the legal attack on Jim Crow laws in Louisiana, when he brought suit for the desegregation of public transportation. The legal subject of this suit is the celebrated *Plessy* vs. *Ferguson* case. The decision in this case led to the famous "separate but equal" doctrine of 1896.

tacts with white "men of power" in the broader New Orleans community. They have been instrumental in helping to elect white candidates to office.

Perhaps, however, their most significant leadership role is that of running for public office themselves. As will be discussed in a later chapter, Negro political candidates have made several significant contributions in the field of race relations. Among the most important are the following:

(1) Through running for public office Negro attorneys have been able to get a considerable number of Negroes registered to vote.

(2) Dissemination of political knowledge to the Negro community has been another of their contributions. This has been one of the most successful means by which knowledge about the whole political process and the responsibility of citizenship has been presented to the Negro masses.

(3) Negro lawyers who have run for public office have, in a sense, become symbols of Negro achievement. They have done much to establish the fact that there are Negroes who are willing and qualified to fill responsible public positions. Further, they have provided stimulating competition for white political candidates, who have frequently adopted important planks of the Negro candidate's platform. These lawyers have often succeeded in forcing white political candidates to take some definite stand on important racial issues which may otherwise have been ignored.

The civil righters. The major leadership responsibility of this group is, perhaps, in the realm of constitutional law. That is, because of specialized legal knowledge, some have been most effective in protecting the civil rights of Negroes through litigation. The outstanding Negro lawyer in the city summarized his leadership role in this way: The legal process is "slow but sure." He is convinced that the Constitution of the United States and federal laws, as they now exist, provide ample opportunities for Negroes to achieve first-class citizenship. Therefore, he considers the education and encouragement of Negroes in the pursuit of their rights within the framework of our existing legal system as his primary community leadership role.

A few of the lawyers in this category have become widely recognized interracial leaders. Their skill in handling federal cases is highly respected by the legal profession and by the courts. The dean of Negro lawyers in New Orleans, who is the legal representative of the NAACP in the state, has an enviable record of successes before the federal judiciary, because of which he is the official and unofficial spokesman on the civil rights of Negroes. He is frequently called upon to speak before Negro audiences when technical points of civil rights are under consideration. In addition, white groups and individuals seek his opinion on race relations issues. He is, consequently, one of the most respected interpreters of the philosophy of race relations as it may be applied to the Negroes' goal of equal citizenship.

It must be kept in mind that at certain points these leadership categories may overlap. Therefore, a number of Negro attorneys may participate to some extent in all areas outlined above, but heuristically it may be assumed that their major or primary activity is in one category.

LABOR

Almost all the recognized community leaders who are recruited from the ranks of labor[4] are labor-union officials. Rarely will a laborer who is not a union official gain standing as an accepted member of the Negro leadership class. The very few who do are usually representatives of some influential lodge, political faction, or women's auxiliary. Therefore, in this analysis, we shall restrict our attention to labor-union officials.

Generally, Negro labor leaders are the most militant and vocal of the better-trained union members. Most were chosen as representatives precisely because they possessed these qualities. A labor leader explained his status in a powerful local in this way: "The men—that is, the rank-and-file Negro members—had known me for a long time as a Negro fighter. When the time came to elect an official, they got together and nominated me because they had confidence that I would fight for their rights. White members in the union went along with me also because they, too, respect a fighter." In a real sense, then, Negro labor officials are selected on the basis of their racial militancy, and some could even be classified as race men.

Basically, all labor officials are leaders in the sense in which the leader is defined in this study. They differ from professional leaders in one major respect: professional leaders lead because that is their main job. Labor officials lead because leadership is their job also, yet theirs is a more special-ized, narrow, self-interested role. Most are primarily interested in the welfare of labor (actually their specific union), not in community betterment or racial uplift. A surprisingly small proportion of Negro labor officials identify with any civil rights organizations or programs that are not essentially labor-union-centered. Consequently, unlike professional leaders, all of whom are recognized as belonging to the Negro leadership class, only eight or ten labor officials in New Orleans are accorded that status.

The labor segment of the Negro leadership class may be divided into three interrelated types:

(1) *Advocates of strong financial support to community agencies.* In this role some labor leaders have made valuable contributions to community betterment. As one outstanding labor leader put it, "Money is with the masses and when the Negro community arrives at some definite plan of action which the masses of Negroes feel to be good and honest, we [labor leaders] can get them to support it." He regarded this as one of the major community functions that labor leaders can perform.

It is largely due to this group of community-conscious leaders that labor unions in New Orleans have given financial support to hospitals, the United Fund, voter-registration drives and, occasionally, to Negro uplift organiza-tions.

(2) *Representatives on important interracial boards and committees.* Labor leaders

---

[4] The term "labor" as used here is intended to include all skilled, semiskilled, and un-skilled workers.

occasionally accept membership on boards of directors or committees concerned with wide community-betterment programs or racial uplift.[5] In this capacity they participate in decision-making on a high level and function as members of the "power-structure." It is true, of course, that their influence is far outweighed by that of powerful whites; nevertheless, their thinking is included in the final decisions of these groups. Whether it is their central desire or not, as Negroes in predominantly white power groups, they become spokesmen for the Negro cause. This fact was voiced by a labor leader who said, "Certainly, I have worked with predominantly white groups. I was invited as a representative of labor, but I knew, and they were also aware that I knew, that I was really invited to represent the Negroes." This labor man was describing a situation in which he had been invited to represent his labor union at a meeting of high-ranking business and labor men. He noticed that a white union colleague was also present. Whenever questions concerning the union, as such, were raised they were directed to his white colleague. Whenever questions concerning the Negro community arose they were directed to him. "This made me know," he said, "that being a Negro was much more important than being a labor leader. In fact, they did not see me as a labor man at all, only as a Negro."

(3) *Political participants.* Labor-union leaders play a significant political role in New Orleans. The major unions have all made it a practice to participate in political campaigns. Actually, besides attorneys, labor leaders are the most politically conscious group in the Negro community. At least four of the major Negro political factions are headed by labor leaders, and the others are subject to strong labor influence.

Although these leaders, as a group, have an active interest in politics, some have observed that their interest is largely a result of their concern for the welfare of labor, rather than civil rights. As a result, though they appeal for broad community support, Negroes outside of labor seldom regard them as their representatives. Perhaps the best illustration of where labor leaders' interest lies was a statement made by an influential Negro labor leader at a mass political rally in 1952, when Louisiana was on the verge of giving its electoral votes to the Republican party for the first time since the Civil War. Many Negro leaders were actively supporting Eisenhower, the Republican candidate, because they felt that the civil rights position of the Republican party was sounder than that of the Democratic party. This labor leader emphasized one basic political principle that he felt labor must follow: "As labor people, we must put the welfare of labor above any other single consideration. Even if the Republican party attempts to do more on civil rights than the Democratic party, we must vote Democratic because that party has the better labor plank."

[5] A union official stated the policy of his union regarding participation in community organizations as follows: "Ours is a policy of infiltration. We want each of our leaders to be active in at least one respected community organization. This is our most important public relations effort."

In their role as political leaders, labor men have served at least three important community needs: They have helped to educate the Negro population on political facts and techniques. They have done much to increase the number of registered voters in the Negro community. They have improved communication between white and Negro leaders through their control of bloc votes that political candidates have had to respect.

BUSINESS

Successful Negro businessmen, like their counterparts in American society generally, are ascribed high social status in the Negro community. Almost all of the more well-to-do among them may be described as upper-class. They own well-appointed homes in desirable Negro neighborhoods, travel extensively, send their children to the "better" schools, hold membership in exclusive clubs, and receive respect from white businessmen. Their styles of life, associations, and prestige become the goals toward which upwardly mobile individuals and families strive.

There are several logical reasons why the Negro community would normally confer high social status upon Negro businessmen. Among them we may suggest the following:

(1) Negroes have always constituted a disproportionately large segment of the economically depressed element in our society. Many social analysts would attribute most of the injustice, discrimination, and low esteem accorded Negroes in American society to their adverse economic condition. The truth is, most of the Negro and white leaders in New Orleans tend to agree that the generally low economic status of Negroes is the primary reason why Negroes are relegated to the bottom rung of the social ladder in our society.

Indeed, some of the outstanding Negro leaders over the years have concentrated on trying to raise the economic status of Negroes as a prerequisite to equal citizenship status. Consequently, the successful Negro businessman has often been pictured as an ideal toward which the Negro race must strive. Some have even advocated that they should become the focal points around which a stable, progressive "Black Economy" should evolve in which Negroes would patronize only Negro businessmen and Negro professionals.

(2) Two or three of the larger Negro business enterprises in New Orleans employ as many as two hundred full- and part-time people. (These are insurance companies). Most of the white-collar positions held by Negroes are provided by Negro businesses. Only a handful of Negro white-collar workers are employed in white business enterprises. Even these are employed in white enterprises only because thay have a Negro clientele on which they depend for a considerable volume of their business.

(3) Negro businessmen often contribute generously to Negro institutions and agencies. This provides them an opportunity to be influential, to some

extent at least, in their policies and programs. Some of their gifts are made to educational institutions with high social status. An identification with these institutions automatically tends to enhance their own social status.

(4) The more successful Negro businessmen usually represent the most stable and respected element in the Negro community. Some of them are offspring of old, well-known New Orleans families who have made significant contributions to Negro education, business, and religious life. They would therefore be respected even if they were not economically well off.

Because the Negro community tends to confer high social status upon successful Negro businessmen, it might appear superficially that practically all of them belong to the Negro leadership class. In actual fact, most are not functional leaders. Upon examination at least three different distinct types of businessmen are revealed insofar as leadership is concerned:

Celebrities. In this category we classify those prominent Negro businessmen who are sought after by individuals and organizations in the Negro community. The celebrities might be described as an important legitimitizing group. That is, socially mobile individuals aspire to be invited to their homes or accepted as members of organizations in which these elite are predominant. Similarly, Negro civic, social, and welfare organizations look up to these more affluent Negroes because they rely heavily upon them for economic support and approval. Prominent Negro businessmen are, therefore, showered with approbation.

It is surprising to find that men in this category seldom identify publicly with any organized effort, movement, or plan to advance the status of Negroes in any area of community life. Even efforts that may at first glance appear to be aimed at raising the status of Negroes or bringing about effective communication between Negroes and whites generally turn out to result from enlightened self-interest or to be by-products of efforts to enhance their own economic or social status.

The basic racial attitude shared by some successful Negro businessmen, or upper-class Negroes in general, was summarized by Myrdal in this way:

> There are many upper class Negroes who try to escape from race and caste. They have arranged a little isolated world for themselves and want to hear as little as possible about their being Negro or the existence of a Negro problem. . . . They try to share the conservative political opinions of the whites of similar class status; they often over-do this considerably.[6]

It is interesting to note that when white men of power were asked to name the three that they considered to be the most outstanding Negro leaders, they usually named at least one or more Negro business celebrities. This, despite the fact that such persons had never been actively associated with the Negro's goal of first-class citizenship.

[6] Gunnar Myrdal, *An American Dilemma* (New York: Harper & Row, 1944), p. 764.

Intraracial leaders. As mentioned before, successful Negro businessmen are highly valued members of Negro organizations. When possible, these organizations literally thrust these people into positions of leadership. Very often they are acclaimed as leaders in the organizations and are elected to offices that are keenly competed for by the rank and file members.

As leaders of important Negro organizations, some businessmen are able to accomplish a good deal toward racial uplift. Their organizations have provided scholarships, sponsored cultural exhibits, and provided the community with eminent speakers and lecturers.

Some of these intraracial leaders behave as though there is no logical connection between the Negro and white communities. At best, they tend to imitate social and economic patterns characteristic of the white middle class. This is perhaps best illustrated by the programs and pronouncements of fraternities, sororities, and social clubs in which they hold important positions.

Interracial leaders. Negro businessmen in this category are potentially the most effective interracial leaders in the Negro community because, as we mentioned before, they tend to be more acceptable to white men of power than are some of the more active interracial leaders. This is to be expected, because most of the decision-makers in the white community are also businessmen. Seen from this point of view, it is not easy to understand why so few Negro businessmen may be classified as interracial leaders. Actually, one of the most frequent criticisms made against Negro businessmen from all segments of the Negro community is that, by and large, they appear to have little interest in race relations. One Negro leader explained this apparent lack of interest in race relations in this way: "They already pass for white and live like white people." He meant by this that they would have little to gain by identifying with the issues traditionally championed by the Negro leadership class.

Despite the fact that proportionately Negro businessmen are under-represented among interracial leaders, those few who are so engaged have made significant contributions. The area of race relations in which they have been most effective is that of negotiation. Since they have both social status and economic security, white men of power seem to respect their opinions and suggestions more than they do the opinions of those of lesser social stature. Thus, one Negro leader observed that "Negro leadership will never be as effective as it might until leaders themselves are economically independent." He added, "The greatest weakness of the Negro leaders in New Orleans is this: They are hungry."

Occasionally, leaders in this category are invited to sit with interracial committees, predominantly white, where the Negro community is an important factor in the success of some project. Important in this connection are United Fund Drives, welfare boards, and certain citizens committees. Also, from time to time powerful white authorities will call upon these businessmen for advice in racial matters.

THE INTELLIGENTSIA

The intelligentsia constitutes a large and influential segment of the Negro leadership class. Individuals who might be subsumed under this category represent several business and professional groups. Nevertheless, for our purpose the intelligentsia will be regarded as composed of professionals whose main occupation it is to impart specialized, technical knowledge. Included in this discussion are the public-school teachers and college teachers.

Public-school teachers. Negro public-school teachers make up the largest professional group in the Negro community. In 1961, there were 1,600 Negro public-school teachers in New Orleans. Consequently, in sheer numbers they are potentially the most powerful Negro professional group. They certainly represent the bulk of the academic elite from which the vast majority of Negro leaders come.

All of the teachers are college-trained, and many of them hold advanced degrees from some of the most highly ranked universities in the nation. A considerable number of them have had wide interracial contacts on a basis of equality as a result of their academic and professional pursuits. Therefore, insofar as training and experience are concerned, public-school teachers on the whole approximate the highest academic and professional standards.

Coming in contact as they do in their daily occupation with all segments of the Negro population, teachers doubtless have great influence in the changing status of Negroes. Since the vast majority of Negro children come from socially and economically deprived homes—unlike their white counterparts, who represent a wide range of economic statuses—in most instances their teachers constitute the only estimable symbol of success that they know personally.

Teachers' salaries, compared with those of other professional groups, are deplorably low. Some laboring groups can boast of higher annual incomes. Yet, despite very modest incomes, teachers enjoy considerable economic security. Their security stems primarily from the fact that they are not subject to fluctuating salaries, as are laborers who might have larger incomes. Consequently, teachers are regarded as good economic risks. Their small, but stable, salaries enable them to enter into long-term contracts. Thus, the style of life of many of them is typically middle class, and similar to that of much higher-salaried business and professional persons from among whom Negro top leadership is normally recruited.

Another characteristic of Negro public-school teachers in New Orleans is that nearly all of them are natives. Since, as we have already pointed out, New Orleans Negroes manifest strong proclivities to follow native sons, we would expect public-school teachers to hold most of the leadership positions in the Negro community. After all, they are numerically strong, well trained, and more or less economically secure, and many have had successful experiences on a basis of equality in race relations. Yet we find that this assumption is not valid. In actual fact, the Negro leadership class has only a few representatives from among public-school teachers.

There may be several logical explanations of why Negro teachers, as the largest professional group, have played such a relatively weak role in the leadership needs of New Orleans. We may consider here three of the most salient.

(1) The teaching profession among Negroes is made up predominantly of women. As pointed out earlier, in spite of the fact that women tend to be socially and culturally dominant in Negro society, only a handful of them evince any active interest in racial uplift. Therefore, whatever factors might be involved in the lack of community interest on the part of Negro women generally would also be operative in this connection and would function to limit the number of teachers who play vital leadership roles.

(2) Negro public-school teachers are economically independent of the Negro community. Unlike typical business and independent professional persons, who must depend entirely upon the economic resources of the Negro community for their livelihood, Negro teachers do not have to depend upon the sponsorship, patronage, or even approval of Negroes for their economic well-being. They are hired by white boards of education, and supervised by white officials. There is, therefore, no necessity for them to cater to the Negro masses, and this is no doubt an important reason why so few trouble to concern themselves actively with community or racial problems.

(3) Closely related to the Negro public-school teachers' lack of dependence upon Negroes is their almost complete economic and professional dependence upon white men of power. Whether a teacher is hired, promoted, or fired; whether a Negro official's program is put into effect, modified, or rejected, depends ultimately upon white boards or officials.

We do not intend to imply that Negroes in positions of authority in the public-school system have no influence or power at all. Some do. What we do mean is that final decisions regarding teachers' welfare and academic programs are made by top officials, and there are no Negro top officials in the public-school system in New Orleans.

Depending as they do upon white officials, public-school teachers have been greatly restricted in their leadership role. As will be considered in another connection, several laws passed by the Louisiana State Legislature, as well as rules and regulations adopted by state and local school boards in recent years, have made it almost impossible for Negro teachers to identify with racial uplift organizations, or even to participate actively in the civil rights movement. This is definitely an important reason why some teachers have remained inactive and silent during heated controversies over civil rights.

Despite widespread lethargy and fear on the part of educators, some have managed to establish themselves as effective community leaders. The extent and nature of their participation have, of course, varied. A few outstanding Negro educators in New Orleans have been honored by both Negro and white people. Perhaps the best indication of this dual honor is the fact that several public schools in New Orleans have been named for them.

The quiet ones. A small number of well-established Negro public-school teachers in New Orleans have chosen to work quietly, without publicity or approbation, for the academic and cultural advancement of Negroes. Some have also played key roles in far-reaching decisions concerning civil rights. Negro leaders of this type rely primarily upon the technique of negotiation. One prominent Negro educator put it this way: "I am convinced that more can be accomplished by an extra-careful, intelligent plan presented to top people, than can ever be accomplished by mass meetings and demonstrations."

Some of the quiet ones are shrewd diplomats. They have developed the art of exerting constant pressure upon white men of power in a subtle, almost imperceptible manner in their role as race relations leaders. They are often successful in getting improved school facilities, greater privileges in the development of academic programs, and better working conditions for teachers.

Not only do they negotiate with white authorities, but some have had notable success as intraracial leaders. They prefer to work with small, selected groups of Negroes rather than with the public. They are, generally, skilled as leaders in small conferences, workshops, and special committees. The most successful seem to have an uncommon sense of timing. They seldom present a proposal or plan that is rejected. Thus, one such leader, in an attempt to account for his success in getting others to cooperate with him, stated: "I never go off halfcocked. I always try to wait for the psychologically propitious moment, then I present my ideas."

The anonymous ones. Teachers who might be included in this category are those who actively participate in Negro uplift, but whose identities are not publicly known. As individuals they become merged in mass race relations efforts. Unlike the quiet ones, whose leadership is largely confined to the achievement of the academic and cultural advancement of Negroes, the anonymous ones are primarily active in community affairs.

Public-school teachers frequently join Negro organizations dedicated to community betterment. Occasionally, they might hold office or serve as a director, so long as these organizations do not participate in direct, public protest against the biracial system. When this is done, such organizations are denounced by white officials. As a result, most teachers in these organizations will simply withdraw their membership and support. The anonymous ones remain staunch supporters of these organizations, but no official or public record is kept of their participation.

During crises in race relations in New Orleans a few school teachers continued to contribute financially to such organizations as the NAACP, the Urban League, the CORE, and the Consumers' League, but they managed to do this in such a way that they could not be personally linked with these organizations. For example, one social club composed primarily of public-school teachers set aside the major portion of its annual budget for the support of uplift organizations. The money was given to a nonteaching member, who made the contributions as though they were his own. Consequently, the teachers' contributions could not be singularly identified.

The anonymous ones often make significant contributions to uplift by formulating plans that would lead to either equality or desegregation. These plans have on occasion been presented in secret sessions where the sponsors negotiated with lawyers, liberal white officials, and other prominent Negro leaders. Some of these plans eventuated in successfully changing the status of Negroes in certain areas of community life, yet the names of the actual social engineers among the educators were never made public.

The militant ones. Throughout the years there have been a small number of Negro teachers who have defied both state and local segregationist school officials by participating in the Negro's struggle for first-class citizenship. Most have engaged actively in bringing about equality within the profession itself. Occasionally, however, some individuals among them have espoused the cause of raising the status of Negroes in other areas of community life by becoming outspoken foes of segregation and discrimination per se. They seize opportunities to protest racial injustices whenever possible. Their protest is likely to be voiced in conferences with white school officials, in meetings with their colleagues, in formal meetings of Negro leaders, and even in mass meetings whenever possible. They also apply pressure in formal meetings of local, state, and national educational associations in order to get these associations to go on record as endorsing some liberal racial recommendation, resolution, or program.

Furthermore, they are always in the forefront of the educator's fight for professional advancement and security. They are among those who advocate fact-finding or research designed to uncover unfair professional practices or racial discrimination as it might exist in the school system.

Since all Negro leaders must identify, at least to some extent, with the Negro cause, the militant teacher frequently uses race patriotism as a potent strategy in getting things done. He knows, first of all, that no leader of a given Negro educational group can afford to go on record as opposing efforts to obtain racial equality. Therefore, he can always ask for a show of hands when liberal measures are being voted upon or when liberal action is proposed. In such situations, elected officials of the organization must keep in mind that the rank and file member can hardly support a candidate who is believed to be an Uncle Tom.[7] Liberal proposals by the militant ones for action or resolutions designed to improve the status of Negroes are seldom, if ever, voted down, but they do often die by default, for lack of sufficient support from a less-militant membership.

In addition to the pressure these teachers exert upon their professional

[7] Negroes who deliberately cooperate with white segregationists in the perpetuation of racial inequalities are referred to as "Uncle Toms."

organizations, they often also bring pressure to bear upon members of civic and social groups in which they hold membership. One characteristic way of forcing their organizations to take positive action on a controversial issue is to appoint a committee headed by a well-known militant. At a definite time this committee will be asked to report. If it recommends that a positive stand be endorsed, or that some action be taken calculated to benefit Negroes, the majority is likely to go along with the proposal even if it is not altogether acceptable.

College teachers. The number of Negro college teachers in New Orleans has always, of course, been small compared with the number of public-school teachers. In 1940, there were fewer than one hundred, and in 1962 there were still only about one hundred and fifty.

Unlike public-school teachers, who are largely native sons, Negro college teachers are recruited without respect to geographic origin. Since all are specialists, they do not have as much freedom of choice regarding residence as do most other professionals. Therefore, in a biracial community such as New Orleans, a Negro specialist in any given academic subject is most likely to find only one or two suitable positions available to him. If for any reason he does not find satisfaction in his position he has little choice but to leave the city in order to continue in his professional specialty. Consequently, one of the most significant social characteristics of Negro college teachers is the fact that they are *potentially* mobile.

In a sense, then, Negro college teachers are sociologically "strangers." Insofar as their position in the social system is concerned, they are similar to the trader as analyzed by Georg Simmel. Accordingly,

> The stranger is thus being discussed here, not in the sense often touched upon in the past, as the wanderer who comes today and goes tomorrow, but rather as the person who comes today and stays tomorrow. He is, so to speak, the *potential* wanderer: although he has not quite moved on, he has not quite overcome the freedom of coming and going. He is fixed within a particular spatial group, or within a group whose boundaries are similar to spatial boundaries. But his position in this group is determined, essentially, by the fact that he has not belonged to it from the beginning, that he imports qualities into it, which do not and cannot stem from the group itself.[8]

Despite the itinerant tendencies[9] or potential mobility of college teachers in general, and Negro college teachers in particular, they are, as a group, accorded high social status. In fact, in the view of Myrdal and other trained observers of the Negro class structure, "practically all Negro college teachers are upper class."[10]

[8] Georg Simmel, *Sociology,* translated and edited by Kurt H. Wolff (Glencoe, Ill.: The Free Press, 1950), pp. 401.

[9] Daniel C. Thompson, "Teachers in Negro Colleges" (Unpublished Dissertation, Columbia University, 1955), pp. 85-91.

[10] Myrdal, *op. cit.,* p. 694.

Reinforcing the high status of Negro college teachers is the prestige accorded college teachers in the nation at large. A well-known study of occupations found that in American society generally college teachers "rank seventh in a rating of prestige of ninety occupations, topped only by the United States Supreme Court Justices, physicians, state governors, members of the President's cabinet, members in the United States Foreign Service, and mayors of large cities."[11] It is only logical, then, that Negro college teachers enjoy high social esteem in the Negro community, since their only serious competitors for social status are the relatively few Negro physicians and successful businessmen. With the exception of physicians, and very recently, members of the Foreign Service, Negroes are not represented in the top-ranking occupations.

As "strangers," with firmly established prestige, Negro college teachers are in a position to render a singular leadership service. They can bring to local issues an objectivity that would be intolerable coming from native sons. Only a few Negro college teachers have taken advantage of their superior learning, prestige, and social immunities by becoming leaders in community affairs. In terms of active community concern we may classify college teachers into three distinct groups.

The indifferent ones. The large majority of college teachers are apparently indifferent to community betterment or racial uplift. They live, as it were, on an island, apart from the problems and issues that are of such great moment to the Negro masses in particular, and the cause of democracy in general.

Some are college-centered. That is, their time is spent almost entirely in the venerable, but narrow, confines of the social world of their particular college. Seldom do they have sustained social or even academic contacts with individuals or groups who are not connected in one way or another with the college in which they teach. Others are profession-oriented. These often develop wide professional contacts that transcend race and region. Therefore, it is not at all uncommon to find a teacher who is nationally respected as a scholar, but virtually unknown in the community where he lives. A few Negro college teachers are avowedly class-conscious. They deprecate the masses, who do not measure up to their particular standards of learning, morality, and success. Their personal friends are scrupulously chosen from among upper-class families or individuals. They attend only the higher status churches, hold membership in exclusive clubs, and only participate in academically or culturally enriching public meetings. They become well-known members of upper-class "society," but staunchly remain aloof from the masses and their problems.

The indifferent ones tend to approach the problem of race relations in the same lofty, objective, academic manner in which they do any other local, national, or international issue with which they have some familiarity. The

<hr />

[11] The President's Commision on Higher Education, *Higher Education for American Democracy,* Vol. IV (U. S. Government Printing Office, 1957), p. 28.

Kennedy-Nixon presidential campaign, for example, came to a climax simultaneously with the climax in the public-school desegregation crisis in New Orleans. During these trying days Negroes were victims of the bitterest vilification by white supremacists, and violence and threats of violence constituted a large proportion of the daily news. Negro leaders were intensely interested in the issue of civil rights, which had been a major plank in both the Democratic and Republican platforms. During this period a Negro academician confided to a few of his friends that he was voting Republican because "Nixon's fiscal policy is sounder than Kennedy's. In my opinion this is the basic issue in this campaign."

The experts. The large number of Negro civic, business, religious, social, professional, and labor groups in New Orleans make relentless demands for the expert services of college teachers, a few of whom accede regularly to such demands. They conduct forums, give analyses of social issues, and serve as consultants under the sponsorship of these groups, thus often rendering necessary community services. They do, in fact, participate directly in the preparation, stimulation, and motivation of community leaders.

The experts themselves will seldom assume a community leadership role. One academician enunciated a cardinal principle adhered to by the experts when he said:

> It is my firm belief that the college teacher has a definite role to play in community leadership. His, however, is a specialized, highly technical role. His main task, I would say his only responsibility, is to provide active community leaders and groups dedicated to community betterment with whatever disciplined insight and knowledge he might have regarding the nature and solution of specific problems. He must never himself engage in the performance of tasks that the nonexpert may do as well or better than he.

Community leaders. From time to time Negro college teachers assume community leadership responsibilities. As a rule they are elevated, so to speak, from the ranks of the experts. Frequently they find themselves in leadership positions more or less by default. That is, they become the only logical, reliable, available persons to execute some plan or program that they themselves have devised. Rarely do they accept the leadership of a group or participate in a movement simply to execute traditional, established, formal programs. By and large, those who become established community leaders may be described as innovators. They do, indeed, import qualities into the Negro's struggle for equality "which do not and cannot stem from the [local] group itself," in almost the same sense that Simmel's sociological form—the "stranger"—has done throughout history.[12]

Both the expert and the community leader among Negro college teachers have served as effective interracial leaders. It is from among them that liberal white civic and professional organizations often seek Negroes to rep-

[12] *Ibid.*

resent the Negro community. They serve on committees composed predominantly of white persons, share panels with white experts, and are occasionally asked to address white groups. In these capacities they become, in actual fact, spokesmen for their people.

It is not easy to ascertain even approximately the extent to which Negro college teachers have contributed to the changing status of Negroes in New Orleans. Generally their influence is subtle, indirect, tangential. Perhaps their most valuable contribution is that they characteristically insist that local racial problems "should be seen," as one professor put it, "in the light of mankind's perennial struggle for life, freedom, and self-fulfillment." In this way local racial problems are given historical dimension. Thus the solution to these problems may stem from the philosophies, strategies, and techniques that have proven fruitful in mankind's long march toward individual dignity and equality of citizenship. As we shall see later, this is essentially the approach that distinguishes the "new" Negro leadership from the "old." The old Negro leadership was essentially expedient-oriented, while the new is essentially principle-oriented.

Professional leaders

Another significant element of the Negro leadership class in New Orleans is composed of a small group of top officials of Negro uplift organizations, particularly the NAACP and the Urban League, journalists, public relations officers, and radio news commentators. These share at least one basic responsibility with the intelligentsia. They are expected to impart information. However, unlike teachers, to whom education or enlightenment is the chief end in itself, professional leaders impart knowledge in order to achieve some concrete, specific social goal. As we shall see, these goals are clearly enunciated in the policy statements of the organizations they represent.

The Negro radio news commentators, though adhering tacitly to virtually the same set of racial uplift principles as do the others, cannot, of course, pursue these ends with as much directness and vigor. They are more restricted in their expression because all of the radio stations are owned and managed by white businessmen, whose interest in the Negro community is primarily financial.

One of the main things that sets this group apart from intellectuals is this: *Leadership is their main job.* All the others who perform leadership functions must do so in addition to their full-time occupational commitments.

These professional leaders render four important, even indispensable, community services: fact-finding, protest, the creation of solidarity, and the formation of public opinion.

Fact-finding. A central service of professional leaders is that of gathering facts. The Urban League, for example, has a long record in connection with vital community surveys. In New Orleans, as in other cities with Urban

League chapters, this organization has gathered facts concerning welfare which often form the basis for intelligent social amelioration.

The NAACP, too, has always maintained a research staff. Though the New Orleans Chapter does not have its own research staff, it does base its program upon facts gathered by the national organization and share in the gathering of facts for the national organization. The NAACP research staff has been able to uncover pertinent facts concerning the many civil rights cases it has handled. Perhaps the best testimony regarding the competence of this staff is the phenomenal proportion of cases NAACP lawyers have won in federal courts.

Since the local white newspapers report only a minimum of facts concerning the Negro's place in community life, and since very little space is given to issues of vital importance to the segregated Negro community, the Negro masses must turn to the local Negro paper for information and guidance in community affairs. The fact is, the local white daily newspapers are obviously dedicated to the defense of the biracial status quo. Over the years, therefore, Negro publications in New Orleans, especially the *Louisiana Weekly*, have done a gigantic job of collecting and interpreting information on vital issues affecting Negroes and the Negro community. There is some feeling among Negro leaders, however, that this information reaches very few white men of power.

Radio news commentators are in some respects similar to journalists. They, too, gather facts of concern to Negro people that otherwise would be ignored. Yet they have made a distinct additional contribution in the realm of education by bringing before the radio public outstanding Negro talent and leaders, and scholarly discussions of issues of interest to Negroes.

Protest. One of the characteristic roles of professional leaders is that of protest. Both the Negro community and the white power structure expect protest from professional leaders. When they do not protest the inequities Negroes experience, Negro intraracial leaders accuse them of being indifferent or Uncle Toms, and some white authorities interpret their silence as meaning that Negroes are satisfied with segregation and discrimination.

At this point a generalization is in order: *White authorities do not effect positive changes in the status of Negroes in any area of community life until professional Negro leaders have voiced long, loud, concerted protest.*

Solidarity. A third function performed by professional leaders is the creation of solidarity and unity in the Negro community. This has been occasioned by times of crisis. This need for unity was succinctly voiced by the executive secretary of the New Orleans Urban League. He said, "We are experiencing a social revolution. In this revolution all segments of the Negro community must participate. There must be protest meetings, sit-ins, mass demonstrations, letter-writing, and negotiation." He, and several other Negro leaders, are convinced that only through unity can the Negro community achieve first-class citizenship. On another level, the president of the Coordinating Council of Greater New Orleans urged unity among community leaders.

He said, "We, as community leaders, must achieve organization and unity among ourselves in order that we might attain a common goal—dignity and freedom."

Not only do professional leaders call for abstract unity, but from time to time they make concrete proposals about how actual unity might be achieved. Thus, they appeal to all segments in the Negro community to unite behind definite programs, such as registering voters, reducing juvenile delinquency, and supporting Negro institutions. These leaders use several techniques in attempts to bring about unity among Negroes. They not only appeal to race pride, but they make deliberate efforts to create it. Those working in communications do an especially noteworthy job in this connection. They emphasize Negro achievements in all fields, and when there are Negro "firsts" in certain jobs or positions they dramatize their success stories. Another technique used by professional leaders to create unity is to point out that all Negroes, regardless of social status, are subject to the same racial indignities. They document the fact that "segregation and discrimination are common to us all."

Public opinion. Professional leaders are among the main creators of a public opinion favorable to advancements in civil rights. This is done mostly through informal education. The leaders frequently make speeches, write editorials, publish reports, and conduct hearings of one kind or another in order to get pertinent information across to the public. A relentless campaign also is carried on "for the minds of men," as one leader stated it.

One of the major points reiterated by professional leaders is that segregation and discrimination, as practiced in American society, especially in the South, do "irreparable damage to the United States's internal strength and international prestige." This thesis is illustrated by examples from various facets of American life—business, politics or government, housing, education, and religion. As a matter of fact, some Negro leaders strongly believe, as voiced by one, that "if white Americans could ever be brought to see and understand the high cost of prejudice and racial discrimination, they would gladly join forces with Negroes and abolish them. Because of ignorance they have turned the struggle for democracy over to Negroes."

Professional leaders are frequently accepted as spokesmen for the Negro people. Their statements and interpretations regarding the status of Negroes and, in a broader sense, race relations, are given national (often international) prominence. Thus, in some measure, they have participated in the creation of a national and international public opinion that is increasingly unfavorable to racial segregation.

MEDICINE

Insofar as social status is concerned, physicians on the whole enjoy upper-class status within the Negro community of New Orleans. There are several reasons for this.

(1) As pointed out earlier, physicians rank second among occupations in the United States. In all societies physicians have been accorded high social status. This is due primarily to the fact that illness is an ubiquitous practical problem. Physicians are expected to be the chief guardians of the health of individuals who comprise a society. Their role is a functional prerequisite for the survival and continuity of society.

(2) They represent the highest average level of academic preparation of any professional group in the community. All have successfully completed rigorous academic and professional training. This training has provided them with highly specialized knowledge unavailable to ordinary citizens.

(3) They possess uncommon authority. No other citizens wield as much personal authority over the lives of others as do physicians. Dealing as they do with the extreme crises in life—birth, suffering, and death—they are associated with individuals and families during times when they are essentially helpless to make their own decisions, and are therefore willing, even anxious, to accept the authority of one who is alleged to be wiser and more skillful.

(4) Negro physicians are generally recruited from middle-class families. Thus, they inherit a certain amount of social respectability.

(5) There are few Negro physicians in New Orleans. Their services, consequently, are in very great demand from Negroes who do not want to submit to the embarrassing segregation practices usually attendant upon visits to the offices of white physicians. The Negro medical profession, furthermore, has been glamorized, so to speak, by Negro leaders as a means of encouraging young people to enter it.

(6) Negro physicians in New Orleans represent the highest income group in the Negro community. They have little competition from other high-income professionals and businessmen, as is the case in the white community.

Because Negro physicians occupy such high social status, practically all of them are potential community leaders. But in fact very few of them, over the years, have earned that distinction. We may divide Negro physicians into three distinct, though sometimes overlapping, categories:

Profession-oriented. A large proportion of the physicians among Negroes are concerned almost exclusively with being physicians. That is, they are so occupied with their very heavy, varied practices that they simply do not have time to involve themselves in any significant community endeavors. One such physician confessed that he did not even have time to keep abreast of basic social issues and problems.

Seldom do physicians in this category find time to attend forums, public meetings, or even meetings of top level professionals, where general community problems and issues are under discussion. Interviews with physicians have revealed an often superficial knowledge of the Negro's struggle for equal citizenship. Many of them even refuse to express personal opinions about trends and practices in race relations.

"Society"-oriented. Practically all of the Negro physicians in New Orleans

participate in setting social standards in Negro "society." Their style of life is usually much more similar to that of the white upper class than it is to that of the Negro middle class. They belong to high-status social clubs and fraternities, and exclusive cliques. These organizations, it should be noted, often make regular financial contributions to racial uplift organizations.

Community-oriented. Over the years an occasional physician has manifested deep concern in the progress toward Negro uplift. Occasionally some one of them epitomizes the highest quality of community leadership. As a rule, they have been respected by both white and Negro people. The high esteem enjoyed by these leaders has been due largely to their exceptional training and wealth, as well as their intelligent community concern.

Very seldom do physicians head uplift organizations or participate in public or mass protest meetings. Generally, they become skilled leaders in areas of high-level planning and negotiation. In these roles, they have made lasting contributions to the growth and development of Negro business, the local Negro hospital, and Negro religious and educational institutions. Occasionally a Negro physician has openly identified with protest and legal action designed to achieve equal rights for Negroes. Yet on the whole they may be said to be class-oriented, rather than mass-oriented. That is, the programs they sponsor, the issues they espouse, and the causes they champion, though if effected they would be beneficial to all segments of the Negro community, are actually designed to achieve professional or business goals of prime value to the Negro upper class. As a matter of fact, they have been virtually silent when problems relating primarily to the Negro masses are concerned. As strange as it may seem, they have seldom participated, for instance, in special efforts or movements designed to improve, directly or indirectly, health conditions in the Negro community.

Finally, most Negro leaders would like to see Negro physicians play a much more active role in the civil rights movement than they have in the past. One of the more active physician-leaders offered the following apology:

> It is true that Negro doctors owe far more to Negroes than they give. After all, just about all of our patients are underprivileged Negroes. Then, too, we are about the only occupational group the white supremacists can't touch. We have been needed badly during the recent school crisis, when teachers, themselves, were afraid to speak up for the children under their care. I know these things. But I, for one, am too busy to do very much about it. Other doctors are in the same boat.[14]

Finally, the leadership class in the Negro community is composed of individuals who actively espouse the Negro "uplift" ideology. Though the vast majority of those identified as leaders come from the middle class, all major socioeconomic segments are represented.

---

[14] Our observations regarding physicians were also found to be true for other Negro medical professionals in New Orleans.

From the discussion above, we may conclude that there are at least three outstanding characteristics of Negro leaders in New Orleans:

(1) In terms of recruitment, they are predominantly self-made, native sons.

(2) In terms of orientation, the large majority are mass-oriented, while a few of the more influential among them are class-oriented.

(3) In terms of central interest, most Negro leaders may be classified as *intraracial*, and a minority whose major concern is to improve the citizenship status of Negroes may be classified as *interracial*. It is this latter group that is of primary interest to us.

5

PATTERNS OF RACE RELATIONS LEADERSHIP

RACE RELATIONS CONSTITUTE an aspect of every social issue in New Orleans. The problem has for generations "disturbed the religious moralists, the political philosophers, the statesmen, the philanthropists, the social scientists, the politicians, the businessmen, and the plain citizens."[1] Practically every recognized leader, both white and Negro, is called upon sooner or later to declare his stand on some question involving the citizenship status of Negroes. The Negro problem is so central to the ethos of the culture that all community leaders are disposed to view all other social issues from the perspective of race. And what is even more fundamental, white "men of power" who would remain neutral in regard to the Negro problem find that almost all of their duties, responsibilities, and actions are enmeshed in it.

Community decisions in New Orleans usually have some serious implication for the citizenship status of Negroes. For example, a certain amount of tax funds will be set aside for a project such as the paving of steeets. Obviously, all streets that need paving cannot be included in the budget. What streets, then, will be selected? Experience tells us that unpaved streets in predominantly white neighborhoods are likely to be first on the priority list. Unpaved streets in Negro neighborhoods are likely to receive secondary consideration, or to be overlooked altogether. Thus, what on its face might appear to be a budget decision turns out to be a decision that reflects a basic philosophy of race relations.

We may say, then, that both Negro and white leaders in New Orleans are inescapably ensnared in this problem. "The white South," observed Myrdal, "is virtually obsessed by the Negro problem. It has allowed the Negro problem to rule its politics and its business, fetter its intelligence and human liberties, and hamper its progress in all directions."[2]

Because whites, in the biracial New Orleans social system, have a near monopoly of social power, it would be meaningless to discuss Negro leadership as though it were isolated from white influence. Actually, in any biracial sys-

[1] Gunnar Myrdal, *op. cit.*, p. 27.
[2] *Op. cit.*, p. 30.

tem composed of a relatively powerless minority and a powerful majority, the patterns of intergroup leadership are determined very largely by the majority group. This is so because the prime role of the leader is to get things done. Impotent leaders must depend upon the favors or concessions voluntarily granted by the powerful.

So it is in a biracial social system that certain *complementary patterns* of race relations leadership develop, wherein each social type of leader among white men of power will choose a complementary type of Negro leader with whom he is willing to negotiate. Consequently, the achievements of Negro leaders cannot be understood except within the total context of the social reality in which they operate.[3]

This chapter will deal with some of the most typical types of leaders who form the characteristic patterns of race relations leadership in New Orleans. A leader's type will be determined by three interrelated criteria: one, his conception of the Negro race and race relations; two, his attitudes toward race and race relations; and, three, his own behavior and actions in the field of race relations. On the basis of these three criteria, we may distinguish the following ideal types. Each type of white leader will be paired with the type of Negro leader with whom he normally has contact.[4]

Segregationist—Uncle Tom

As conceived here, a segregationist is one who expresses belief in the morality, legality, and workability of a biracial social system. He is essentially a reactionary, who dreams of a society in which there is complete separation of the races. He would reject all changes that might lead to social intercourse on a basis of equality between Negroes and whites. He would revert to a social situation akin to slavery in which all Negroes would be socially inferior to all whites. According to the best available evidence (political elections, legislative actions, administrative policies, referendums, polls, "letters to the editor," public and "private" statements, and the editorial policies of mass media) the majority of white people in New Orleans appear to be segregationists. We find that segregationists differ in terms of the rationales they give for their beliefs, attitudes, and actions in regard to race and race relations. Accordingly, there are three distinct, though overlapping, subtypes of segregationists.

The white supremacists. White supremacists are those who hold that all Negroes, regardless of how worthy their achievement, should be permanently relegated to the bottom rung of the social ladder. They categorically deny the validity of the principles of equal citizenship, the central tenet of the Ne-

[3] The dependency of northern Negro leaders on white leaders was noted by James Q. Wilson, *Negro Politics* (Chicago: The University of Chicago Press, 1960), p. 100.

[4] Leaders of the Black Muslim movement are not included in this study because they constitute a very small and, so far, uninfluential segment of the Negro leadership class in New Orleans.

gro uplift ideology. They tend to rationalize the doctrine of white supremacy in terms of the alleged "inherent inequality of races."

Perhaps the main characteristic of this group is *closed-mindedness*. They refuse to accept any scientific finding, logical interpretation, or concrete achievement on the part of Negroes as in any way a contradiction to their belief in white supremacy. Thus, they seek to revive and perpetuate scientifically rejected Negro stereotypes. They persistently hold that the Negro is biologically and psychologically inferior to whites, and that "racial integration would be a fatal blow to civilization as we know it." A highly vocal woman segregationist in New Orleans, for example, insists that "it is just as sinful to integrate racially as it is to commit murder or adultery. . . . The New Testament clearly established that the Law of Segregation is immutable and that it is therefore just as binding upon man today as it was before the incarnation and the redemption."

In short, white supremacists defend the biracial system in New Orleans because they claim to be convinced that the Negro is biologically and psychologically inferior to whites. This position has been reiterated in one way or another by all of them. Perhaps the best summary of it was given in a leaflet passed out to the public by an anti-Negro group. The author of this pamphlet contended that

> There must be no defilement of race. . . . Blood mixture and the resultant drop in racial level is the sole cause of the dying out of old cultures. . . . It is the quintessence of folly to suppose that the nigger can emulate the white in progressive civilization. . . . We will never accept equality with these animals.

In the eyes of the white supremacist, therefore, the Negro cannot achieve the equality of citizenship that is inherent in the American Creed and the Negro's uplift ideology.

The states' righters. The main argument of the states' righters is legalistic. They rely mainly upon the Tenth Amendment to the Constitution for their authority. According to their interpretation of the Amendment, each individual state is a sovereign power, and as such it has the right to make any laws its state legislators deem necessary in regard to civil rights. The only criterion by which a given legislature can be limited in this respect is by the will of the majority of its white citizens. Thus, certain high-ranking officials in Louisiana have actually held that the state has the right to deny Negroes civil privileges which the federal courts insist that the Constitution guarantees in the Fourteenth Amendment. This group relies strongly upon the belief that the only limitation of a state's power should be a referendum in which its own white citizens register their desires.

It was this relatively small, but powerful, group of states' righters in Louisiana that led the movement for that state to interpose itself between the "people" and the federal government in November 1960. The Interposition Bill that passed the State Legislature unanimously cited the Tenth

Amendment to the United States Constitution as authorizing the state to prevent any

> government agency, judge, marshal or other officer, agent or employee of the United States (from) undertaking or attempting the enforcement of any judgement, decree or order of any federal court, nor make or attempt to make service of any citation, summons, warrant or process in connection therewith predicated upon the United States Supreme Court's decision and decree in the case of *Brown* vs. *Topeka Board of Education* upon any officer of the State of Louisiana or any of its subdivisions, agencies or school boards, or upon any of their agents, employees or representatives in the maintenance of the public schools of the state, or who may be engaged in carrying out the provisions of this act, or other law, right or power of the State of Louisiana.

Carried to its logical conclusion the states' rights doctrine, as interpreted by segregationists in Louisiana, would set up a confederation of fifty sovereign states. Each individual state would have the exclusive right to establish any system of race relations deemed desirable by the majority of its white citizens. It would regard *state citizenship* as *primary* and *national citizenship* as *secondary*. And, despite the fact that the United States Supreme Court unanimously held that the doctrine of interposition is "without substance," some segregationists still persist in the right of Louisiana to determine its own racial policies without regard to their constitutionality.

A few states' righters will even admit that there is a serious racial problem in New Orleans and that Negroes are often treated unjustly. Yet they insist that white New Orleanians understand this problem better than outsiders, and should be left alone to solve it in their own way.

The culturists. The basic position of the culturists is that Negroes are not yet ready for full citizenship. They base their contention primarily upon alleged immorality and a high crime rate among Negroes. This argument is expressed in every meeting of the white Citizens' Councils, by many state and local officials, and by numerous individuals in other public meetings, and in "letters to the editor." The fact is, this seems to be the unstated race relations editorial policy of the daily newspapers in New Orleans. Every effort is made by these papers to emphasize Negro crimes and all negative Negro news, and frequently even editorial space is given over to propagandizing the views of the segregationists. On the other hand, Negro achievements and progress are either ignored or given the most superficial attention.

The outstanding trait of the culturists is their deliberately overlooking the fact that many white people do not measure up to the social and cultural standards that they assume to be basic in "our great white civilization," and that many Negroes could be given the highest ranking according to these standards. In other words, they tend to judge all white people according to the highest achievements of which that race can boast, while all Negroes are judged according to the lowest achievement level of their race, usually the criminal element among them. They make no distinction among Negroes.

They propagandize exaggerated stereotypes of Negroes as if they were actual physical, social, and psychological realities.

Even allegedly "liberal" whites often cite the cultural backwardness of the Negro masses as an apology for their segregationist stands. Thus, one of the most respected writers in the South, who achieved the reputation of being "another liberal voice," held in an interview with a *Life* reporter that "Negroes in this area are still not ready for integration because of the cultural disparity that still exists, largely through economic causes . . . as evidenced by the vast differences by race, in such cultural indices as crime commission, illegitimacy, illiteracy, venereal disease, and general social standards."[5]

We may conclude that, though the rationales differ, segregationists are dedicated to the proposition that the biracial system in New Orleans is moral, legal, and workable. With what type of Negro leaders will white segregationists, who have a virtual monopoly of social power, negotiate?

The Uncle Toms. According to the most reliable evidence in history and in contemporary social life, white supremacists are willing to do business with Negro leaders who are disposed to accept their "place" in the biracial system. The "place" of Negroes in New Orleans society is defined by segregationists in terms of what might be called a parasite-host relationship. According to this pattern of race relations, white men of power regard themselves as hosts and Negroes as parasites. Put in another way, the relationship segregationists accept with Negroes is paternalistic. Consequently, the Negro leaders with whom white segregationists will do business may be described as "Uncle Toms."

The most characteristic trait of the Uncle Tom is his acceptance of the parasitic status assigned him by white supremacists. He never demands on the basis of the Negro's rights, but instead begs for favors. Always underlying his requests is the assumption that something not necessarily deserved may be given. A vivid example of this type was related by a white lawyer describing what he regarded as a great Negro leader: He came "hat in hand, stood at my desk, waiting for an invitation to be seated, as was his custom . . . as an humble, but great supplicant for the friendship of the white man for his race."

Not only does the role of Uncle Tom prescribe that he should be a supplicant, but it also entails his bringing other Negroes to appreciate what some white authority has done for "our people." For example, a white school-board authority may accede to a Negro educator's request for funds to expand a program in his school. A similar program might already be in effect in all of the white schools, yet when such funds are granted to the Negro educator's school, he will try to find some occasion at which the white official responsible can be recognized publicly as "our friend." On such an occasion, the white authority will also play a familiar role by declaring himself a "friend of the Negro people." As a matter of fact, the most avid segregation-

[5] September 17, 1956, p. 120.

ist interviewed for this study likes to picture himself as the "best friend Negroes have." Among white segregationists tremendous prestige seems to be attached to "the friend of the Negro" role. They actually compete among themselves, at least verbally, at being a friend of the Negro. This, then, is the most effective technique employed by Uncle Toms: white men of power are challenged to qualify as the "friend of Negroes." It is expected that the highest prestige in this regard will go to the wealthier, more established, and most powerful among the white supremacists. We can see then why Uncle Toms almost always "go to the top men, don't bother about straw bosses," as one such leader put it.

Myrdal saw Negro leaders of this type as functioning primarily as instruments in the hands of white people. In this capacity they were used, he concluded, to keep other Negroes in line. This, of course, is one of their major functions. Yet, it must not be overlooked that they do get things done. Just as white people use Negro leaders of this type to control the Negro masses, so the Uncle Toms manipulate white authorities to serve their own purposes. Thus the Uncle Toms have often been responsible for persuading Negroes not to join labor unions or to engage in mass protest, and generally they are able to stifle Negro radicals. However, through the Uncle Toms Negro workers may receive also some benefits, such as somewhat higher salaries or better working conditions. Uncle Toms are also frequently granted certain personal favors in return for their role as liaison between the Negro and the white communities.

Most of the favors the Uncle Toms receive are due to the fact that in order to be serviceable to the white community, they must maintain prestige among Negroes. They must, therefore, evince some influence with white authorities. This the white community understands. As a result, the trusted Negro liaison leader is often allowed to "get away with murder." That is, he is permitted, so to speak, to engage in what sometimes appears to be almost radical social action. Yet such radical behavior is really a kind of social catharsis, without which a leadership vacuum would be created that might be filled by a really radical Negro leader, who is not under the control of white authorities. So, even in an apparently radical role, the Uncle Tom proves to be an invaluable preserver of a biracial system which perpetuates white paternalistic men of power in their status as hosts and Negroes as parasites.

MODERATE—RACIAL DIPLOMAT

There are two distinctly opposite points of view or philosophies toward the biracial system in New Orleans. On the one hand, segregationists hold that the best, certainly the most desirable, social system is one that adheres religiously to the principles of racial segregation. On the other hand, integrationists insist that the basic principle inherent in our republican form of government is equal citizenship. Accordingly, racial segregation is logically untenable and a legal contradiction.

Ideally, the moderate occupies a position somewhere between the segregationist and the integrationist. He may be described as a "middle-of-the-roader," a kind of eclectic. Actually he has no definite, defensible philosophy of race relations. Sometimes his racial views on certain issues are similar to those of the avowed segregationist. At other times, even on the same issues, the moderate may take a stand very much like that of the integrationist. Therefore, the moderate is usually indefinite and vacillating when it comes to the question of equal citizenship rights.

Most moderates create the impression that they try to hold fast to a belief in equal citizenship, while "realistically" hanging onto the conviction that individual differences and inequalities are important. They seem never to resolve this conflict in their basic ideology. This ideological contradiction often leads them into a kind of legal legerdemain. Thus, while acknowledging certain "unalienable" rights inherent in American citizenship, they manifest at the same time a willingness to entrust the securing of these rights to the uncertain will of city and state authorities who have repeatedly pledged to maintain segregation and inequal citizenship at all costs.

A few moderates attempt to resolve their ideological dilemma through education and persuasion. That is, they gather, interpret, and disseminate facts designed to encourage local men of power to formulate plans and to map out courses of action "best suited to local needs," whereby "certain racial injustices" might be eliminated.

There are perhaps three distinctly different degrees of moderation insofar as race relations are concerned:

The lukewarm. Those who fall into this classification are ostensibly neutral in regard to the racial segregation-integration controversy. This is the traditional stand of most white businessmen, independent professionals, and academicians. When possible, they avoid making any statement about "the problem." They can seldom be persuaded to take any public stand on the race issue, and they almost never join racially militant organizations, either those advocating racial uplift or those advocating racial segregation.

When asked to express his views on race relations in New Orleans a high-ranking public official made the following statement:

> I have made a policy of saying nothing. I know your work is confidential [meaning the interview], but this is a rule which admits no exceptions and that's why I've been able to stay out of trouble. . . . Some people accuse me of being stupid and having no guts, but I don't see it that way at all. I think it is my duty to do my job [naming his profession] and keep away from emotional disturbances. I'm hired to administer under established policies and this sets the limits upon my activity.

When circumstance makes the need to respond to some racial issue inevitable, the lukewarm moderate is likely to respond "objectively." As a rule, the question of equal citizenship rights will be equated with some other value, such as good business, a good civic reputation, or high academic standards.

Thus, when an outstanding businessman was pressed to express himself on the school-desegregation crisis in New Orleans, he finally stated, "One thing I am sure of, we simply cannot afford to let our city become another Little Rock. Look what happened to business after the riots and everything. They may never get over the mess they made of the school business." Again, a college professor expressed this fear—

> I think that the politicians are making far too big an issue about four little girls [referring to the four Negro girls in New Orleans who were admitted to the first grade in two formerly all-white schools]. If this keeps up recognized scholars will begin to avoid the South. Already I know of a few professors who plan to leave southern colleges. I hope our leaders will soon show a little more sanity.

Because some of the lukewarm moderates are persons of great influence, their opinions on race issues are diligently sought and highly valued. Therefore, in New Orleans, where a white person is assumed to be a segregationist unless he indicates otherwise, persons in this category are often unwittingly included among "the vast majority of white people who regard racial segregation as a sacred heritage," in the often-repeated phraseology of segregationist leaders. In this way their lukewarm attitudes on race relations give tacit sanction to the biracial social system as it now exists.

The gradualists. The characteristic trait of the gradualists is their insistence that Negroes must "qualify" for equal citizenship status. In some respects they are similar to the segregationists who hold that "Negroes are not yet ready for equality." They differ from the segregationists, however, in that they are much more willing to acknowledge that *some* Negroes are "ready" for equality with white people. They are less likely than the segregationists to participate in movements designed to impede the progress of "qualified" Negroes, because other Negroes happen to have a high crime rate or behave in an unseemly fashion. In fact, some gradualists seek out opportunities to promote or enhance the prestige of certain qualified Negroes.

Sometimes gradualists make important and far-reaching contributions to Negro advancement. They have been known to donate substantial sums to segregated Negro institutions. One Negro leader expressed the belief that "practically all white people on boards of directors of Negro institutions, or who are assigned special duties in the Negro community as representatives of white authorities in the field of public education and 'Negro affairs,' are gradualists."

Much of the progress Negroes have been able to make during the last twenty years in New Orleans has been due directly or indirectly to gradualists. This is so primarily because gradualists tend to view race relations more or less in terms of enlightened self-interest. That is, they are much more likely than the segregationists to understand the ubiquitous nature of disease, crime, and poverty, and to attempt to eradicate them without regard to race. As one gradualist labor leader put it:

I have always insisted that Negro workers should be treated the same as white workers, because after all we need them to help us raise the general standard of living in our community. Nothing gives us a stronger argument in our own ranks than demonstrating that organized labor is interested in all of its workers. Do you know that the most loyal members we had during [our last strike] were our Negroes?

A favorite technique used by the gradualists to get things done in the Negro community is the threat of "total integration." The argument, for example, that a high city official gave for expanding certain recreational facilities for Negroes was that if improved facilities for Negroes were not provided, Negroes would seek to break down segregation patterns "protecting" white facilities. He insisted that when Negroes have adequate public facilities "of their own" only a few of them attempt to use facilities set aside for whites, even when all legal barriers have been removed. He even boasted that certain "white" public facilities had been legally desegregated for a considerable length of time, yet only a "token" number of Negroes had ever sought to use them.

Perhaps the best illustration of the gradualists' position is the stand taken on the desegregation of the public schools. Gradualists tend to accept "limited integration," such as was attempted through a program of "pupil placement." According to this placement program in New Orleans, Negro first graders had to qualify for white schools by passing a long comprehensive examination intended to test their mental aptitudes, cultural achievements, and social adjustment. This test was admittedly designed to "eliminate all but a few of the Negro pupils who might apply" to attend hitherto white schools.

The rate of change in race relations acceptable to gradualists was pointed up by a Negro attorney representing some Negro children seeking to attend nonsegregated schools. The lawyer for the Negro plaintiffs filed a motion that held that pupil placement effectively limits the number of Negro children who should be receiving nonsegregated education. He contended that "the plaintiffs and the class they represent—approximately 50,000 Negro students, save four—are still effectively denied their constitutional rights to nonsegregated education."[5] ("Pupil placement" in New Orleans was eventually declared unconstitutional by a federal court.)

Gradualists were asked, "How long do you think it will be before Negroes are generally admitted to participate in civic organizations, such as the Chamber of Commerce, Rotary, and the Lions Clubs?" They usually predicted that it would be "a long time." When pressed for a definite answer they mentioned fifteen, twenty, twenty-five years.

The borderline liberals. The most stable element among the moderates is composed of well-to-do white people, generally women, who make a career

[5] The four referred to in this Brief applies to the four Negro children admitted to formerly all-white schools in November 1960.

out of helping Negroes. Some of them are convinced that they are absolutely indispensable to Negro progress. These are the ones who serve on important welfare boards where "Negro interests" are of major concern. They are called upon by Negro leaders to plan fund-raising campaigns, and to negotiate with white men of power, from whom certain favors are sought and whose offices are necessary for the success of some project. As one outstanding woman leader phrased it, "I walk in two worlds."

Persons in this category, more than any other type of white leader, manifest a strong sense of community pride. This may be the main reason why they would prefer to have "local problems solved by local people," as one of them said. She maintains that if she could get the Negro community and the white community to work together on common projects, "then there would be no race relations problem. We could cut through the lines to get some things done." She gave as a specific example a project on which she had worked in the Negro community. It was successful, she said, because "we had teamwork. If this had been an all-Negro project, then we could not have gone to the [white] papers with our publicity and had it accepted the way it was."

Their strong sense of community pride leads most of them to take the position that New Orleans should be left alone to solve its own problems of equal citizenship for Negroes. One leader said, "I am optimistic about this. I know that if a few of the truly respected men in this city could be convinced that our public schools must be kept open, and Negroes generally should be accorded more respect, then it would be done." This statement revealed two important basic attitudes held by individuals who are classified in this category.

First, they have an almost child-like faith in the integrity of "truly respected" authorities. In all of their public pronouncements, as well as in private interviews, they tend to project their own sense of community pride onto others. They refuse to believe that a responsible authority would allow racial discord or injustices to exist, "if he understands their nature and consequences." Thus, they see themselves as "advisors" to city officials on Negro affairs.

Second, they manifest optimistic faith in the leadership of powerful authorities. During every discussion of possible racial strife, they reiterate that certain city officials must be apprised of the seriousness of the situation so that they can "tell the people what to do." Thus, as we shall see later, this attitude of trust on the part of these race relations leaders was primarily the reason why almost no preparation was made to meet the public-school-desegregation deadline ordered by the federal courts. These leaders simply could not visualize a situation in which the mayor would be unwilling or unable to "handle the situation in the best interests of everyone." They felt that whatever line of action the mayor proposed would be followed without question by the vast majority of citizens.

To them, "The Embarrassment of Louisiana," as characterized by the

Saturday Evening Post (May 27, 1961) and popularly referred to as the "Shame of New Orleans," was not due basically to what the *Post* writer described as "the integration conflicts [that] broke out in all their ugliness," but rather to the fact that local authorities refused to handle their own problems and the federal government found it necessary to intervene. Sympathizing with this point of view, Helen Fuller, writing in *The New Republic* (February 16, 1959), prophetically lamented: "New Orleans Knows Better."

Segregationists and moderates have at least one basic attitude in common: both strongly resent outsiders. Consequently, when it comes to the problem of equal citizenship, they are likely to invoke the doctrine of "home rule," or local autonomy. This doctrine springs from confidence and faith in the ability of people, on a local level, to work together in the solution of their own common problems. There is, of course, one important fallacy in this belief: it presupposes that men of power are also men of good will, who are willing to sacrifice personal, political, and economic gain for the welfare of the total community.

Moderates tend to place too much faith in the doctrine of community autonomy. They manifest a willingness, they even prefer to entrust the securing of equal citizenship rights to local authorities who, in the name of "law and order," are, ironically, pledged to maintain the same biracial system that the segregationists consider sacred.

Again, with what kind of Negro leader will moderates negotiate?

The racial diplomat. The racial diplomat is usually class-oriented. He is highly skilled in dealing with white leaders. However, unlike the Uncle Tom, he does not accept segregation as right, but as an effective diplomat, he does manifest an astute understanding of the "ways of the South." Like the white moderate, he has a strong feeling of belonging in the local community and a keen sense of community pride. He identifies with the problems of the total community and he talks about the welfare of human beings, as one racial diplomat put it, and not just about "what is good for the Negro." This leader emphasized one point he always makes when working with white people on some committee or project: "I let them know to begin with," he said, "that I am not just concerned about doing things for Negroes, but rather, about how I can benefit mankind. I refuse to serve on any committee where they regard me as simply a Negro representative."

This, then, is the primary role of the racial diplomat. He essays to interpret the peculiar needs of Negroes in terms of general community wellbeing. For example, on this basis one Negro leader appealed for funds to support a Community Fund agency. "I did not ask to have this [institution] supported simply because Negroes needed it," he said. "I went on record as supporting three such projects, only one of which would be for Negro youth."

Another familiar role played by the racial diplomat is that of advising moderates on the "best way" of promoting uplift in some specific area of life. A powerful white labor union leader said that when he first came to New Orleans he wanted to bring drastic pressure to bear on white businessmen who refused to employ Negro union members in positions for which they qualified or to pay them salaries commensurate with their work. In the most positive "union language" he said that he would have followed through with actions calculated to "break the backs of the employers" in regard to the rights of Negro members, but a Negro official of the union "taught me better." The Negro official had advised a diplomatic approach rather than pressure tactics. Therefore, instead of the union's taking direct action in regard to equal membership status to Negroes, it adopted a diplomatic approach calculated to minimize resistance on the part of white employers.

The racial diplomat can always be depended upon to *protect* white race relations leaders from being embarrassed by other Negroes. For instance, a white moderate will hardly accept an invitation to speak before a Negro group, or to serve on an interracial committee, unless he is invited by a well-known racial diplomat. The latter will, first of all, select the Negroes to be present and then serve throughout the meeting as a buffer or "friend" when untoward situations develop. In some instances, the racial diplomat will simply explain away embarrassing questions which might be put to the white moderate. In other instances, he will deliberately select the kind of questions that should be answered regarding some specific action engaged in, or position taken by, the moderate present. In other words, regardless of his personal feelings in the matter, his most important function in a group the membership of which is predominantly Negro is to protect the white moderate (the visitor) from any unpleasantness.

A few of the most skilled racial diplomats can be trusted to participate in traditionally all-white groups. This is occasionally arranged by moderates in order to achieve two interrelated ends:

(1) To demonstrate to segregationists (whom they would like to persuade) that some Negroes do, in fact, "qualify" for equal citizenship. Needless to say, when their "exhibit number one" measures up, they are gratified and happy. One white leader described a racial diplomat in these glowing terms: "A great Negro leader," "perennial optimist," "skilled in getting things out of others," "unusual capacity for understanding," "patience like unto a saint," "in touch with reality," "always alert," and a "great capacity for work."

(2) To enhance the prestige of the racial diplomat in the eyes of other Negro leaders and in the community at large. This is, indeed, an important reward for his "understanding service" in helping them to accomplish racial uplift in the framework of a biracial system. Furthermore, such an assignment functions to advise other types of Negro leaders that this is the kind of Negro with whom influential white moderates are willing to do business.

It is very probable that if the actual achievements of Negro leaders in race relations were compared, those of the racial diplomat would rank highest. Unlike the Uncle Tom, who is not respected by either the white or the Negro community, the racial diplomat is respected by both because he fits well into the success pattern inherent in our national ideology. And, in the true

Machiavellian tradition, he chooses respect in preference to love. Actually, the racial diplomat is often hated by other Negro leaders because there is always a feeling of suspicion on their part that he "sells out to white people." Nevertheless, he does get things done.

One of the best insights into the philosophy of the racial diplomat was provided by a Negro leader who ranks high in that category. He said

> It is my belief that the main job of race relations organizations is keeping race relations on an even keel. Therefore, my organization surrounds itself with white leaders who are willing to support this approach to race relations. We believe in the scientific approach. We first gather facts . . . then we sit around a table and on the basis of these facts we seek to secure change. Undue sentiment and emotion should not be involved in our deliberations.

Another prominent racial diplomat gave a projected appraisal of a colleague in these words

> A good leader should have genuine concern for the group, should be active rather than offering mere lip service, should have racial consciousness, and a keen sense of social change. I know of no one who measures up to this standard better than [Mr. ———]. He approaches white people in the right manner. He can discuss issues intelligently with moderation, tact, and poise with them. The prestige of his position helps him out. He demonstrates social graces, culture and refinement. He is on big boards.

We may conclude that racial diplomats are generally *middle-class oriented*. To them, a successful Negro leader is one who possesses all of the traditional middle-class traits. These traits were summarized by one such leader in this way: "The essential qualities of a leader should be: . . . altruism, humanitarianism, appreciation for the principles upon which our government was founded, the ability to do long-range planning, economic independence and security, and high social status."

LIBERAL—RACE MAN

The concept of the liberal as used here is intended to classify individuals who would rank national citizenship above state or local citizenship. The most characteristic attitude held by liberals is that inherent in American citizenship is equality of status. They insist that second-class citizenship is in fundamental contradiction with the principles of equality and freedom upon which our government is founded.

Liberals maintain that all persons, regardless of race, religion, or national origin, should have equal opportunities to develop to the fullest extent of their individual capacities unhampered by laws and traditions. Therefore, no matter how difficult or unpleasant a given situation may be, the liberal insists that the basic principle of the American Creed—equality of citizenship—should never be compromised.

Generally, liberals in American society have favored movements to expand the electorate, to get stronger civil rights legislation, and to equalize economic and educational opportunities. Specifically, liberals renounce the biracial social system. They take the position that racial discrimination in any area of our national life is "undemocratic, unjust, and undermines our national strength and international prestige."

Basically, the liberals' argument against a biracial system is this: Every individual citizen has a heritage bequeathed to him by a republican form of government. This heritage includes equal rights and opportunities. They point out that when the majority sanctions political or social techniques designed to abridge these rights for a minority in any way (no matter how despised the minority in question might be), they also sanction the techniques that will eventually destroy the equal rights and opportunities of the majority as well.

One liberal explained his conception of equal citizenship in this way:

> I feel that all laws restricting Negroes from enjoying full citizenship privileges should be abolished. Just removing restrictions, however, is not enough. It should also mean employing Negro personnel in public facilities without discrimination. Also, I think that there should be laws passed, like in New York, to make it illegal to discriminate in public facilities, such as hotels, restaurants, parks, and so forth. Complete desegregation of the school should only be a first step.

Very few white people in New Orleans may be classified as liberals. There are no manifest liberals, at the moment, in positions of authority in the city. Why are there so few liberals in the area of race relations in New Orleans? This is a difficult question to answer, because the reasons white persons offer as answers to this question usually stem from complex psychological sources. However, if we were to give the single most pervasive reason it would be *fear*. This emotion has been expressed by practically every white leader or official who has been called upon to face up publicly to problems in race relations. Three examples illustrate this.

(1) A wealthy realtor opposes "open occupancy" in housing because he is *afraid* that certain businesses that traditionally cater to white patrons would be seriously hurt if the predominantly white community were to become a mixed neighborhood. He is particularly concerned about an old, well-established mortuary. This business has catered to moderately wealthy white people in his neighborhood for several decades, and he wondered "what would happen to this business if the neighborhood becomes black? I tell you what I am afraid would happen—this business would just fold up."

The fear expressed here is typical of a large number of white businessmen. In one way or another, all of them when pressed indicated that they were afraid to take a liberal stand on race relations. A wealthy department store manager, when asked to employ Negroes in sales positions, expressed his fear in this way:

> I am sure that there are Negroes who would do an adequate job as sales people, or on any other job they had a chance to learn. I would like to be able to employ people for what they could do, not because of race, yet I feel that I would lose more white customers if I employed Negroes as sales people than I would gain Negro customers. I am not in business for my health.

(2) Some of the younger politicians who would like to function as liberal confide that they are *afraid* that if they are reputed to be liberals (or integrationists) they would be committing "political suicide." When, therefore, the Louisiana State Legislature was passing scores of bills, resolutions, and amendments designed to maintain racial segregation despite federal court orders to the contrary, the alleged liberals in the legislature from New Orleans voted for almost every "anti-Negro" measure presented. When explaining their contradictory behavior as legislators, they all agreed that they took the stand they did because they were *afraid* to do otherwise.

(3) A prominent head of a wealthy law firm was entreated to make a public statement warning the state legislature against the passing of obviously unconstitutional laws aimed at preserving segregation. This lawyer agreed that "most of this current legislation is not even legal on its face." He further acknowledged that such laws tend to heighten negative race relations and "will serve to bring us national and international disgrace." He refused, however, to make the public statement some citizens desired of him because, he said, "most of my law partners are young, ambitious, capable lawyers. Whereas I am a wealthy man, I don't think it would be fair for me to jeopardize their future on such a controversial issue as race relations is at present in New Orleans."

The examples given above are only a few of the many that might have been selected from interview materials, newspaper reports, and public statements by leading white citizens. All of these indicate a fear of taking a positive stand on the question of equal citizenship status for Negroes. When we tried, painstakingly, to ferret out the sources of this fear, we encountered great difficulties. Individually, a large proportion of the men of power expressed their belief in equal citizenship, and the reasons they gave for not expressing these beliefs publicly were seldom logical, consistent, or sound. Their responses tended to remind the researchers of the much-quoted statement of the late President Franklin D. Roosevelt summarizing the psychological condition of the American businessman after experiencing years of depression. He said, "We have nothing to fear, but fear itself."

On numerous occasions representatives of powerful political, economic, civic, social, and religious groups meet together to consider, among other things, the question of race relations. Personally, almost to the man, they express concern about the "race problem." They generally agree as individuals that something should be done. But, when the question arises regarding what specifically is to be done and who is to do it, fear takes over. It is at this point that such expressions are heard as, "If this course of action is taken, we might have violent reaction from *them*"; "If I stick my neck out, *they* will promptly cut it off"; "I just don't think New Orleans is ready for that action yet"; "Members of my organization wouldn't go along with this, because *they* would be afraid of losing business"; or, "*They* just wouldn't stand for it."

One significant thing stands out in the quotations above: there is seldom any attempt made to define who "they" are. Thus, after listening to a long discussion as to whether or not an Interracial Human Relations Council should be appointed by or legitimitized by the city government and certain powerful city organizations, a white liberal summarized his impression in this way—

> I got the idea that these hard-headed businessmen and politicians all agreed in their minds and in their hearts that we need such a committee operating in our community. Yet, each one who spoke continued to use the word fear over and over again. Then it occurred to me that there were no real people they feared because they, among themselves, had the power to control or even outlaw any group in the community that would dare challenge them. I also knew that even if they were prejudiced that they would not be so stupid as to allow their personal prejudices to ruin their businesses or disgrace our city. So I had to conclude that their fear was based upon ghost-like images of their own creation.

There is, of course, some basis in reality for this fear syndrome so frequently expressed by "men of power." After individuals have made liberal statements or participated in liberal action, a few have actually lost business, been harassed by cranks who called on the telephones at all hours of the night or been forced to endure public criticism by segregationists. Yet, even this is often instigated more by fear than by any other consideration. One business man suggested this in a statement to a white interviewer. He said—

> Mr. [———] lost all of his business when he got on the wrong side of the school desegregation issue. Before this, I was one of his main customers myself. I cancelled my orders with him, not because I disagreed with his stand, I think that he was a perfectly honest man and did what he thought was right, but if I had not cancelled my orders with him, with the climate of opinion what it is now, I am sure I would have lost business myself.

It seems, then, that fear is compounded by fear so that "a perfectly honest" man is persecuted, not for what he has done, but because his persecutors are afraid not to persecute.

Whatever may be the reasons, or imagined reasons, there are very few white persons in New Orleans who are acknowledged liberals. Those who are publicly regarded as liberals must endure persecution, ostracism, and "investigations." The systematic harassment to which they are subject is apparently calculated to make them anathema. The most effective technique is to declare them "Communists" or "fellow travelers." When this is done, other liberals, who actually know of their staunch Americanism, often refuse to associate with them personally, in groups, or on committees. One liberal, in analyzing the reasons why an interracial committee disbanded in New Orleans, cited as the main cause the fact that a member of the committee had been investigated by the House Committee on Un-American Activities. He said that the accused was never "proven to be a Communist, but a shadow was cast over him. This man knew that the members of the group wanted him to resign, but he refused to do so." This informer concluded, "I am inclined to believe that it was because he was naïve. He believes that each man has a right to his own beliefs. I would say that men can believe as they please, but that they do not have the right to jeopardize the rights of the others. All rights are thus conditioned." According to him, then, the committee disbanded, not because one of its members was a *proven* Communist, but because he had been *accused* of being a Communist. This is only one example of how insidiously effective the technique of name-calling is in limiting the number and influence of militant liberals.

Although there are no acknowledged liberals in municipal or state government posts in the city, there are a few white liberals who represent wealthy respected families with entree to city and state authorities. Using this advantage, some have been able to make significant contributions to the changing status of Negroes. In most cases, liberals negotiate with local authorities as preliminary steps in accomplishing some definite goal in race relations. The ultimate, most reliable, and certainly the most frequently used strategy is appeal to the federal government—that is, to Congress, the President, or the federal courts. These appeals generally come after a long period of skillful propaganda based upon evidences of discrimination and injustice. These evidences are compiled and analyzed in terms of the basic principle of equality of citizenship.

With what type of Negro leader will white liberals do business?

The race man. Perhaps the best insight into the personality of the race man is offered by Robert Johnson. According to him

> The "Race Man" is generally the spearhead of militant race leadership. . . . He has achieved a measure of personality adjustment on racial matters, but sees the world through race colored glasses and interprets most events in their racial context—how they will affect the Negro. . . . The "Race Man" is bitter not only at whites, but also at more accommodating Negro leadership, at the indifferent Negro masses who won't support him, at the more disorganized areas of Negro life, and at all persons who are able or qualified to help in the struggle for Negro rights, but refuse to do so.
>
> On the other hand, "Race Men" are favorably disposed toward all liberal elements in the community. . . .[6]

[6] "Negro Reactions to Minority Group Status," in Milton L. Barron, Editor, *American Minorities* (New York: Alfred A. Knopf, 1957), p. 207.

There has been no period in the history of Negroes in American society when there was not recognized militant Negro leadership, such as characterized here by the race man. In order to appreciate and properly evaluate the role of the race man in history, it is necessary to see him in his proper social context.

One of the distinguishing traits of the race man during the Negro's struggle for equal citizenship has been his unwillingness to compromise the basic principles of freedom and equality inherent in our American Creed. Historically, he has disagreed with such celebrated compromises as the all-Negro army unit, the "separate but equal" doctrine of race relations, and "token" integration. Though he realistically worked within the biracial framework, he has prophetically looked forward to total participation in American life. His greatest contribution is likely to have been his insistence that Negroes should unceasingly prepare to accept first-class citizenship, whenever it might be secured. Thus, in the most fundamental sense the race man never accepted racial segregation as a proper or workable way of life. He has always insisted that a biracial society is ethically and legally inconsistent with our democratic commitment.

One race man averred that he felt that the main purpose of all Negro organizations—colleges, churches, and particularly the NAACP—is to "improve race relations to the extent that they will no longer be necessary in American society." The fact is, this is the position formally taken by Negro lawyers in New Orleans who found it necessary to organize the all-Negro Martinet Legal Society, because they could not participate in the Louisiana Bar Association.[7] One of the stated objectives of this society is—

To encourage and promote the full and complete integration of all lawyers irrespective of race, creed or color in the professional life and activities of the Louisiana Bar Association.

From this Guillory concluded that—

As these objectives clearly suggest Negro lawyers regarded this segregated institution as first a temporary organization designed primarily to foster the integration of Negro lawyers into the professional life and activities of the Louisiana Bar Association.[8]

The race man differs significantly from both the Uncle Tom and the racial diplomat. The Uncle Tom, through his actions and public pronouncements, tends to accept the biracial system in the South as right. Therefore, he begs for the crumbs that fall from the tables of the dominant white majority. He is apparently satisfied to accept second-class citizenship if it is made

[7] The Louisiana Bar Association accepts only dues from Negro lawyers. They are not permitted to attend its meetings or otherwise participate.
[8] *Op. cit.*, pp. 66-67.

at all tolerable. The Negro diplomat never quite accepts the biracial system as right or just. He has learned, however, to *work well* within the framework of the "separate but equal" doctrine. Accordingly, he has been successful in founding and maintaining influential institutions through which members of his race have greatly benefited. As a rule, however, his pronounced class prejudices have functioned to separate him from the masses and mass movements.

The race man, on the other hand, *has been a perennial enemy of the biracial system.* He has insisted that racial segregation of any kind is psychologically harmful, socially unworkable, and a legal contradiction. He has constantly voiced his protest in literature, music, public utterances, and organizational objectives. At all times he expresses a restlessness and declares his impatience with second-class citizenship. Examples of this attitude are legion. The following are typical:

A Negro minister expressed a militant "charisma"[9] at a "loyalty rally" just prior to the desegregation of buses in New Orleans. He said—

> God has given me a mission and I cannot be content until that mission is accomplished. I cannot sit idly by and see my people oppressed on every side and remain silent. I would rather be dead than to spend the balance of my days on my knees begging for what rightfully belongs to me and my people as human beings and as citizens of the United States of America. As soon as this cup passes, we will strive to register every eligible man and woman, so that we may boast of a citizenry of first-class citizens.

The ideology of the race man is well stated in the editorial platform of *The Louisiana Weekly*:

> *The Louisiana Weekly* shall work relentlessly for human and civil rights for all citizens and will expose those who appeal to prejudices rather than reason in their approach to problems concerning human relations. *The Louisiana Weekly* shall strive to mold public opinion in the interest of all things constructive.

When asked what he thought Negro uplift organizations should endeavor to achieve, an official of the NAACP answered—

> The first step should be to abolish all laws designed to discriminate against Negroes. Laws may not change the hearts of men, but they do affect what they will do. If there were no segregation laws, communication between the races could take place on a different plane—a plane of mutual respect. What Negroes want is not necessarily social equality—they want this too—but more than that they want human dignity.

[9] According to Talcott Parsons, *The Social System* (Glencoe, Ill.: The Free Press, 1951), p. 402, "The charismatic leader plays an expressive leadership role where moral authority is claimed."

In a prepared speech before a conference of Negro leaders, the chairman of an influential Negro organization summarized what he regarded as a creative approach to racial uplift. His statement also summarizes the ideology of the race man.

The historical experiences through which the Negro has come are unparalleled in regard to deprivation and success; pain and pleasure; degradation and respect. This multitude of varied, unmatched experiences have uniquely prepared us for the kind of intelligent, courageous, understanding leadership our community, our nation and the free world so desperately needs. We have been conditioned by our own struggle for survival to the point that we are able to identify with the universal struggle now going on for freedom and dignity. Perhaps no other race or ethnic group in history, not even the Jews, has ever been so inextricably involved in man's struggle for freedom and dignity as is the Negro race today.

At this moment in time, Negro leaders have two interrelated challenges:

1. We must recognize, first of all, that as Negro people we have a common goal and a common destiny. History, experience, and our enemies have made us one people. This we cannot escape. This we should not want to escape. Consequently, the success or failure, the suffering or joy of any one Negro anywhere on the face of the globe affects me and you because we are one with him.

2. As Negro leaders we are also challenged to transcend the narrow confines of race and realize our involvement in mankind. Therefore, Negro leadership must raise its sights above the issues and problems of Negro people only. It must come to realize that the Negro's struggle for full citizenship, though the most dramatic and perennial in modern history, is only one phase of the social revolution of our time. This revolution will continue until freedom and dignity can be claimed by all men regardless of race. . . . Therefore, we must have a solidly organized Negro leadership class whose primary goal will be the complete abolition of racial segregation in our community.

The quotations cited indicate that the race man has a vital concern for the welfare of Negro people. He insists upon equality of citizenship. His ideology is based fundamentally on the American Creed. He constantly reminds America that it "must either live up to its democratic commitments or continue to be shamed before the world." More and more, he is coming to equate the Negro's efforts to attain first-class citizenship with the perennial struggles of mankind for freedom and dignity.

A clear statement of this position was made by Dr. Ralph J. Bunche, the Undersecretary for Special Political Affairs of the United Nations and winner of the Nobel laureate as mediator in the 1948-49 Palestine conflict. Speaking before the National Convention of the NAACP which met in Atlanta, Georgia in July, 1962, he said that he granted to anyone

the right to find me unacceptable as a person, as an individual; but never to indict my group and slur my ancestry as the reason for rejecting me.

The point is that no individual Negro can be free from the degradation of racial discrimination until every Negro is free of it.

There is no emancipation and no escape for the individual Negro American until the entire group is emancipated, there can be no dignity for one without dignity for all; no Negro can ever walk down any American street with full security and serenity until all Negroes can do so in every town; old or young, black, brown, or high yellow, the axiom applies to all alike.

Until all racial discrimination is ended here [Atlanta], the progress can never be fast enough and every deprived underprivileged Negro will be immensely impatient or he isn't worthy of the rights to which he is entitled and wishes to exercise.

The race man is *not a racist*. He is *not chauvinistic*. Instead, he sees himself as the Negro symbol of mankind's struggle for dignity. He does not apologize for his Negro-ness, yet he continues to insist that he is an American and feels that being Negro should not in any way limit the rights, duties, and opportunities inherent in American citizenship. He is, therefore, at ease when working with white liberals, to whom he is a natural complement.

It is true, of course, that most of his energy has been devoted to the Negro problem.[10] This has been a deliberate choice and race men often express guilt feelings because they would like to concern themselves with the broader problems of mankind. Some have felt compelled to spend practically all of their time in the unmasking of Negro stereotypes, fitting Negroes for full citizenship, and defending the Negro cause in courts and before a critical public opinion. This compulsion to dedicate himself to his people was dramatically expressed by an outstanding Negro writer. He said that he had devoted about twenty years to writing on Negro life and problems. During that time he had several widely read books published. In the last of these books, he lamented that he had felt compelled to dedicate himself to the Negro cause. He vowed that he would make no further statement about the problem because he had earned the right to a commitment to something outside himself which is necessary to human and humanistic development.[11]

We may conclude, then, that in the biracial society of New Orleans, the type of Negro leader who can get things done is determined very largely by the type of white leader with whom he must do business. Consequently, if we would properly understand and evaluate the changing status of Negroes we must take into consideration at least three basic race relations leadership patterns: Segregationists who prefer to work through *Uncle Toms*, *moderates* who work well with *racial diplomats*, and *liberals* who find ideological kinship with the *race man*.

We do not imply that only one of these patterns operates in race relations at a given time. Actually, in New Orleans, and perhaps throughout the

---

[10] This has been true, also, of southern white liberals.

[11] J. Saunders Redding, *On Being A Negro in America* (Indianapolis: Bobbs-Merrill Co., 1951), pp. 25-27.

South, all of these patterns can be detected, especially when racial crises are imminent or present. It is true, however, that in different social contexts one pattern may be more prominent and effective than other patterns.

It should be clear that the patterns of race relations leadership discussed above, in a strict sociological sense, involve complementary roles certain leaders elect to play. These patterns are not meant to describe the personalities or character of the leaders. Though personality factors do tend to limit the different roles an individual may play, theoretically an individual may, at one time or another, play the appropriate complementary role in each of the three major race relations patterns analyzed. For example, the race man is occasionally pressured into playing the role of the racial diplomat because the Negro community needs things done, and there are no liberals in authority with whom he can do business. Therefore, out of expediency, he is sometimes led into negotiations and compromises that fall short of his desired goals. Thus, for example, some race men in New Orleans accepted the "pupil placement" plan for school desegregation and tried to make it work, though their goal was still total integration. It is in this regard that the race man is often absorbed by the racial diplomats in order that he may do business with influential moderates.

It should be pointed out that the race man is seldom flexible enough to adjust to the Uncle Tom role. This is an important reason why there have been several crises in race relations in New Orleans since 1956. Specifically, segregationists in positions of authority have had no reliable Negro complements with whom they were willing to negotiate because their natural complements, the Uncle Toms, are generally discredited. More and more the Negro community rejects the Uncle Tom, and since white men of power tend to refuse to do business with Negro diplomats and race men, an impasse in race relations has developed. This impasse can only be countered by what Dr. Mays refers to as "straight talk" between Negro and white leaders.[12] This communication must not be based upon wishful thinking or half-truths, as has been characteristic of the segregationists and the Uncle Toms in the past, but must be honest communication based upon mutual respect.

In the pages to follow, we shall see how different types of race relations leaders employ various strategies and techniques in their efforts either to accelerate or to impede the advancement of colored people.

[12] Benjamin E. Mays, "A Plea for Straight Talk Between the Races," *The Atlantic*, December 1960.

6

CITIZENSHIP

The Issues

THE FOURTEENTH AMENDMENT states:

> All persons born or naturalized in the United States, and subject to the juris-
> diction thereof, are citizens of the United States, and of the State wherein they
> reside. No State shall make or enforce any law which shall abridge the privileges
> or immunities of citizens of the United States; nor shall any State deprive any
> person of life, liberty, or property, without due process of law; nor deny to any
> person within its jurisdiction the equal protection of the laws.

The story of the Negro's struggle to attain first-class citizenship is one of
the epic chapters in American history. Basically, it is an account of the
strategies and techniques employed by an almost powerless minority to
achieve rights and privileges traditionally monopolized by a stubborn,
powerful, and often arrogant majority. Thus, every "stride toward freedom"
(to use Dr. Martin Luther King, Jr.'s phrase), no matter how modest, is
met with stern, often violent, resistance from entrenched segregationist forces.
And, as we shall see, some opponents of the Negro's advancement have
demonstrated a willingness to use every legal, extra-legal, and occasionally,
illegal means at their disposal to prevent Negroes from achieving the citizenship status they seek.

The story of the Negro's bid for equal citizenship in American society
began to unfold in 1619, when the first Negroes landed in this country. At
that time, they were free; then they became indentured servants; and later
they were forced into slavery. During the period of slavery the United States
Supreme Court, in the 1857 Dred Scott case, declared them to be "chattel."
From these depths began the slow, frequently frustrating, ever difficult, climb
toward equal citizenship. The first decisive step in that direction was *de jure*
freedom, which came as a result of the Emancipation Proclamation and the
Civil War Amendments (the Thirteenth, Fourteenth, and Fifteenth). Since

then the *de facto* citizenship status of Negroes has constantly undergone changes. These changes, sometimes positive, sometimes negative, have varied significantly in time, situation, and geographic location. The truth is, the status of Negroes as a group is so varied, complex, and unstable that Negro leaders differ widely in their opinions about whether or not Negroes have made actual, or even relative, citizenship gains since World War II. Some leaders in New Orleans feel that advancements toward equal citizenship have been noteworthy; about the same number feel that the gains in some areas are canceled out by losses in other areas; and a few Negro leaders are convinced that Negroes, at least in New Orleans, have actually lost ground insofar as citizenship is concerned.

Since first-class citizenship is such a highly valued goal on the part of Negroes, they tend to expect all of their leaders and organizations to take some definite part in the "advancement of colored people." In this sense, practically all successful Negro leaders are engaged, directly or indirectly, in race relations, and at one time or another, all Negro organizations engage in programs designed to improve the status of Negroes. This, again, is perhaps what Myrdal means when he observes that "the Negro genius is imprisoned in the Negro problem."[1]

The concept of first-class citizenship is used by Negroes to cover a wide variety of rights and privileges. However, as used here, this concept is meant to include only equal protection of the law, equal rights of political participation, and equal access to public facilities.

Equal protection of the law

Negroes have relied heavily upon the Fourteenth Amendment in their contention for equal citizenship. This amendment provides that no state may deny any person within its jurisdiction "equal protection of the law." In a broad sense, this phrase has been interpreted to cover inequalities in housing, economic opportunities, transportation, education, and even segregation per se. It is applied here in the narrow, literal sense which involves arrest, court procedures, and punishment for crimes.

Arrest. One of the most vexing problems with which New Orleans Negroes have had to deal is that of hostile policemen. Since 1940 Negroes have registered numerous complaints regarding punitive police actions. The various incidents of punitive behavior registered by Negroes may be summarized under four general headings:

(1) *Indiscriminate arrest.* There is widespread belief by Negroes that police officers habitually arrest Negroes on the slightest pretense. It is not uncommon for "police roundups" to include persons walking the street, waiting for transportation, and otherwise going about their routine business. The usual reason police give for such arrests is that they are attempting to solve some

---

[1] Gunnar Myrdal, *op. cit.*, p. 28.

crime and are "taking people in" who might in any way be suspect. When this reason has basis in fact, the Negro community is tolerant. Yet there is evidence that at times harassment is the only motive. This situation was summarized by a minister who said that—

> I have known them [the police] to arrest people walking along the street minding their own business. If the police had only been professional enough to ask for their identities they could have known immediately that those they arrested were innocent of crime. They didn't do this. They often prefer to drag Negroes down to the station and have them questioned and insulted like common criminals, and sometimes even jailed for several hours, before they bother to establish their innocence. . . . I remember a man coming from work who was stopped in front of his house. He tried to get the officers to call his parents who would establish beyond doubt his identity, and the fact that he was at work during the day. He demanded that they show him a warrant. They beat him unmercifully and charged him with resisting arrest. It was later established that he had no criminal record and, of course, did not commit whatever crime the policemen had in mind.

The incident described by the minister is typical of scores of such incidents reported by Negroes throughout the years. Negroes are frequently subjected to mass arrest. This ordinarily occurs when some Negro is involved in a fight or otherwise "disturbs the peace." On such occasions the police are likely to arrest "every Negro in sight," whether these people have any connection with the crime or not.

An important consequence of the disrespect that white police express toward Negroes is the hatred many Negroes have come to feel, not only for the police, but for the system of law enforcement itself. A *Louisiana Weekly* editorial best sums up this problem: "The treatment the Negro receives [at the hands of policemen who make arrests] is not making a better citizen of him, it only embitters him, makes him resentful, sullen, ready to explode."[2]

(2) *Discourtesy.* The most widespread criticism Negroes have had of the police in New Orleans is that they are generally discourteous to them. Even when Negroes have been stopped for simple traffic violations, they have often been subjected to insults, and not infrequently they are addressed as "nigger," "boy," or "girl."

One Negro physician, for example, hurrying to the bedside of a patient, was stopped by the police for speeding. The officer evidently resented the Negro's referring to himself as "Doctor," and he reminded him that he was "just another black nigger in my book." When the physician objected to the abusive language of the officer, he was arrested and kept in jail for some hours. Similar incidents are so common that most Negroes have come to *expect* discourtesy on the part of policemen, and express surprise when they are treated courteously.

(3) *Unfair treatment of Negro women and juveniles.* Time and again the police

[2] August 28, 1943.

have been accused of mistreating Negro women and children. A Negro lawyer,

> gathered a mountain of evidence which would prove that one of the most serious problems in New Orleans is the way white policemen take unjust advantage of Negro women. Sometimes, Negro women are arrested on the slightest pretense, forced to accompany them to some secluded spot, and raped.

Such a case as the lawyer described became a *cause célèbre* when a Negro woman filed formal charges of rape against three uniformed officers. Another related aspect of police brutality has been the manner in which some of them have treated juveniles. Periodically, there are reports of beatings, unfair punishment, and even murder of Negro children. Since 1940, there have been several formal investigations into such incidents. Policemen involved are usually exonerated.

(4) *Cruelty.* As a rule, police cruelty has been committed during the apprehension and arrest of logical suspects who are often subsequently found guilty. Unfortunately, this type of behavior has not caused as much negative publicity as it might have if the suspects had been law-abiding citizens. Ordinarily, cruelty to proven criminals is only brought to light by their lawyers. Some incidents of cruelty have been so flagrant, however—such as the beating to death of Negroes already under arrest or in jail—that formal investigations were launched. Most often these investigations were conducted by the police department itself, and they usually ended in an announcement that the policemen involved were blameless. On rare occasions, when the evidence was overwhelming, some policemen have been suspended for acts of cruelty.

There is ample evidence that insofar as Negroes are concerned, police officers characteristically treat them as second-class citizens. This thesis is validated by a reported conversation between two policemen "knocking off from duty." One said to the other, "I didn't hit him because he had his hat pulled down over his face and I couldn't tell whether he was a 'nigger' or not."

Court procedures. Until recent years—actually until about 1950—Louisiana courts were "lily white." Not only were all officials white, but the juries were as well. The practice of using all-white juries has been a major legal contention. On the basis of this practice federal courts have reversed numerous decisions as a violation of "due process of law." It was only during the 1950's that Negro lawyers became a significant element in the Negro community. This has been documented in a manuscript done for this study. The author points out that—

> At the close of World War II there was only one Negro lawyer practicing in New Orleans, and not more than three in the entire state. . . . Many reasons may be offered to explain this. . . . Perhaps the most important reason is that

until recently, the courts were "lily white." Historically, the courts were the basic instruments used by southern whites to validate segregation, to prevent any form of integration, and to discourage any effort of social mobility on the part of the Negro masses.[3]

Even now, where decision-making is concerned, the courts in Louisiana may be described as "lily white." Negro leaders still generally feel that "insofar as the civil rights of Negroes are concerned, southern courts have served mainly as filters through which civil rights violations may come in due process, to the attention of federal courts."[4]

In regard to court procedures, Negro leaders have called attention to two glaring discrepancies: one, the fact that at one time Negroes were systematically excluded from jury service; and two, that all court officials are white and are believed to have a more or less careless attitude toward Negroes. "Certainly," a Negro lawyer asserted, "they can hardly be expected to understand the social background of Negroes who appear before the bar of justice."

Punishment for crimes. In regard to punishment for crimes, Negro leaders have called attention to three general inequalities in the administration of justice: one, Negroes often receive considerably harsher punishment for crimes than do white persons who commit the same crimes; two, in their view, Negro crimes against Negroes are often treated too lightly; and three, Negroes are more severely punished for crimes against white people than are whites for the same crimes against Negroes.

For years, Negro leaders have complained that Negroes are meted out heavier sentences by courts than are white criminals. "It is almost a truism in the Negro community," one leader phrased it, "that Negroes receive stiffer fines and longer prison sentences than do whites who commit the same crimes." He initiated an investigation recently in which it was found that Negro prisoners in the state penitentiary were, in fact, serving considerably longer terms for crimes than were white prisoners for the same crimes.

A white supremacist attempted to establish the fact that "all Negroes who are not criminals tend to condone crime. This is the main purpose of the NAACP. Instead of trying to improve Negroes, like it ought, it spends its time trying to defend Negroes who ought to remain in jail." This statement overlooks a basic attitude on the part of Negro leaders: Perhaps no other Americans are as ashamed of crimes committed by members of their group, and are more determined to curb crime, than they are. All established Negro leaders at one time or another have complained about the crime rate in the Negro community. One leader voiced what he believed to be a majority opinion among Negroes when he denounced certain socioeconomic classes of Negroes for

[3] Barbara M. Guillory, *op. cit.*, p. 18.
[4] Daniel C. Thompson, "The Role of the Federal Courts in the Changing Status of Negroes Since World War II," *The Journal of Negro Education*, Spring 1961, p. 97.

betraying everything your leaders have fought for. While your leaders fight for equality you attempt to give the lie to everything they say. I see Negroes hanging out on [————] street every day. They are determined to undermine all the prog- ress we have made since slavery. Sometimes I wish they were all herded together and kept in jail until they learn some sense.

In actual fact, then, most Negro leaders are hypercritical of what they regard as socially reprehensible behavior on the part of members of their race. They have constantly pleaded with the Negro masses to consider the social consequences of their behavior. They try to convince them that they, like other Negroes, should help to "uplift" their people.

Some leaders minimize the Negro crime rate. They hold that "Negroes do not commit more crimes than others, they are simply more frequently arrested." Others point out that Negroes commit "precisely the kind of crimes for which there are highest arrest rates. Many white criminals are so-called 'big-wheels.' They have other people to take the rap for them." These leaders often contended that "Negroes are no more criminal than are other individuals who are subject to the same negative social forces."

The various apologies offered by class-oriented Negro leaders reflect that they would like to disassociate themselves from the "criminal element" in the Negro community, and that they are intolerant of Negroes who commit crimes. Thus, the *Louisiana Weekly* published several editorials some years ago calling for stiffer punishment for Negroes who commit crimes against other Negroes. One of the editorials voiced approval when a Negro was given the death penalty for the murder of another Negro, and pointed out that this kind of justice was long overdue, because it had been ten years since a Negro in New Orleans had been given the death penalty for an intraracial murder. All evidence seems to bear out one important conclusion: all Negro leaders are anxious to reduce the crime rate among Negroes, and some of them do not approve when courts treat Negro crimes against Negroes lightly.

Negro leaders concur that a Negro is more severely punished for crimes against whites than whites are for crimes against Negroes. This double standard of justice has been attacked numerous times over the years. Our findings suggest that it is applied to various criminal acts from traffic violations to murder. No crime so dramatically points up the practice of differential justice as much as do cases involving rape. Negroes have held protest mass meetings about it, petitioned public authorities on the state and national levels, and appealed to the federal courts.

The history of the Negro's experience under a double standard of justice was summarized in a *Louisiana Weekly* editorial of April 29, 1961. It called attention to the fact that—

Approximately 50 Negroes have been put to death for the rape of white women since the crime was defined in 1892 as a capital offense. During the same period only two whites have been executed—the last in Orleans Parish 54 years ago.

Ironically, no male—Negro or white has paid the extreme penalty for violating a Negro female. A half dozen Negroes are presently awaiting execution in Louisiana for this crime against white females. . . . The worse that has happened to any white accused is that he received a mild jail sentence.

This is not an attempt to justify the crime of rape nor to say that persons found guilty should not be punished according to law. This merely points out the undeniable fact that the severe penalties in Louisiana's rape law are reserved exclusively for Negroes accused of assaulting white females.

EQUAL RIGHTS OF POLITICAL PARTICIPATION

According to the Fifteenth Amendment:

The right of citizens of the United States to vote shall not be denied or abridged by the United States or by any state on account of race, color, or previous condition of servitude.

The right to vote is a cornerstone of our republican form of government. It is inherent in the proposition that in a democracy public decisions should reflect the majority will. This principle of decision-making has never been seriously questioned by Negro leaders. In fact, every organization in the Negro community, like those in the white community, relies upon majority vote for the determination of its policies, goals, strategies, and techniques. Thus, there is no evidence that the Negro community objects to the principle of "the people's choice." What Negroes insist upon is that all segments of the community, and Negroes specifically, should participate in public elections, so that elected candidates are, in fact, "the people's choice."

Negro leaders have launched any number of drives to increase voter registration. There is hardly a single recognized Negro leader, or effective Negro organization, that has not gone on record as a sponsor or participant in one of these drives. "Top" Negro leaders have been attempting to mobilize other leaders and organizations to make all-out efforts to increase Negro voting strength to near its maximum each year since 1950. Before then, they realistically attempted to get a token number registered. They knew that the tradition of Negro disfranchisement and opposition from powerful segregationist forces would not permit more than a token number of registrations. Yet, even before 1950, as now, some Negro race men used every strategy and technique available to them to encourage Negroes to become registered voters.

The various means Negro leaders have employed in their drives to increase the number of Negro registrants were always given maximum publicity in the local Negro press. Looking back over the years, the *Louisiana Weekly*, for example, has been a sort of unofficial coordinator of the various strategies and techniques leaders have advanced in attempts to convince the Negro masses that voting is a good thing.

Negro leaders have made several kinds of appeals in order to stimulate voter registration. They have presented data to show that only registered voters are actively included in the running of government; and that all decision-making concerning appropriations for city improvements, welfare programs, education, and recreation are made by persons who are directly or indirectly responsible to those who hold elective offices. Consequently, Negroes are often reminded that it will do little good to protest unfair treatment in the dispensation of public funds so long as they are not counted among those participating in making "the people's choice."

They point out that some of the best jobs in the state, and some of the most promising business opportunities available, are directly controlled by elected officials; and that the money appropriated for certain jobs is collected from them, as taxpayers, and that they, along with others, *deserve* equal consideration. Yet, from a realistic political point of view, such opportunities will continue to be open to those who are able to determine the security of professional politicians. Leaders have attempted, on any number of occasions, to establish the fact that equal protection of the law is a direct function of the voting strength of the individuals or groups in question. Thus, during each of the many meetings to protest police brutality, this proposition has been hammered home by practically every speaker.

This position was stated by a prominent minister in a 1959 "loyalty rally." He said, "The ballot is the only concrete symbol that politicians fully understand. With it he sees you as a man and woman, not as a boy and girl; he sees you through the eyes of respectability." Others have called attention to the fact that in communities where the Negro voting strength is significant, Negroes enjoy a great deal more respect than they do in New Orleans, where their strength is considerably weaker; and that not only does voting strength eventuate in respect from politicians, but it is also reflected in business associations and civic improvement leagues, as well as in personal courtesies on the part of white "men of power." As one Negro put it, "When you are a registered voter, you don't have to demand respect, you are, in fact, respectable." Thus, the Negro masses have been constantly reminded that it is morally and ethically expedient to become registered voters. In this connection, some ministers have done a creditable job of getting their church members to register and vote. A few have also attempted to stimulate other ministers to include civic responsibility among the Christian virtues they advocate.

All of these appeals were summarized in a handbill circulated by the Frontiers' Club of New Orleans just prior to the 1960 gubernatorial election in an effort to encourage Negroes to register:

ASK YOURSELF—

CAN YOU get a job in your city government as a clerk, a stenographer, a maintenance worker, supervisor, a sanitation worker, a mechanic, or any other job you can do?

YES, if you register and vote!

CAN YOU get decent housing in desirable neighborhoods?

YES, if you register and vote!

CAN YOU get better parks, playgrounds and recreation centers for you and
your children?

YES, if you register and vote!

CAN YOU get fair and equal police protection?

YES, if you register and vote!

CAN YOUR CHILD get equal educational opportunities?

YES, if you register and vote!

On the opposite side of this handbill a sample ballot was printed for the convenience of those who might wish to learn how to fill it out correctly.

Despite constant efforts on the part of Negro leaders, the number of registered Negro voters has increased very slowly. In 1940, there were only about 400 Negro voters in Orleans Parish, and by 1942 just 660.[5] At present (1962) the number of Negro registered voters is about 36,000. However, this is still less than a third of the 125,000 or more eligibles. This proportion is very small indeed compared with the more than 176,000 white voters registered, who represent 69 per cent of all white eligibles.

The Negro masses are well aware of the differential treatment they receive in this biracial society. They are convinced that their rights and privileges will continue to be limited unless they become a significant part of the electorate. Why, then, is it that the many drives to increase the number of Negro registrants have had so little tangible effect? There are, of course, many reasons. We call attention here to some of the most salient.

The white primary. The "lily white" primary was designed to serve the same purpose (to prevent Negroes from voting) as the "grandfather clause" and the poll tax. That is, it was conceived as the safest and most effective "legal" means of disenfranchising Negroes, while at the same time not limiting the franchise of white people. Specifically, it was based upon the assumption that the primary had the same legal status as a private organization. Therefore, leaders of the Democratic party contended that they could adopt any rules they wished, including those to exclude certain persons from its membership. In effect, the Negro could not register as a Democrat under this system of regulation. The few Negroes who did register had to do so either as Republicans or Independents.

The "lily white" primary was an ingenious method of disenfranchisement because, in a state politically controlled by the Democratic party, it auto-

[5] Report of Secretary of State, State of Louisiana, January 1, 1941 to December 31,. 1942.

matically barred Negroes from participation on a local level. Seldom do Republicans or Independents have a chance to vote except in national elections. This kind of token voting on the part of non-Democrats could bring little more than psychological satisfaction to the voters, since there are never enough of them to eventuate in any tangible political consequence.

This method of disenfranchising Negro people was finally outlawed in 1944 in the *Smith* v. *Allwright* case, in which the United States Supreme Court ruled that the defendant, as a citizen of the United States, had been illegally denied voting privileges because of exclusion from the Democratic primary. Since the Democratic primary, according to the United States Supreme Court's ruling in the *Classic* case, was tantamount to election, Smith had been denied his constitutional rights to participate in public elections. Justice Reed, who read the decision, was emphatic on this point. He held that the white primary violated both the Fourteenth and Fifteenth Amendments, and that "when primaries become a part of the machinery for choosing officials, state and national, as they have here, the same tests to determine the character of discrimination abridgement should be applied to the primary as are applied to the general election."[6]

This decision did not affect the political status of Negroes in Louisiana to any significant degree until after it had been definitely validated by the *Elmore* v. *Rice* case in 1948. As a result, by 1950 the Secretary of the State of Louisiana reported 26,029 Negro registered voters in Orleans Parish. This means that the many voter registration drives by Negro leaders have resulted in adding a mere 10,000 Negroes to the rolls over a ten-year period, or an average of 1,000 per year.

The one-party system. For all practical purposes, there is only one political party in Louisiana—the Democratic party. Democratic nomination is tantamount to election. Within the party itself there are some political factions, but they all come under the auspices of the State Central Committee. Many citizens, both white and Negro, have protested that under such a system the voter has very little choice in regard to issues. Actually, the most important "issue" in primary elections is what candidate has the best personality. As a rule, the major distinction between the platforms of the recognized political factions lies in the means they promise to use to accomplish virtually the same objectives. For example, the race issue is never debated in terms of whether there will be continued segregation or some program of desegregation. This is already decided by the State Central Committee. What is debated is what strategies and techniques will be employed to maintain the status quo in regard to the races.

It is the lack of real issues in state and city elections that tends to discourage citizens, regardless of their race, from voting. This attitude was expressed succinctly by a Negro leader when he was prevailed upon to

[6] For a summary of federal court decisions regarding the civil status of Negroes see Rayford W. Logan, *The Negro in the United States* (New York: D. Van Nostrand Company, 1957), pp. 106-182.

participate in a registration drive: "What's the use?" he said. "Whoever runs for office will be designated by the same gang. I don't have time to worry about which candidate is the lesser evil." In other words, many voters feel that there is little purpose in voting because, in terms of issues, there is actually no contest. As we shall see, this is the main reason why Negro political leaders appear so inconsistent and contradictory in their endorsements of candidates.

Voter restrictions. The voting laws of Louisiana, and all interpretations of these laws by the courts and by elected officials, make it clear that voting is regarded as a *privilege* and not a *right*. Actually, all branches of the state government have held, at one time or another, that the state has the "exclusive authority" to decide who should or who should not be eligible to exercise the privilege of voting.

This philosophy of voting makes it logical for a state to set up any voting laws it pleases, as long as they can be applied "without discrimination." Consequently, the relatively powerless Negro masses are in the undesirable position of trying to qualify according to laws that were designed specifically to *prevent* them from qualifying for the "privilege" of voting.

The several voting regulations intended to prevent Negroes from qualifying in large numbers include "standards of morality," "Americanism," and "literacy." The specific Louisiana law regarding voter registration, as adopted in 1959, provides that citizens applying to register as voters shall be of "good character," "shall understand the duties and obligations of citizenship," and "shall also be able to read any clause in this Constitution (Louisiana) or the Constitution of the United States and give a reasonable interpretation thereof."

In order to determine the literacy of applicants the state legislature approved twenty-four separate tests, a total of seventy-two questions (three questions for each test). Among the constitutional laws to be interpreted are the following:

The right of the people to keep and bear arms, shall not be infringed (U. S. Constitution, Second Amendment).

Full faith and credit shall be given in each state to the public acts, records, and judicial proceedings of every other state (U. S. Constitution, Article IV, Section 1).

The powers not delegated to the United States by the Constitution, nor prohibited by it to the states, are reserved to the states respectively, or to the people (U. S. Constitution, 10th Amendment).

The citizens of each state shall be entitled to all privileges and immunities of citizens in the several states (U. S. Constitution, Article IV, Section 2).

The judicial power of the United States shall be tested in one Supreme Court, and in such inferior courts as the Congress may from time to time ordain and establish (U. S. Constitution, Article III, Section 1).

No power of suspending laws of this state shall be exercised unless by the legislature or by its authority (Article 19, Section 5, Louisiana Constitution).

Perpetual franchise or privileges shall not be granted to any person or corporation by the state or by any political subdivision thereof (Article 13, Section 7, Louisiana Constitution).

The legislature shall provide for the registration of voters throughout the state (Article 8, Section 17, Louisiana Constitution).

The exercise of the police power of the state shall never be abridged (Article 19, Section 18, Louisiana Constitution).

The military shall be in subordination to the civil power (Article 1, Section 4, Louisiana Constitution).

No ex-post facto law, nor any law impairing the obligation of contracts, shall be passed (Article 4, Section 15, Louisiana Constitution).

Nor shall any vested rights be divested, unless for purpose of public utility, and for just and adequate compensation previously paid (Article 4, Section 15, Louisiana Constitution).

In a debate concerning test questions in the state legislature, one legislator pointed out that any registrar in the state could apply these tests in such a way that "no one of us in this room could qualify to vote in Louisiana." What he evidently meant to call attention to is this: even the United States Supreme Court Justices have rendered quite different opinions arising from their interpretations of certain of these constitutional laws. And even if there were an established uniform interpretation of each of these codes, any registrar of voters can "flunk" any applicant he chooses since answers are to be given orally, and the registrar has the "legal" right to determine (without witnesses) whether the answers are satisfactory or not. These tests, then, are used to limit the number of Negro registered voters whenever and wherever it is deemed desirable. This is, indeed, their avowed purpose.

The exponents of the so-called literacy tests claim that when they are applied by segregationists "according to the letter of the law," all Negroes except a very small percentage can be rejected. Knowing this, a Negro lawyer predicts that "the voting strength of Negroes will always be kept down by segregationists in state politics until the federal government sets a definite standard of literacy—say a sixth-grade education."

Louisiana legislators have also perfected other ingenious techniques to limit the Negro vote. Among the most effective are the "slowdown," a technique that permits a registrar to take an unspecified amount of time to register a single applicant; and "tricky" questions, such as the one on the registration form that reads "My color is ———." The voter cannot know whether this refers to the pigmentation of his skin or to his race, or even whether he is supposed to use the designation "colored" or "Negro."

Another such ambiguous question asks for precise age in terms of years, months, and days. The applicant has no way of knowing, and is not told by the registrar, whether he is to use the legal thirty-day month or the calendar month. The simple question of age becomes extremely difficult as it is asked on the official registration form of Louisiana. This fact was dramatized before the United States Supreme Court in a 1960 hearing, when the State of Louisiana was summoned to answer charges on the constitutionality of its voter-registration procedures. "At one point," reports the *Louisiana Weekly*, "the state's attorney was asked to compute the age of the Negro school teacher who failed the literacy test because she was one day older than she reported, by not including in her computation the date of registration. . . . The state's attorney worked at it for nearly ten minutes, counting on his fingers in plain view." These "tricky" questions have proved to be so effective in limiting the number of Negro registered voters in New Orleans that it has seldom been necessary to ask Negro applicants to interpret constitutional laws in order to "flunk" them.

The literacy tests and "tricky" questions function to discourage would-be voters at several points. First, any Negro desiring to register, regardless of the degree of his literacy, would hardly undertake such an ordeal without some previous instruction. Not only must he learn "the letter of the law" and how to read and write any portion of it, but he must also acquaint himself with the various interpretations that might be satisfactory to different registrars. Second, in effect, the potential voter must not only find time to register, but he must also find time for considerable schooling. This schooling is very important, because if an applicant makes the slightest error in filling out the registration form the registrar of voters is permitted by law to require him to wait up to ten days, conceivably more, before being eligible to try again. There are instances where applicants have made six or more unsuccessful attempts to register. Therefore, a large number of potential Negro voters simply cannot take enough time off from their jobs to wait in line for their turn when the "slowdown" is being used, or to return to try again and again, only to be refused by registrars who are forbidden by law to tell them why they are rejected.

Third, it is psychologically upsetting to submit to a test, even for those who are accustomed to being tested. Such an experience is, of course, doubly disturbing to persons who have taken few if any tests in their lives, particularly when they are aware that the tests are intended solely to disenfranchise them. Among the test terms the applicant may be asked to explain are: "ex post facto," "insubordination," "franchise," "infringe," "original jurisdiction," "judicial proceedings," "immunities," and "vested and divested rights." These are some of the most sophisticated concepts used by trained lawyers to express themselves, and they could hardly be in the everyday vocabulary of even highly trained specialists in other fields. Ordinarily, then, it would take long, intensive training to prepare the average citizen to the extent that he would feel comfortable in using these concepts in a situation where he knows full well his answers will be scrutinized by hypercritical registrars. Small wonder that an investigation by the Civil Rights Commission discovered that Negroes with the most advanced university degrees had been denied registration because they had "flunked" literacy tests presumably passed by illiterate whites.

Lethargy. Martin Luther King, Jr. has accused the Negro masses in some places of being "too apathetic and lazy to exercise the franchise." This has been a recurrent contention of Negro leaders interviewed for this study. The majority of them expressed great dissatisfaction over the apathy of potential Negro voters. A few insisted that Negro apathy "is primarily the reason why Negroes have made no more progress in New Orleans than they have. They are too shortsighted and lazy to secure the ballot, which is the most potent weapon we can use to gain first-class citizenship."

Just saying that Negroes do not take advantage of the franchise because of "apathy and laziness" is too simple a summary of the complex problem Negroes must solve in exercising the right to vote. In addition to the many "legal" restrictions, several aspects of Negro life and history should be taken into consideration.

First, there is no political tradition among Negroes in New Orleans as there is among whites, where there are a number of distinguished political families. All Negro politicians in New Orleans are first-generation, and they are regarded, more or less, as mavericks by whites and Negroes alike. Consequently, in the absence of Negro political families, the Negro masses do not have a tangible symbol of political success and achievement. Negro political leaders are not accorded the respect enjoyed by some white politicians. What social esteem they do have stems from their business or professional success and not from their political achievements. Generally, as political leaders, they do not have the high social status necessary to inspire large numbers of Negroes to aspire to political careers. This lack of aspiration for political careers among young Negroes may, indeed, reveal itself as political apathy to the casual observer.

Second, there are no full-time Negro politicians in the state. Actually, only one Negro in recent history has held a full-time political appointment, a four-year term as assistant district attorney. He was discharged after two and a half years. This means that Negro politicians are, in fact, only political aspirants. The few Negroes who have held political jobs got them through appointment, never election. These positions are always separate from decision-making, and they are part-time, peripheral, and temporary. These appointees simply have not had time or the sustained incentive to give dedicated attention to the cultivation of potential voters, as do many full-time white politicians. About the only time Negro political leaders make special efforts to cultivate potential voters among the Negro masses is the three months or so before some municipal, state, or national election. Usually during this period they are employed by certain white politicians to "deliver" the Negro vote or, occasionally, they volunteer to assist some Negro candidate who runs for political office.

Between political campaigns little is done by Negro leaders to reach potential voters. It was precisely this lack of foresight that led the editor of the *Louisiana Weekly* to deliver a scathing criticism of Negro politicians. He said—

> Negro political leaders in New Orleans would do well to take note of what is happening in . . . [other cities]. In New Orleans there are 84,000 Negroes who have not been convinced that they should become registered voters.
>
> Of course, the Negro political groups are aware that there are municipal elections slated: but they apparently do not realize that now is the time to begin gathering voter strength for these elections. Any political leader who is worth his salt should be up and doing now.
>
> The Negro vote registration total in New Orleans has fluctuated around the 35,000 mark for several years despite the potential of 120,000. This is proof enough that Negro political leaders are not doing the job; and until more than 50 per cent of the eligible Negroes are registered voters in New Orleans, each—without exception—should hang his head in shame.[7]

It would seem that until the Negro community has developed some full-time politicians whose security is based upon election to public office, the Negro potential electorate is likely to remain small.

Third, Negroes are traditionally excluded from political jobs. In the white community literally thousands of jobs are held by persons who have in some small way, directly or indirectly, been responsible for electing someone to political office. Each of these jobholders is a potential political campaigner. Some will campaign only among friends and relatives, while many others will campaign only in the broader community. This they do for their own economic security because the continuation of their jobs, or new jobs for relatives and friends, may depend upon who is elected to public office. The Negro community, on the other hand has few, if any, informal political campaigners. In other words, there are large numbers of white voters who can expect to receive tangible rewards for voting, while for Negroes about the only incentive for overcoming stubborn barriers to registration is the indefinite promise of first-class citizenship made by Negro political aspirants.

Fourth, there is a definite lack of faith in Negro political leaders. In order to have any political success, Negro political leaders have felt it necessary to ally themselves with white politicians. Since white politicians, so far, are all avowed segregationists, Negroes tacitly or openly classify most Negro politicians as Uncle Toms. As one Negro reasoned, "Governor (————) has already gone on record as being one thousand per cent for segregation, now I ask you, what kind of Negro do you think can cull favors from him except an Uncle Tom. In my book all of the so-called Negro politicians in New Orleans are back-door boys."

Another Negro leader called attention to the fact that "our leaders [politicians] are latched onto different white segregationists. Did you notice this week's paper [the *Louisiana Weekly*]? Each of our top men had his picture made with a different white supremacist. I can't see, to save my life, how

[7] July 29, 1961.

they have the nerve to go around asking us—their own relatives and friends —to elect some white Citizens' Council segregationist to public office."

Although Negro politicians have tried repeatedly "to get the Negro masses to understand the strategy behind their support of white supremacists," as one Negro politician complained, there is reason to believe that the vast majority of Negroes agree with the labor-union member who confided, "From what I can see, Negro politicians, except one or two, are in that racket for what they can get out of it personally. I think they actually hate some of the men they support." From statements like these, we may conclude that so long as most Negro politicians are widely regarded as Uncle Toms, they will have little significant influence in persuading Negroes to register and vote.

Finally, Negro voters are subject to periodic purges. The registrar of voters is appointed by the governor of the state. During some recent administrations registrars in New Orleans were apparently somewhat less dedicated to keeping the number of Negro registrants low than during other administrations. As a result, the Negro registration in the state in 1956 reached a high of 160,892, with 31,980 in Orleans Parish. Of the total number of Negroes registered in the state, 19,346 were classified as illiterate, compared with 30,661 white voters. One governor's opponents accused him of increasing the Negro vote and making it easy for white illiterates to vote because these two overlapping elements helped him maintain his political power. According to a Negro politician who was a loyal Earl Long supporter—

> Long's opponents knew that the only way they could possibly break his political back was to find some legal means of preventing a large number of Negroes and poor whites from voting. It was not surprising that just prior to the gubernatorial election the arch segregationist in the state invented the purge. He insisted that he intended the purge to affect mostly Negroes. He said that his intention was to purge 90 per cent of the Negro voters from the registration rolls.

The segregationists' main technique was to have registrars throughout Louisiana, particularly in parishes where there was a sizable Negro electorate, check through all registration forms filled out by Negroes to see if they had been completed correctly. The registrars were ordered to challenge the registration of any person whose voter application showed the slightest discrepancy. One registrar charged that the Joint Legislative Committee on Segregation was trying to remove all Negroes from the rolls. She said that at first it had instructed the registrars to confine themselves to "major errors," but later they were instructed to challenge on "minor errors" as well. She concluded that if they challenged Negroes and whites impartially, "they'll get 92 per cent of my [white] people." This committee made it clear, however, that purging would not be done impartially.[8]

[8] Report of the United States Commission on Civil Rights (U. S. Government Printing Office, Washington, D. C., 1959), pp. 105-106. Reported also in the *Times Picayune*. August 4, 1959.

Throughout the latter part of 1959 and early 1960, registrars continued to issue challenges to Negro voters over the state. One day challenges were issued to more than 2,500 voters in Orleans Parish. It is not known exactly how many Negroes in Orleans Parish were actually disqualified by the purge. However, despite the fact that some Negroes continued to register as a result of registration drives, there were fewer on the rolls in 1959 than in 1956, when there were 32,578. Thousands of Negroes were stricken from the rolls throughout the state. The percentage of eligible Negroes registered to vote in Louisiana decreased from 31.7 in 1956 to 27.5 in 1959. The purge was most diligently applied in certain rural parishes where the percentage of Negroes registered or potential voters was relatively high. For instance, in Red River Parish, where Negroes constitute about 45 per cent of the potential electorate, the number of registered voters was reduced from 1,512 to 15.

Wholesale, indiscriminate purges by segregationist forces in Louisiana finally resulted in an investigation by the United States Attorney General's office and the Civil Rights Commission. In March, 1960, the state was summoned before the United States Supreme Court to answer charges that it had illegally removed Negroes from the registration rolls. At the end of the hearing that court unanimously upheld a key clause in the 1957 Civil Rights Act, and ordered that 1,377 Louisiana Negroes be restored to voting rolls. Again, in August 1961 the United States District Court ordered 570 Negro voters reinstated to the rolls. These represent only a small proportion of those who had been purged, yet these actions by the courts do validate the Negro's constitutional right to vote. They have also made the registrars of voters a good deal more discriminating in their purge campaigns.

EQUAL ACCESS TO PUBLIC FACILITIES

Another of the most stubborn fights Negroes have had over the years is for the unsegregated use of public accommodations. It is a well-established fact that public authorities use the lion's share of taxes to provide public facilities for the use of whites only. Actually, ever since Reconstruction the system of "black codes" in the South has covered almost all types of public and private facilities and has restricted the better of them for whites. In New Orleans, these "black codes" cover such facilities as the municipal auditorium, transportation, recreational facilities, eating establishments, hotels, and so forth.

Until 1950 Negro leaders had made no apparent dent in the impregnable wall of rigid racial discrimination in the use of public facilities. Most white authorities stubbornly ignored the inequalities existing in this area. Those who did recognize these inequalities did little more than express belief in the fairness of the "separate but equal" doctrine and the hope that some day equality actually might be attained. There is still seldom any admission on their part that Negroes deserve equality in regard to public accommodations. Apparently white officials still give little thought to the need for unsegregated use of available facilities; until recently most Negro leaders tended to accept the "separate but equal" approach, and only once in a while did a race man demand integration of public facilities. However, as early as 1940 a few "radical" Negro leaders did go on record as totally opposed to segregated facilities. Today, practically every Negro organization endorses outright or tacitly the principle that "segregation must go." They have joined in the fight to end segregation in every area of community life. Some of these organizations are militant, but most of them work quietly, yet relentlessly, to accomplish this goal. This effort to end racial segregation in the use of public facilities has gained momentum since 1954. Since then, the drive to end segregation in private businesses has reached almost the same strength as that against segregated public facilities.

Negro leaders are nearly unanimous in their insistence that segregation in any area of public life is an affront to the dignity of Negroes as individuals. It is also interesting to note that all Negro leaders interviewed were optimistic about the ending of segregation in New Orleans. They agreed that it would come first in the use of public facilities, but they felt that once segregation in public life is abolished, it would soon disappear in all areas of community life. For example, a Negro lawyer predicted that Negroes would be permitted to use all public facilities within five years, and would be admitted freely to white churches and even social clubs within a decade. He reasoned, "Once we have public facilities desegregated, Negroes and whites will have an opportunity to get to know one another as persons. They will then organize clubs of their own choosing, which will not use race as a criterion for membership."

Underlying this optimism on the part of Negro leaders is the conviction that most of the racial frictions, fears, and stereotypes are due to state and city regulations preventing Negroes and whites from getting to know one another. Some of the leaders expressed great hope that when Negroes and whites have opportunities to know one another as persons negative attitudes about Negroes will soon disappear. This hope undergirds the strategies and techniques Negro leaders use in their attempts to achieve equal citizenship, which will be discussed in the next chapter.

7

CITIZENSHIP

Strategies and Techniques

IN ATTEMPTS TO achieve equal citizenship, Negro leaders and uplift organizations have relied upon five basic strategies: *protest*, which is largely verbal in nature; *negotiation*, which usually emphasizes persuasion; *litigation*, intended primarily to have legal barriers to equal citizenship declared unconstitutional; *political action*, designed to achieve civil rights through bloc voting and other political maneuvers; and *direct action*, calculated to force state and local governments to abandon "Jim Crow" laws.

PROTEST—POLICE BRUTALITY

The strongest and most consistent protest the Negro community has voiced has been directed at police brutality. The problem was well summarized in a memorandum sent to Negro leaders by a "Committee to Prevent Police Brutality to Negro Citizens." Dealing with "recent beatings of Negroes by police without justification," it called attention to—

> A matter of grave and extreme importance that cries out for our *support;* for the *support* of every key Negro leader in the Parish of Orleans. This matter concerns itself with the increased *wave* of Police beatings of Negroes who have become the subject of arrests.
> Because of the fact that numerous persons have contacted various Negro leaders to do something about this dastardly thing, we have found it necessary to call a "SUMMIT CONFERENCE OF NEGRO LEADERS" to discuss the grave issues involved herein and to develop a *program of action* to prevent the recurrence of this violation of human rights.[1]

Protest by Negro leaders of "unequal protection of the law" is designed primarily to inform Negroes of the facts regarding this problem, and to

[1] Dated July 7, 1960.

arouse the "conscience of white men of good will" who have the power to intercede in the Negro's behalf. This latter purpose was suggested as early as 1940 in a *Louisiana Weekly* editorial. The writer presented the case against police brutality and concluded with the recommendation that "the most satisfactory solution . . . would be to have a higher selective police force, properly and effectively trained."[2] A year later, the *Louisiana Weekly* again found it necessary to call attention to police brutality. Lamented the editor—

> Everytime a Negro is shot to death in such a manner for resisting arrest and allegedly attempting to escape, as was the case of Wilbur Smith, Willie Buggage, and 15-year-old Jesse Walton, it lessens our faith in this so-called "democracy" we are being conscripted to defend and serves to make us less and less willing to put such matters in the hands of the Lord, as we have done for the past 75 years.[3]

Another type of response registed by Negroes is mass protest. During the early 1940's, when there were fewer than 400 Negroes registered to vote in New Orleans, a militant Negro labor leader called mass outdoor meetings to protest repeated instances of police brutality. It was his custom to present to those gathered the actual victims, who would describe their ordeals in their own way. On these occasions representatives of the police department were usually present. After such mass meetings Negro leaders often received verbal pledges from police authorities that "the situation will be promptly investigated and whatever action deemed necessary will be taken."

This labor leader relates an interesting technique of direct protest that had some effectiveness, after the mayor had refused repeatedly to see him on this matter. He finally got several "thuggish-looking" Negro men to accompany him to the mayor's office. He is still amused when he recalls the excitement and frustration of the receptionists "when they looked up and saw all of us rough-looking Negroes waiting to see the mayor." At first they attempted to have the visitors wait outside in the hall until the mayor had concluded a "high level" conference. When they refused, the mayor's secretary rushed into his office and within seconds the mayor was out asking them what he could do. Whereupon, the leader told him that this was a committee from the Third Ward and they wanted to talk with him about police brutality. The mayor agreed to talk, but requested that the other members of the group wait outside. The leader refused, and all of them went into the mayor's private office. This leader reported that the mayor was so anxious to get them out that "he promised us anything we asked for." He interprets this manifest concern of City Hall as a "fear of race riots, not the Negroes' votes, because we had none."

Still another kind of mass response is the "protest funeral" for Negroes who are killed by the police. On such occasions a number of prominent Negro leaders make speeches intended to appeal to "all Negro and white

[2] February 3, 1940.
[3] *Ibid.*, May 31, 1941.

people who believe in the principles of equality and justice that are so fundamental to our Christian and democratic society," as one speaker said at the funeral of an eleven-year-old boy who had been killed by an officer "in the line of duty."

Since speakers at "protest funerals" are often leading citizens, their statements are widely circulated. Knowing this, one leader revealed an important purpose of this technique by remarking that—

> This funeral will shake up City Hall quite a bit. I don't think it will arouse any sympathy, but it may eventuate in some definite action. You see the mayor likes to sweep all the dirt in New Orleans under the carpet, so when the tourists come everything will look nice and clean. He knows now we don't plan to keep quiet about continual police cruelty to our people. If we keep on hollering loudly enough he is afraid we will be heard in Washington. He doesn't want that.

A new type of protest in New Orleans is picketing. On August 25, 1961 a group of Negroes, led by a Protestant minister, was arrested for picketing a district police station. Their action was meant as a protest against the police "murder" of Ezell Ward, twenty-one-year-old Negro, who had just been beaten to death by police officers after being arrested for simple burglary. This was the second such protest within a week.

For several years Negroes protested discrimination in the hiring of policemen. At first, Negro leaders gathered information relative to the practices of other southern cities, and endeavored to show that wherever used, Negro police had been instrumental in significantly decreasing the incidence of crime among Negroes. This line of reasoning has been summarized from time to time in the *Louisiana Weekly* as a basis for its protests. Thus, in a 1943 editorial, the editor poses the rhetorical question:

> Why a southern city of the size of New Orleans doesn't have Negro police is a fitting question to ask in the light of the high homicide rate among Negroes in this community with apparently nothing being done to halt its apparent upsurge. [4]

In retrospect, protest against police brutality has been focused on these issues: more humane treatment of Negroes suspected of crime, hiring of Negro policemen, and the need to curb crimes among Negroes by "substituting scientific methods of detection for ruthlessness and cruelty."

Equal justice. Insofar as the courts are concerned, Negro leaders have not voiced quite the same level of continual protest as they have in regard to police brutality. Their criticisms were originally directed at the absence of Negroes on juries. For several years the Negro community protested this periodically, particularly when some Negro was convicted of a crime against a white person that received wide publicity. Therefore, protest against court procedures is almost always linked with what the Negro community regards as differential justice. The thorniest problem is that of Negroes who are sen-

[4] *Op. cit.*, June 6, 1943.

tenced to be executed for the rape of white women. This subject has been the basis of numerous mass meetings and formal resolutions sent to local and federal authorities. Sometimes at mass meetings substantial sums are raised for the appeals of those so convicted.

Interestingly enough, the most effective protest directed at all-white jury convictions has been organized by a group of Negro women who have manifested little concern about other racial issues. This association has been active primarily in seeking justice for Negroes accused of rape. The most celebrated case in which this organization played a major part was that of Edgar Labat and Clifton Alton Poret, sentenced to die for the alleged rape of Helen Rajek in 1950. These two Negroes were given national publicity in *Look Magazine*.[5] In an interview with a Louisiana lawyer the author was told bluntly that "the law says you have to prove a man guilty beyond a reasonable doubt. But, the plain fact down here is that if a white lady accuses a Negro of raping her, *he* has to prove that he is innocent beyond any doubt." Therefore, despite the fact that the federal courts have seen fit to order several stays of execution and the United States Supreme Court remanded the case to the federal district court because of "systematic exclusion" of Negroes from the trial jury, these two men are still awaiting execution for rape, twelve years after the alleged crime.

The conflict over equal justice in this case was summarized by Mars in two quoted statements. One is that of a Louisiana state official who said, "This is just a question of two niggers against the integrity of a white lady." The other is in the comment of an expert on United States Supreme Court actions: "For a capital case, this is one of the shakiest I have ever seen."

Years of protest against "lily white" juries and differential justice was summarized in a *Louisiana Weekly* editorial in March, 1960. It attacked all-white juries which had found—

"Three white ex-cops not guilty in the alleged rape of a 23 year old Negro mother . . . thus upholding an old 'Southern custom' of reserving the death penalty for Negroes only who have been charged with rape involving women of the 'master' race."

The editor pointed out that—

There is no question that there is a double standard of justice for the crime of rape in the South. . . . In other words, according to southern customs rape of a Negro woman is not as vicious and ugly as when a white woman is raped. . . . The Communists do not have to raise a finger. "Southern justice," WCC (White Citizens Council) race haters and demagogues are doing a better job than they could ever hope to do in stirring up unrest. . . . The stench of injustice has become too strong to stomach any longer.[6]

[5] Peter Mars, "The Man Who May Break Chessman's Death-Cell Record," *Look Magazine*, July 19, 1960, pp. 19ff.
[6] March 1960.

In March 1961, a "Citizens Committee for Concerted Action" urged Negroes to protest segregation in the courts of the city. It called attention to certain of the most objectionable indignities: segregated rest rooms in the civil district court building, and segregated seating in the juvenile court. The committee asserted, "Municipal courts are the most notorious ones. They have segregated everything."

The committee suggested that citizens write letters, draw up petitions, delegate committees to wait on individual judges and the mayor, and threaten wide publicity and political censure for judges who live in wards with large numbers of Negro voters. They feared that racial discrimination in the use of court facilities would lead inevitably to differential justice.

It is not easy to evaluate the effect Negro protest has had in securing equal protection of the law. But one might ask: With relatively little voting strength, what would have been the story of the courts' treatment of Negroes if they had not protested apparent injustices? One thing is clear: protest has been an important strategy used by Negroes to create a national public opinion unfavorable to differential justice. Local court decisions have had to withstand the glare of a critical United States citizenry. This, no doubt, has functioned to make local courts somewhat more careful in their administration of justice. Thus, according to a prominent Negro lawyer, trial judges often "bend over backwards because they fear that Negro criticism might eventually lead to appeals which could result in reversals from federal courts."

The right to vote. When it comes to protest against voting restrictions, Negro leaders in New Orleans have joined forces with Negro leaders throughout the South. They have insisted that voting rights are federal, not state prerogatives. Thus, all protests against local or state restrictions have been directed toward the stimulation of federal action. As one Negro leader stated the problem—

> White politicians are not fools. They know that if a large number of Negroes are registered to vote, their first show of power would be to vote them out of office, because most of them are known segregationists anyway. Negroes would be wasting time trying to get southern politicians to liberalize voting regulations where they are concerned. All of them boast about their perfect records in fighting civil rights, particularly voting rights. Our position is clear: we must call voting injustices to the attention of the federal government. This is our only hope.

All types of Negro leaders concur on at least one point: the Negro electorate in New Orleans, and throughout Louisiana, must increase to 75 or 80 per cent of its potential before Negro citizens can expect to enjoy equal citizenship status. They seldom pass up an opportunity to denounce local and state authorities who are dedicated to keeping the Negro politically powerless, in the "sacred" tradition of the Solid South.

An NAACP field director reported to the Civil Rights Commission on Negro voter purges in Louisiana—

The most potent weapon available to citizens today is the ballot. We believe that the Commission on Civil Rights and others in the Government concerned with human freedom and justice should foster a "Voice of America" program for Americans, so that political leaders and citizens alike, knowing the promises of democracy, might work toward the fulfillment of those promises.

In the meantime our Federal Government must continue to work, in every possible way, to secure for all of its citizens those basic rights which some states and individuals would usurp. We believe this because we believe that America must first guarantee to its own their heritage of freedom before we can be fully worthy of carrying forward the democratic concepts to peoples abroad. . . .

The essence of the Negro leaders' protests against voting restrictions was captured in a *Louisiana Weekly* editorial—

The oft heard expression of the "professional" Southerners "Leave us alone. . . . Let us solve our own problems. . . . We love the Negro and treat him fairly" has worn pretty thin after 80 odd years or more. In fact, it has worn so thin in some Southern areas that the U. S. Justice Department announced last week it will file more court suits where Negroes are denied the right to register and vote.

It is now time for leaders and statesmen of this so-called democracy of ours to move against the "political hoodlums and racketeers" that infest Southern politics and deny Negroes the rights to register and vote.

Said Roy Wilkins [National NAACP Secretary] in a recent speech: "The right to vote is a basic American right. . . . Through trickery and threats and even violence, Negroes have been kept from the polls. . . . If democracy is precious in Hungary, it is precious in the South."

Meager and slow as this action by the Justice Department might be, it gives most Negroes in the South a boost in morale and renews their faith in democracy.[7]

Public facilities. Negroes in New Orleans have long protested against segregated public accommodations. Their denunciations of segregation have taken several forms. Individuals have protested in public addresses, "letters to the editor," poetry, newspaper articles, scholarly papers, and books. During the early 1940's one teacher expressed his condemnation of segregation on intracity carriers by paying his students small sums to remove "screens" (the signs that partitioned Negro and white passengers) from buses or streetcars.

At one time or another, all Negro organizations in New Orleans find some means of expressing their objections to segregated public facilities. Occasionally, this protest is expressed in their bylaws, constitutions, or formally adopted objectives. Even when this is not the case, Negro organizations denounce segregation indirectly in their public meetings, at which speakers are expected to defend the rights of Negroes to enjoy equal citizenship status. Such speakers, as a rule, will also register strong disapproval of certain white individuals and organizations that attempt to prevent Negroes from attaining civil rights.

[7] *Op. cit.*, November 28, 1959.

Perhaps the most significant protest technique employed by Negroes has been the carnival "blackout" movement. This movement brought to focus practically all of the grievances Negroes have had in regard to racial segregation. It was sponsored by an organization of social clubs. This organization is composed of representatives of the several Mardi Gras clubs and a musicians' union. Just before the 1957 carnival season, leaders of the united clubs appealed to all of its member clubs to cancel their annual balls to indicate sympathy with the Montgomery and Tallahassee bus boycotts. They coined the slogan, "It is immoral for Negroes in New Orleans to dance while Negroes in Montgomery walk." Member clubs were asked to contribute whatever amounts they had budgeted for their balls to uplift organizations that are "in the fight for freedom and first-class citizenship."

Although the request to cancel balls was made rather late in the year, after some clubs had already made cash deposits on bands and ballrooms, the effort did meet with surprising success. Most carnival clubs either canceled their balls altogether or held them on a much more modest scale than was their custom.

For three years after the 1957 carnival blackout, the Negro clubs went back to their traditional practice of having elaborate annual balls. Then came the school desegregation crisis of 1960, which was characterized by punitive legislation and vilification of Negroes by white supremacists. This was done so blatantly and viciously that one Negro leader summarized the attitudes of Negroes thus—

> During the last several weeks segregationist forces in this state have left no stone unturned to show how much they despise Negroes. The state legislature, with its obviously unconstitutional anti-Negro laws; newspapers, that sound like the official organs of the White Citizens Council; and television stations, that have broadcasted Negro stereotypes in homes to poison the minds of children; all have made the Negro mad.

This speaker went on to endorse the 1961 blackout movement "as one way we can show white supremacists, and the nation, that we are tired of being segregated."

Not only did Negro leaders ask for a cancellation of balls, but they also called for a total carnival blackout in protest against all forms of segregation in New Orleans. This time they included such activities as attending balls given by others, participation in small parties, and attendance at carnival parades. Some leaders even suggested that Mardi Gras should be set aside as a day of prayer. As a result of the wide publicity given this blackout movement, every major ball was canceled; Negroes were noticeably absent from parades, and some actually attended church on that day of traditional festivities.

Immediately after this Mardi Gras the *Louisiana Weekly* observed—

For all who were willing to look, the Negro was conspicuous by his absence [at carnival parades]. Negroes, spearheaded by the United Clubs, Inc., are to be congratulated for the manner and spirit in which they shouldered almost to the man, woman and child the burden of protesting against second-class citizenship.[8]

The frustrations often experienced by Negro leaders in their attempts to secure the full rights and privileges of citizenship are summarized in a formal protest adopted by the New Orleans Chapter of the Frontiers' Club at the height of the school desegregation crisis. The state legislature was in the midst of its fourth special session. It had passed scores of Jim Crow laws and numerous resolutions calculated to preserve the rigid pattern of racial segregation throughout the state. The behavior of this legislative body caused Negro leaders grave concern. A special committee of the club drew up the following protest:

> Today Louisiana is controlled by a handful of power-mad segregationists who are determined to keep Negroes relegated to an inferior citizenship status. All efforts to stem the tide of punitive legislation, economic pressures, and character assassination have failed. It has become necessary for Negro leaders to appeal to the conscience of well-meaning people outside the South to come to their aid, because—
> One, Negro citizens cannot depend upon elected officials to uphold their civil rights.
> Two, enlightened white individuals and groups in Louisiana who disagree with these "Black Codes" are subject to many of the same punitive measures as are Negroes.

The above statement indicates that one important focus of Negro protest is to create favorable civil rights opinion in other parts of the nation. It is an expressed hope that when the North is sufficiently disturbed about what is happening to Negroes in the South, their congressional representatives might be encouraged to take a more definite stand in supporting legislation designed to secure equal rights for all American citizens.

NEGOTIATION

Another of the strategies Negro leaders have used in order to get things done is negotiation. Though the techniques have varied somewhat according to the type of leader, negotiation, as such, generally follows a predictable pattern. It is closely related to protest and is usually carried on by selected members of protest movements and uplift organizations.

Groups that espouse some civil rights issue will gather the facts and then attempt to devise methods by which Negroes might receive equal rights in

[8] February 25, 1961.

that particular area of community life. The Negro community, thus, is informed of the nature of the problem under consideration. If the investigating group is mass-oriented, the next step will be public protest. If the group is class-oriented, negotiations will follow fact-finding and propaganda.

Therefore, as an adjunct to protest, Negro organizations, notably the NAACP, have engaged in negotiations with white men of power in order to achieve equal citizenship status for Negroes. Negro negotiators generally find themselves playing rather awkward roles, since bona fide negotiation presupposes the equality of the parties involved. With practically all political and economic leaders in New Orleans pledged to maintain racial segregation and inferior citizenship status for Negroes, the racial diplomat and the race man are likely to be maneuvered into playing some version of the Uncle Tom role if they are to get things done. It is primarily this noncomplimentary role-playing that prevents negotiation from being a more successful strategy in the Negro's struggle to become a full participating citizen in New Orleans.

Looking back over the past twenty years, *Negro leaders in New Orleans have accomplished little in the advancement of colored people through negotiation.* The Negro community has felt keenly the need to use negotiation to a much greater extent than has been possible in the past. All civic groups among Negroes have petitioned public officials and civic and business organizations in the white community to find some better way whereby fruitful negotiations between the races might be established. Although mayors, for example, have been petitioned time and again to appoint "human relations" or "race relations" committees, just two aborted attempts have been made to do so. Both ended unsuccessfully because Negroes complained that they had not been properly represented or that the mayor had selected Uncle Toms as Negro representatives. Therefore, nothing concrete has resulted.

As far as we are able to ascertain, Negroes in New Orleans have received only two definite citizenship gains as a result of genuine negotiation (without threat of legal or direct action). These are access to the municipal auditorium, and desegregation of the public libraries.

For many years the municipal auditorium was unavailable for Negro use. Negro leaders protested to no avail. Finally, a highly respected Negro diplomat requested the use of the auditorium for a "cultural program." When it was refused, he secured the services of an influential white lawyer, who assisted him in getting information about the use of city auditoriums in other southern cities. They found that all of the forty cities responding had adopted policies whereby certain "trusted" Negro groups could obtain use of their auditoriums. The white lawyer, armed with this information, went with the Negro leader to see the mayor. After receiving the information they had gathered, the mayor proceeded to establish a policy that would permit selected Negro groups to use the auditorium on a segregated basis.

Even now the city auditorium is not available for equal use: just prior to the school desegregation crisis in New Orleans, the NAACP was denied use of the auditorium for a meeting in which Thurgood Marshall, chief attorney for that organization, was to be the main speaker because they allegedly feared racial disturbances might ensue. Yet Negro leaders point out that only a few weeks later, in the midst of the school crisis, this auditorium was let to the white Citizens' Council to hold a segregation rally on the night of the first day of school desegregation. This rally is generally credited with having abetted the riots that occurred after the first peaceful day of desegregation. Again, in early 1962, the white Citizens' Council was permitted to use the auditorium to present an address by a Protestant minister entitled "Why I Believe in Segregation." This mass rally was picketed by a Negro group protesting the fact that only a few days earlier the auditorium had been denied to Martin Luther King, Jr. on the basis that he was controversial. Furthermore, Negroes who attend concerts or other public programs in the auditorium where white people are in attendance are still segregated in "reserved" seats in the balcony, or "buzzard roost."

The desegregation of the public libraries was carried out in a quiet, even secretive manner. There were no public protests or fanfare preceding it. After a group of Negro and white leaders simply "sat down with the proper authorities and talked sense," certain Negro groups in the community were advised that they might use public library facilities without discrimination.

One thing might be pointed out in regard to the two successes achieved by negotiation: The Negro negotiators were class-oriented diplomats, and the white authorities "were intelligent white people who understood that Negroes could use these facilities with the same kind of care as anyone else," according to a Negro leader who played a prominent part in the limited use of the municipal auditorium and the desegregation of the public libraries. There are still vestiges of the old pattern in the use of these public facilities, however. Drinking fountains and rest rooms are still designated by race, and the staffs continue to be all white.

LITIGATION

A third strategy Negro leaders have employed in attempts to secure equal protection of the law has been litigation. It is, in fact, their most successful strategy. Thus, when Negro leaders were asked: "Suppose a law is passed by the Louisiana State Legislature or Congress that a large number of people believe to be contrary to their best interests, or even unjust—what do you think they should do about it?" they usually concurred that any such law should be obeyed, regardless of hardships, until that law can be changed or declared unconstitutional.

One leader, commenting on "constitutional" laws, pointed out that "there has never been a time when Negroes were not called upon to obey laws they regarded as unconstitutional." He mentioned such laws as those designed to limit the rights of Negroes to vote, to live wherever they can afford to buy or rent, to use tax-supported facilities indiscriminately, and to participate freely in community affairs. He concluded, "No matter how unjust a law is, we must seek to remain law-abiding citizens. This, I believe, gives moral and spiritual strength to the Negro's continuing struggle for equality and justice."

Police brutality. Negro leaders have used whatever legal means available to them to curb police brutality. They have filed numerous complaints in the district attorney's office and with the United States Justice Department, naming policemen who had committed crimes against Negroes and acts "unbecoming an officer." In most instances, such cases were either dropped "for lack of evidence," or the accused officers were allowed to plead guilty to some lesser offense.

In one year, 1949, the NAACP handled ten charges of alleged police brutality. An official of this organization confided that this was only a very small proportion of the actual number of complaints his office received regarding the "Gestapo-like" methods police used with Negro suspects. He feels that despite the fact that only a few policemen have been temporarily suspended for criminal action against Negroes, legal action taken by the NAACP has served an important purpose. He contends that—

> The mere fact that we bring legal charges against these officers lets them know that if they do not show more humane treatment to Negro people, the police department in New Orleans might eventually be subjected to a federal investigation, which would uncover a whole lot more illegal activities than just police brutality.

According to the above statement, at least one basic logic underlies Negro leaders' use of the courts: This action is a tangible threat to local authorities that "if we do not receive proper consideration from you, we will make our complaints to officials of the federal government." Actually, in almost all legal actions taken by Negroes to achieve equal citizenship status, the local courts become significant only in their relationship to the federal judiciary. As one Negro leader interpreted, "Were it not for the fact that our state courts are a part of the federal system (whether segregationists like it or not) the Negro's fight for justice would be so much wasted energy."

Voting rights. Most of the litigation regarding unfair registration and voting practices to which Negroes have been subjected has been handled by the NAACP's national office. No local test case has reached the United States Supreme Court, though evidences of such practices in New Orleans have been noted by federal authorities.

Since voting is regarded as a basic constitutional right, any test case anywhere in the United States that leads to validating this right results in improving the citizenship status of Negroes in New Orleans. Thus, Negroes in New Orleans have shared, with Negroes throughout the South, in the citizenship gains provided by the *Classic* case,[9] in which the United States Supreme Court ruled that Congress has the authority to regulate primaries as well as elections when primaries effectively control the choice of congressmen; and

[9] *United States* v. *Classic*, 313 U. S. 299, 318 (1941).

by the *Smith* v. *Allwright* decision,[10] which outlawed the "white primary" as a violation of the Fifteenth Amendment. These rulings have been sustained several times, but most importantly in *Elmore* v. *Rice*,[11] in which the district court and the court of appeals ruled that the party and the primary were instruments of the state and functioned to elect public officials, and that as such they were subject to the same regulations as stipulated in the *Allwright* case.

Legally, Negroes in Louisiana have not been forced to fight voter restrictions through the courts. Instead, their main task has been that of insisting that state officials abide by the constitutional "law of the land," as interpreted in decisions involving Negroes in other sections of the country. The litigation, then, involving Negroes in New Orleans (or Louisiana) has stemmed from the constitutional right to vote as set forth in basic federal court decisions.

Public facilities. Negro leaders in New Orleans are aware of the fact that the most effective strategy available to them in their bid for equal citizenship has been litigation or the threat of it. Most gains made through protests and negotiations fall within the scope of a biracial society. That is, though rights are gained, the system remains segregated. *Whenever segregation is broken down, it is almost always as a result of federal court orders, not the voluntary action of state and local authorities.*

Negroes protested segregated transportation facilities for decades. Also, there was hardly a year when some group did not seek to negotiate with responsible officials in attempts to get unsegregated accommodations for Negroes on public carriers. These efforts were fruitless. Negroes were forced eventually to initiate suits intended to bring about federal action. It was in 1958 that a New Orleans physician and a Protestant minister-politician won their suit in the United States Supreme Court, which ruled that "segregation in local buses and trolleys in New Orleans is unconstitutional and unlawful."

Another suit brought by New Orleans Negroes in 1949 involved the unsegregated use of City Park facilities. After nine years of litigation, the Supreme Court affirmed a lower court ruling barring segregation in golf courses and other public park facilities. On December 21, 1958, the park's general manager announced resignedly that segregation in City Park had come to an end. He said, "We have reached the end of the rope. This means that Negroes are now permitted to use all park facilities—the tennis courts, the baseball fields, the golf courses, the amusement rides . . . all facilities."

Since the Supreme Court decisions cited have reference to the total Negro population, except for the cases involving segregation in education, they mark the most significant gains in the citizenship status of Negroes in New Orleans since the adoption of the Civil War Amendments.

For many years Negro leaders insisted that one of the most estimable ways of securing more equal protection of the law would be the employment of

[10] *Smith* v. *Allwright*, 321 U. S. 649, 661 (1944).
[11] *Elmore* v. *Rice*, 333 U. S. 875 (1948).

Negro policemen. Hardly a year passed when individual leaders and various organizations in the Negro community did not petition the mayor to appoint Negro policemen.

One of the most frequently offered excuses for not employing Negro policemen was that a Civil Service examination had to be passed in order for the applicant to qualify, and from some quarters it was suggested that Negro applicants could not hope to compete successfully with white applicants on such an examination. Whether this propaganda was intended merely to discourage Negro applicants or its advocates actually believed in the mental inferiority of Negroes, cannot be determined here. In any event, Negro leaders took the challenge seriously. They encouraged a capable young college graduate and war veteran to take the required Civil Service examination. He was officially informed that he had passed with a high score. Some say that his was the highest score made by an applicant at that time. According to some informed leaders this Negro applicant was "given the brush-off." It was done in this way: According to Civil Service regulations, if one appointment is to be made, the administrator in charge may select any one of the three top candidates according to examination scores. And so, despite his high score, the Negro applicant was "picked over."

Sensing the weakness of making demands under such circumstances, Negro leaders encouraged several highly qualified Negroes to apply for the Civil Service examination required by the police department. Six of them passed the examination, also with high scores. None was appointed. This fact gave the sponsoring organizations, particularly the NAACP, legal evidence of discrimination, and a court case ensued. It went through several hearings, and finally in 1950 two Negroes were appointed. Since 1950, after the initial breakthrough, several other Negroes have been appointed to the police force.

Although Negro leaders still insist that "Negroes do not fill anywhere near their deserved quota of policemen," there is now no litigation in progress to increase their number. The main issue since 1950 has been the restricted authority of Negro policemen. For a time, they served mainly on "special assignments," that is, with the juvenile division and at Negro public gatherings. Eventually, they were given uniforms and assigned beats in predominantly Negro neighborhoods. Later, they were occasionally assigned to traffic duty during rush hours. Even now, after eleven years on the police force, Negro policemen are not thought of as regular patrolmen. Only infrequently are they assigned patrol cars, and none is with the motorcycle corps. It is still generally believed that Negro policemen are expected to keep order among Negroes only.

Negro leaders have limited themselves to two primary techniques of litigation to secure equal justice in the courts. They raise money to employ able lawyers to ensure that equal justice in federal courts is received by Negroes, and they remind local court officials, particularly elected judges, that the "Negro people must have fair treatment in the courts." They promise political support to the man who is able to convince them that they will be treated like all other citizens. Thus, a politically ambitious Negro lawyer summarized the attitude many Negroes have regarding court officials when he told a candidate for a judgeship, "We don't want any special sentencing; no special fines; no special courtesies. Give us your promise to be a judge of all of the people according to law, and my people will support you."

Since the Negro vote has always been weak, needless to say, the most trusted of the two techniques has been that of remanding questionable local court action to federal courts. There is no doubt in the minds of Negro lawyers that this technique is the more effective. Most Negro lawyers agree that except in cases involving assaults against white persons by Negroes, "most judges attempt to be fair." They acknowledge, of course, that when there is a minimum and maximum punishment for a crime, Negroes are more likely to get the maximum punishment than are whites. As one lawyer said, "This is not a miscarriage of justice, rather it is the prerogative of the trial judge. In such cases they are not threatened with reversals from federal courts."

Finally, during the twenty or more years in which Negro leaders and organizations have used every strategy and technique at their disposal to guarantee Negroes equal protection of the law in New Orleans, there is no record of white leaders or white "men of power" allying themselves with them in this cause. The vast majority of them apparently ignore the importance of the Negro's efforts to attain equal justice. It may be said, then, that whatever progress has been made in this area has been due entirely to the insistence of Negro leaders and organizations, and to federal intervention. *All evidence indicates that without constant prodding from Negro leaders, and what segregationists call "interference" from the federal government, Negroes cannot hope to achieve equal protection of the law in New Orleans.*

POLITICAL ACTION

In order to make the Negro ballot a potent weapon in their fight for "full freedom" or equal citizenship, Negro leaders use the strategy of political action, along with protest, negotiation, and litigation. Thus, in addition to voter-registration drives and registration schools, sponsored regularly by various uplift organizations, by far the most promising instrument has been political organizations. These organizations have adopted every strategy and technique available to them in attempts to expand and influence the Negro electorate, including programs and slogans which reflect dedication to the highest ideals of Americanism. One such organization founded during World War II has as its central purpose "to promote an interest among its members in civic, social, educational and governmental affairs; to work to improve housing, streets and drainage in all parts of the community."

From time to time these organizations have sponsored voter-registration drives and protest meetings, along with their sporadic political programs.

Most of the political activities engaged in by Negro political factions have been designed to get some white segregationist elected to public office. Occasionally, these political factions have sponsored Negro candidates for public office, but their efforts have never been as united behind Negro candidates as might be expected. There were always one or two factions among the eight or so that refused to give unanimous support.

Despite the fact that Negroes have had the legal right to participate more or less freely in the Democratic primary since 1948, and Negro political leaders have given unswerving support to the Democratic party (except for some defection in the 1956 national election), only one Negro political leader has held a public office, that of assistant district attorney. This appointment came as a result of a combination of two factors: strong support given the Negro candidate in the first primary, and the fact that the white candidates going into the second primary had about the same political strength. The Negro candidate thus offered the balance of power that barely ensured the election of the district attorney. For his support the Negro was appointed assistant district attorney, the highest political office held by Negroes since Reconstruction days. Except for this appointee, Negro political leaders and their followers have had no official voice in influencing the policies or practices of the Democratic party in Louisiana. They are excluded from the Democratic Parish Committee and the powerful state executive committee, where the qualifications of Democratic candidates are passed upon.

Unlike the Democratic party, which ignores Negro political leaders in state and national policy-making, the Republican party, with only about 250 Negro members in the city, has consistently included its single Negro leader in its policy-making. Though powerless in local elections, he has served as secretary of the Orleans Parish Republican Executive Committee, and as a delegate to the party's national conventions.

During the last twenty years, Negro political organizations have made at least two important contributions to Negro advancement. First, their leaders, in connection with political campaigns and mass meetings, have been able to create among the Negro masses some definite awareness of the role of politics in our modern industrial society. All segments of the Negro community have been brought to see that directly or indirectly their welfare will be determined in large measure by the type of leaders who are elected to public office. Second, though the Negro electorate is still weak, Negro leaders in New Orleans generally agree that it would be even weaker had there not been political factions upon whom white political aspirants could depend to muster a balance-of-power vote. One of the most successful Negro political figures contends that "the only Negroes who are registered in many sections of the state, New Orleans included, were permitted to do so because I, and a few others like me, promised the governor [who appoints the registrar of voters] that I would register enough Negroes to guarantee him victory in a close election."

Under this permissive system of registration, Negro political leaders have not been able to marshal enough Negro votes to present a serious challenge to the *status quo*, but they have been able to register just enough Negroes to ensure the political security of certain white supremacists who are dedicated to the preservation of the biracial system in Louisiana. Much of the increase in Negro registration is also due directly to Negro political candidates who have run for office during the last decade. It is a well-established fact that in their efforts to win political office, Negro candidates have done a better job of convincing the masses of Negroes to register than is done at any other time. The best example of this is the accomplishment of an independent Negro candidate, who ran for a seat in the state House of Representatives in 1960.[12] After qualifying for the second primary he knew that he needed a substantially larger number of Negro votes from his ward than those already registered. Though repeated voter drives in past years had resulted in a Negro registration of only 7,299, his efforts added 1,000 or more Negroes to the rolls within a five-week period.

The career patterns of Negro political leaders present a study in contradiction. All of them began their leadership in the role of race man. Most were literally pushed into political leadership by hopeful Negro followings. Several of them acknowledged that in the beginning they had no political ambitions. One said,

> When I looked out before me and saw all of those black faces depending upon me to represent them to the white folks, I was struck with the idea that if I could get them to stick with me I might become governor. From that moment I stopped talking so much about how we have been treated and started talking about voting. Man, I had myself a vision.

"Neo-Uncle Tomism." When we look at the careers of such race men, turned politicians after they have gone through what Max Weber termed "routinization,"[13] or a coming to grips with reality, it is sometimes surprising to see the transformation. In some cases they have been conditioned to play roles similar to that of the traditional Uncle Tom. They tend to beg for favors rather than demand rights. They develop this technique because practically all of the powerful white politicians in the state are segregationists. And, as we have already noted, the Uncle Tom is about the only type of Negro leader with whom segregationists will do business.

A sobering fact to be considered by Negro politicians is that legal codes in Louisiana are sufficient to prevent any Negro from voting if the registrar elects to keep him from doing so. Therefore, segregationists have demanded that former race men play Uncle Tom roles as a price for allowing certain Negroes who have been well screened to register. As one Negro politician put it—

---

[12] Local white Democrats have never endorsed Negro candidates. However, a few Negro candidates have placed certain white candidates on their ballots.

[13] See H. H. Gerth and C. Wright Mills, *From Max Weber* (New York: Oxford University Press, 1958), pp. 53, 54, 262-264, and 297.

The only way I could persuade the governor to pass the word to the registrar to let my people register, was by pledging him my loyalty and promising him that I would not intercede for any Negro who might vote for . . . candidates.

Another Negro politician revealed his orders covering the support of even Negro candidates. He said that the head of a white political organization—

. . . expects me to support all of its candidates. The only exception I am allowed is when a Negro is running against them. And, then only when in my best judgment the Negro has a chance of winning.

He went on to explain that officials of this organization realize that he can be valuable to them only if he maintains the good will of the Negro masses, and that the masses expect him to support Negro candidates. To be successful, race relations leaders must have the confidence of two polar-extreme groups: equalitarian-oriented Negroes, and powerful segregationists. Faced with this dilemma, some Negro political leaders behave in very inconsistent ways. For example, there have been occasions when a Negro candidate might have won if he had been able to get the support of certain Negro political leaders. This sets in motion a kind of "self-fulfilling prophecy," because predicting that a Negro candidate cannot win is tantamount to voting against him, thus ensuring his failure. In such a situation, the conduct of Negro leaders is precisely that of the traditional Uncle Tom, who for personal gains identifies with white authorities in opposition to the welfare of his own people. This is what one educator termed "Neo-Uncle Tomism."

Perhaps the greatest single weakness of Negro political leaders in New Orleans is their lack of organizational ability. Though they have been trying sporadically for two decades to establish an effective city-wide organization of Negro voters, none of them has as yet achieved his goal. Instead, their efforts have resulted in numerous rival organizations. The constant bickering among themselves functions to undermine the confidence the Negro masses would probably place in them under other circumstances, and to isolate from them groups that would be necessary to their success. Most of these organizations remain one-man organizations insofar as decision-making is concerned.

Bloc voting. All Negro leaders interviewed, including those primarily interested in politics, agree that about the only way Negro voters can significantly influence political affairs in the city is by bloc voting. Fear of the Negro bloc has been expressed by most white candidates. Time and again, the NAACP, Communists, and Negro "troublemakers" have been accused of cementing the alleged Negro bloc. It is referred to as something sinister, un-American, and dangerous. Segregationists are apparently unaware of the fact that the most potent weapon the South has used to prevent civil rights has been the use of the bloc vote of its representatives in Congress and its legislators in the several southern states.

Actually, bloc voting among Negroes is widely misunderstood and misinterpreted. In the first place, as we have noticed, Negro political leaders have been far from unified in any political campaign; some of them have refused even to campaign for one another when they have run for public office. During the last gubernatorial campaign some supported candidates who were avowedly "100 per cent" for segregation, others supported a candidate who boasted of his loyalty to sacred southern traditions and estimated that he was "1,000 per cent" for segregation, and another prominent Negro political organization backed a candidate who attempted to prove that he was "1,000,000 per cent" for segregation. One of the candidates who received the unswerving support of a "militant" Negro political leader, assured the Louisiana Association of Registrars of Voters that he was "a billion per cent" for segregation.[14] Such divisions among Negro political leaders, themselves, are hardly conducive to bloc voting.

In the second place, the majority of Negroes who cast their votes for a given city or state politician did not do so because their votes were "controlled" by some organization. They voted the way they did mainly because the candidates had become well known for certain "favors," and they were regarded as the less rabid of the segregationists seeking office.

Perhaps Negro political leaders were responsible for propagandizing what one called the "gentlemanly qualities" of their respective candidates, yet in the end Negroes voted for those they considered the lesser evils. There is reliable evidence that most Negro voters follow their individual wills and vote for the candidates of their own choosing rather than following the dictates of some organization.

Since the beginning of the crisis in public-school education in New Orleans, Negro leaders have been trying to find some means to bring all of the warring political factions in the Negro community together. This is proving to be an extremely difficult task because there are so many forces mitigating against it. The most significant of these factors is that most of the leaders with political ambitions are already "married" to various white factions.

DIRECT ACTION

Negro leaders advocate direct action as a strategy in the achievement of equal citizenship only after protest, negotiation, litigation, and political action have proven ineffective.

The sit-in movement. One of the most significant and far-reaching results of the 1956 Montgomery bus boycott is that it established the strategy of direct action as an accepted means of obtaining equal citizenship. Previously, the NAACP had handled test cases of individuals who deliberately violated local or state laws as a first step toward having them eventually declared uncon-

---

[4] These statements were actually used repeatedly by the candidates to describe their racial views.

stitutional by a federal court. The only objective in the deliberate violation of a law was to get concrete evidence of its unconstitutionality for federal courts.

Such forms of direct action as "sit-ins," "kneel-ins," and "freedom rides" are not calculated as a step toward having "Jim Crow" laws declared unconstitutional, although this might be a result. Instead, the central purpose of this movement is to force state and city officials to abandon such laws. Thus, whereas a Negro sponsored by the NAACP might sit at an "all white" lunch counter for the purpose of getting evidence for a test case, a Negro member of the Congress of Racial Equality (CORE) would sit at the same counter in order to get served.

The essential motivation behind the direct-action strategy was expressed eloquently by Roy Wilkins, Executive Secretary of the NAACP. He said, in part—

> American Negroes have been stirred deeply by events in the past few years. They are restless and frustrated. They are tired and snappish. They remember the lynching of Mack Charles Parker . . . defiance of the Supreme Court . . . filibuster in the Senate.
>
> Negro citizens are weary of the old-time promises and excuses. Young Negro students have served unmistakable notice that they are through with the old order of segregation and racial insults.

He predicted that—

> The minute Negro young people agree spontaneously that they will go to jail rather than submit to the old practices, those practices are dead. . . . white people can be "tough." . . . It will not affect the final outcome: Segregation in public places must go![15]

Direct action was officially launched in New Orleans on September 17, 1960 when an interracial group of four CORE members was arrested at a lunch counter of a downtown five-and-ten-cents store. Since then there have been consistent efforts to break down segregation at various types of eating places—restaurants, bus and train stations, and the dining room at the airport. Also, there have been several "kneel-ins," and picketing incidents by members of CORE, the youth chapter of the NAACP, and by individuals acting independently.

This strategy shocked the established leadership in New Orleans—both Negro and white. Individually, Negro leaders at first tended to criticize such methods of direct action and to underestimate their potential effectiveness. After the initial shock passed, most Negro organizations endorsed the strategy as appropriate in the Negro's struggle to break down Jim Crow laws. These organizations contributed funds and provided space for mass

[15] *Louisiana Weekly*, April 16, 1960.

meetings, and Negro leaders in all walks of life, particularly ministers, gave moral support by publicly lauding those who participated in direct action. One minister said, in a speech before a large mass rally where freedom riders were honored, that—

> There has not been in modern history as true a demonstration of Christian suffering as we see here tonight. Those who were beaten because they dared to act like first-class citizens have set for us an exceptionally high standard of Christian behavior.

Although CORE is interracial in nature and practically all of its direct action has been shared by white participants, its strategy has been unequivocally condemned by all white organizations expressing themselves on the issue. White segregationists have been particularly vituperative of white CORE members. One white youth participating in the first series of sit-in demonstrations received the most abusive treatment, and was the only one of the demonstrators charged with criminal anarchy. The district attorney interpreted his action in refusing to desist from sitting with a Negro companion at a lunch counter "to be a statement against the state of Louisiana." He was placed under a $2,500 bond.

The direct-action strategy to desegregate public places was condemned by white persons in newspapers, editorials, resolutions passed by civic organizations, and from pulpits. The demonstrators were accused of instigating riots, creating racial tension, disrespecting laws, being "headline-seekers" and "invaders," and indulging in "childish and foolish behavior."

After virtually ignoring the problems of race relations in its editorials for a decade or more, on April 3, 1960, the New Orleans *Times-Picayune* took issue with what it termed "sitdowns" by college students:

> The tragedy is that all the effort is so grossly misdirected while the tensions growing out of it lead toward hatred, fear and violence. This accomplishes nothing. Certainly it can gain for the Negro students only the contempt of the majority.

At this time it is not possible thoroughly to evaluate the significance of the direct-action strategy in the Negro's struggle for equal citizenship. However, there have been at least two instances in which it has brought about definite Negro advancement.

First, throughout the South generally, and in New Orleans specifically, there has been some measure of desegregation of public places that can be attributed to direct action. Negroes have received service in eating facilities once reserved for "white only" in bus stations and train stations, and in the coffee shop of the airport.

Secondly, direct-action strategy has done more to facilitate communication between segregated southern Negroes and others outside the South than has any other strategy. This era of positive communication was begun during

the Montgomery bus boycott. Action makes better headlines and more interesting reading for the masses than do other strategies Negroes have used.
Mass media in other sections of the United States have made the Negro's
plight in the South common knowledge to all segments of the American
population, and indeed throughout the world. Unlike the protest strategy,
which seldom reaches beyond the Negro public[16] and almost never has any
publicity in media outside the South, organized direct action on the part of
Negroes is usually fully reported with accompanying pictures. As one Negro
leader put it—

> Negroes in the South have always been persecuted and treated worse than
> foreign enemies. So called "good people" in the South choose to ignore our situa-
> tion, and the busy people in the North have no time to concern themselves. What
> we are doing now [reference here to the freedom riders] is shocking the whole
> world. Our President pointed out yesterday that our international security may
> depend upon how we solve this problem. The conscience of the world has been
> touched.

One of the clearest statements of the motivation, dedication, and strength
of the direct-action strategy was enunciated by a college student in answer
to the *Times-Picayune* editorial cited. He said—

> We have just as much right to this country as any other people.
> We fought, toiled and died for this country.
> We will strike the moral conscience of the white man and not his physical body.
> No longer can we endure the back door of public places; the denial of equal job
> opportunities, the right to vote, or any privileges granted to a full time citizen.[17]

According to the statement quoted, the sit-in movement is a great deal
more complex than what most southern authorities have been willing to
acknowledge. For example, one segregationist was "amazed that a person
will spend sixty days in jail and pay a stiff fine for a hamburger and a cup
of coffee." Actually, lunch counter demonstrations are only means whereby
Negro youths have expressed dissatisfaction with the total biracial system.

To summarize, since the end of World War II, Negro leaders in New
Orleans have engaged in an intensive drive to achieve equal citizenship.
They have employed five basic strategies: Protest, Negotiation, Litigation,
Political Action, and Direct Action. Thay have used practically every tech-
nique available to them. These have met with only limited success.

As the goal of Negro leaders has shifted away from the "separate but
equal" doctrine toward integrated use of public places, the race man is

---

[16] In most instances, Negro mass rallies are attended by Negroes only. On occasions,
when outstanding Negro personages such as Martin Luther King and Thurgood Marshall
have spoken, just a few white people may attend. White newspapers usually give only the
briefest summaries of such meetings.

[17] *Louisiana Weekly*, April 9, 1960.

becoming more and more the spokesman for the Negro "cause." He is essentially an idealist who visualizes a completely integrated society. He enunciates the philosophy of "first-class" citizenship; points up the fallacies and disadvantages in "second-class" citizenship, and sets up what he regards as the ultimate, democratic goals to be attained. The racial diplomat espouses essentially the same social philosophy and goals of the race man, yet he differs from this type in that he is far more realistic on how to "get things done." He is more apt to realize that the process of attaining goals may require certain intermediate steps. Therefore, the racial diplomat brings to the Negro's struggle his skills as negotiator, "peacemaker" and organizer. The Uncle Tom is rapidly passing from the leadership scene.

The shift in Negro leadership is the basic condition underlying the crisis in race relations. Pointedly, Negroes have come to rely upon the race man to set goals to be achieved and upon the racial diplomat to map out ways and means of achieving these goals, while white segregationists continue to rely upon the Uncle Tom who has characteristically demonstrated loyalty to the biracial social system. There is, then, little effective communication between accepted leaders of Negroes and the official leaders of white people in New Orleans. As might be expected, every strategy and technique employed by the "new" Negro leadership is met with stern, often violent resistance from segregationist leaders. Consequently, one fact has become increasingly clear since 1954: *left to itself New Orleans* (indeed all of the deep South) *does not seem to have the will, the courage, the "morality," or the leadership required to voluntarily grant Negroes equal citizenship status.*

8

EARNING A LIVING

IN AMERICAN SOCIETY, equality of economic opportunity is assumed to be an inherent aspect of citizenship. Accordingly, all Negro leaders included in this study are of the opinion that the widespread economic discrimination Negroes experience is a most serious contradiction to the principles upon which our American government is founded. They are convinced that in our highly competitive economic system, Negroes can never achieve full citizenship so long as they are hampered in their economic participation.

Although Negro leaders are unanimous in agreeing that first-class citizenship means essentially equal economic rights, there is some difference of opinion among them as to the importance of economic discrimination relative to other forms of racial discrimination. About 20 per cent would rank economic discrimination as the number-one problem Negroes must solve. They contend that equality of economic opportunity is a prerequisite to all other citizenship prerogatives. This point of view was expressed by a prominent Negro leader in a keynote address before a consumers' group which met to protest racial discrimination in employment. He said—

Negroes will only attain equality in education, government, housing, health facilities and social recognition when barriers to equal, full, economic participation have been removed. Let's face it, no servant class in history has ever been accorded the same privileges and responsibilities as those claimed by the owner or business class. The problem is clear: We must first put forth every effort to gain equal citizenship by removing all inequalities in our economic life. When we can work, buy, and sell as do white Americans, all other citizenship rights will follow in due course.

A small number of Negro leaders, perhaps 5 per cent, would rate economic inequality somewhere below certain other forms of discrimination. They regard economic equality as a result, not a means, of equality in other areas of our national life. They tend to hold, therefore, that Negroes must first achieve equality in such areas as education (particularly technical and professional), potential political strength, and general social respect before they can logically expect to share equally in the economic advantages to be found in the United States. A Negro educator expressed this central idea in a commencement address. He predicted that—

> You [the graduating class] will never achieve the economic success of which you are capable until you can measure up, man for man, and woman for woman, with other so-called more fortunate Americans. You must combine the educational philosophies of Booker T. Washington and W. E. B. DuBois. The former advocated education of your hands to do the necessary skilled and technical work needed in our society. The latter would have you educate your minds so that you might do the thinking, planning and directing essential to a great nation such as ours. I say you must do both. And when, and only when, you measure up academically and have gained respect in some chosen field, will you be able to break the economic fetters in which our people have long been ensnared.

The vast majority of Negro leaders, perhaps 75 per cent, are reluctant to rank economic discrimination in relation to other problems stemming from race. Rather, they see the problem of earning a living as inextricably interwoven with all other facets of the Negro's status in American society. Some of them acknowledge that they find it extremely difficult to say which form of racial discrimination should be given priority of solution. These leaders concur that first-class citizenship presupposes the right to participate in the total institutional life of a community or nation. They feel that at a given time in a particular community economic discrimination might be more dangerous than another form and might require greater attention than any other single problem. Even then, they feel that it would be unwise for all Negro leaders to focus attention upon that specific issue. This point of view was emphasized by the chairman of a citizens committee organized to discuss racial problems with some powerful white officials. He insisted that—

> Equal citizenship for Negroes will only be achieved when we Negro leaders are well-organized to fight discrimination on all fronts. The great weakness with so many movements to improve the status of Negroes is that each tends to emphasize one goal at the exclusion of all others.
>
> The time has come when we must achieve sufficient unity among ourselves so that we might wage a strong fight against all forms of racial segregation in our society. Segregation in any phase of our national life inevitably leads to discrimination in all other phases. Our fight is not simply against a given expression of segregation, such as that existing in employment, but against the principle of white supremacy, no matter in what guise it might be manifested.

In a general sense, we may say that "class-oriented" Negro leaders advocate a rank-order approach to problems of racial discrimination. They conceive the various forms of racial discrimination as having two distinctly different orderings. One, as social problems, they may be ranked in terms of their negative effects upon Negroes on the whole. Two, they may also be ranked according to how difficult they are to solve. Class-oriented leaders usually acknowledge that the economic discrimination experienced by Negroes is a social handicap of the first order. However, most of them are quick to point out that achieving equality in this area is the most complex and difficult racial problem to be solved. Consequently, only a few of the most influential class-oriented leaders have actively engaged in attempts to achieve equality of economic opportunities for the Negro masses in New Orleans. Those who have concerned themselves with this problem have usually done so indirectly as members of national "uplift" organizations whose programs included some specific action to be taken against economic discrimination. Rarely has any class-oriented leader personally identified with the Negro's struggle for fair economic privileges. Instead, over the years, most of them have preferably engaged in movements designed to solve what mass-oriented leaders regard as some lesser racial problem. Thus, on the one hand, efforts to secure the right to "separate but equal" use of the city auditorium, and the desegregation of public libraries and golf courses were led by "class-oriented" leaders. On the other hand, these leaders have discreetly shunned open support of labor's efforts to achieve fair employment and consumer movements to break down segregation in the hiring practices of business enterprises catering to Negroes. The rationale they offer for concentrating on some lesser racial problem is that the solution of a major problem, such as economic discrimination, will be made easier when other, simpler interrelated problems are solved first. Thus, one leader defended his near anti-labor-union attitude in this way:

> Look at how little organized labor has actually done to elevate Negro workers. There is still the worse kind of discrimination in the ranks of labor itself. Negro workers would have been much better off if their leaders had had the sense to improve the general educational level and skills of the workers first, then press for equality of all union members. Such efforts would have met with less resistance from white members and employers.

As a rule, class-oriented leaders can be expected to take the initiative in the solution of racial problems of primary concern to upper-class Negroes and in those that happen to be the pet projects of wealthy white liberals. They are much less likely to support efforts to raise the economic level of the Negro masses, particularly when such efforts are defined by influential white businessmen as being "against the best interests of the community." Consequently, some of them are outspoken critics of a consumers' movement to get white-collar jobs for Negroes by picketing and boycotting certain stores that have a large number of Negro customers. One Negro leader complained: "Why can't they wait until we have nailed down gains in education and the use of public facilities before they take on this project. Their timing is bad, their goals are unclear."

Unlike class-oriented leaders, mass-oriented leaders complain most about unequal employment. They rank inequalities in opportunities to earn a living as the most serious racial problem.[1] Yet, since mass-oriented leaders are not on the whole highly skilled in race relations, they tend to make many blunders in their efforts to raise the economic status of the masses. This may be an important reason why all leaders, white and Negro, interviewed for this study expressed the belief that Negroes have made fewer relative gains economically than in any other area of community life. And, according to United States Census reports they have in fact made few relative economic gains in New Orleans since 1940. At that time, the median income of Negro families and unrelated individuals in New Orleans was somewhat less than 60 per cent of that of whites. In 1960 it was still only about 65 per cent that of whites.

The two main reasons for the economic gap between Negroes and whites in New Orleans remains great despite twenty years of unprecedented prosperity are the very narrow range of employment opportunities available to Negroes, and the fact that Negroes are virtually excluded from participation in the business world.

THE NARROW RANGE OF EMPLOYMENT OPPORTUNITIES

Blue-collar employment. The range of job opportunities for Negroes in New Orleans is very narrow when compared with that of whites. The vast majority of Negroes in New Orleans, about 85 per cent, may be classified as blue-collar workers. (Only about 35 per cent of white workers may be so classified.) About half of the Negro workers in this category may be designated as menial laborers. They hold what has been traditionally considered "Negro jobs"—jobs that pay the lowest wages and provide the least security. Negroes are indeed "the last hired and the first fired." Whenever automation is introduced, they are the first to be replaced. Whenever there are cutbacks, even due to temporary recessions, they are the ones who suffer most. When prosperity comes, they are the last to benefit from it.

Negro blue-collar workers are almost invariably employed in jobs where there are white supervisors, and however competent they may be, there is little opportunity for advancement. In the hauling industry for instance, most of the vehicles are operated by driver-salesmen and helpers. Rarely are Negroes employed as driver-salesmen; rather, they are generally restricted to the position of the helper, whose pay is seldom more than half that received by the driver. Yet some Negro helpers are efficient drivers, and often do assume that responsibility informally. The Local Teamsters Union has proven ineffective in changing this unfair pattern of employment. This record is not atypical, for labor unions in New Orleans, with few exceptions, have been

[1] This ranking is in keeping with Myrdal's thesis. See his *An American Dilemma*, pp. 587-588.

unable to reduce discrimination against Negroes. And even though the National AF of L-CIO has gone on record several times as opposing racial discrimination in its ranks, it has not been able to eliminate some of the most glaring unfair labor practices in New Orleans. It is no secret that the union has allowed certain of the more desirable jobs to be monopolized by white persons, despite their avowed dedication to upgrading according to tenure and merit. There are also many instances in which Negro workers are paid lower salaries for the same work as that done by white workers. The most classic cases of discrimination, however, are due directly to union policies of exclusion. Thus, in New Orleans certain craft unions, particularly the plumbers, electrical workers, and machinists, maintain rigid policies of racial exclusion. Therefore, Negroes are prevented from entering many blue-collar occupations simply because they are excluded from certain craft unions.

White-collar employment. In 1940 only about 8 per cent of Negro employed persons could be classified as white-collar, compared with approximately 32 per cent of white workers so classified. By 1960, the percentage of Negro workers in this category had increased to about 10 per cent of those employed. Nevertheless, the percentage of white workers in this category has increased much more rapidly, and is now at about 55 per cent of employed white persons. Relatively, then, Negroes have actually lost ground in this category. This is a serious lag, because it indicates that Negro workers generally are not keeping pace in the rapidly changing United States economy, which is relying increasingly upon white-collar workers. There are several reasons for this in New Orleans:

One, practically all Negro white-collar workers are employed by Negro firms or institutions, and these have remained more or less stable, or have actually declined in importance, in comparison with white-controlled enterprises. Thus, whereas a generation ago, when only a few Negroes were able to obtain insurance from the better-established white agencies, Negro insurance companies and burial-aid societies had little white competition. Since in recent years Negro economic conditions are generally improved and Negroes are healthier and live longer, white insurance companies find them a better risk. As a result, Negro insurance companies are encountering stiffer competition from white companies. This means that Negro insurance agents and clerical workers, though increasing in actual numbers, are not increasing nearly so rapidly as whites in this category, who now profit by their companies' expansions into Negro communities. As a matter of fact, southern traditions tend to prevent the employment of Negro salesmen and clerical people in white insurance establishments, so that actually much of the white expansion is done at the expense of qualified Negro white-collar workers.

Two, there is a tradition in New Orleans that Negroes are not to be employed in such capacities as would put them over white persons, as many white-collar positions would do. This in itself automatically narrows the job opportunities for Negroes who would qualify as supervisors, foremen, managers, technicians, salesmen, business-machine operators, bill collectors, and numerous other jobs that may be classified as white-collar. Even Civil Service appointments, which are supposed to be awarded on the basis of merit, bow to this principle and are often awarded to whites in preference to Negroes. This is done cleverly, in keeping with a Civil Service rule previously described, according to which a department head is given the right to select one of the three highest scoring eligibles.

Three, a large number of jobs in New Orleans in the white-collar category are politically controlled. The local Urban League estimates that approximately 2,500 such jobs are available in New Orleans. These jobs include clerks of court, inspectors, deputy registrars, adjusters, telephone operators, supervisors, and scores of clerical workers on all levels. As government becomes bigger and bigger, the number needed in these categories naturally increases. Since Negroes have been politically weak they have not been able to demand their "fair share" of these jobs. Thus, up until now whites have had a virtual monopoly upon all political jobs in New Orleans.

Four, Negroes have had little opportunity to prepare for white-collar positions. There are no "top-rank" schools in New Orleans where Negro business-machine operators, technicians, designers, interior decorators, and salesmen can be trained. Nor are Negroes generally accepted for on-the-job or apprentice training in these and other such white-collar positions. Consequently, they lag greatly in this area of employment, despite the fact that opportunities in this category are ever expanding. They have been almost completely stymied by laws and traditions designed to keep whites segregated from Negroes and Negroes relegated to an inferior social and economic status.

Negro professionals. Negroes in professional pursuits, like Negro white-collar workers, usually are circumscribed within the Negro community. Laws and traditions function to prevent them from earning a living as equal competitors with white professionals. Their white counterparts are expected to compete with them for economic opportunities in the Negro community, but they are not expected to compete with their white counterparts in the general economy. This situation, of course, puts Negro professionals at a distinct economic disadvantage. Therefore, compared with the white population, relatively few Negroes are engaged in professional activities. For example, in 1940 only 2.8 per cent of the employed Negro population could be classified as professional and semiprofessional. At that time, approximately 10 per cent of white employed persons were so classified. Even as late as 1960, after twenty years of economic growth and unusual emphasis placed upon education in our national life, the proportion of Negroes engaged in professional pursuits still lagged behind the proportion of white professionals to about the same degree as was true twenty years before. At the present time the proportion of Negroes classified as professional or semiprofessional has increased to 4.7 per cent, yet the whites in this category have increased to about 11 per cent of all white employed persons. This is largely a result of the fact that the range of opportunities for Negro professionals in New Orleans is relatively as narrow as it is for other classifications of Negro workers. Actually, about 85 per cent of all Negro professionals are teachers and ministers, and the only opportunities open to them are in Negro institutions.

Unlike public-school teachers and ministers, Negro college teachers do not have a monopoly on their professional positions. It has always been customary for white teachers to be employed in private Negro colleges. Thus, the private Negro colleges in New Orleans employ a large proportion of white teachers. During the period of research for this study, several Negro college teachers were asked to express their feelings about the competition they experience from white teachers. All of them agreed that such competition is wholesome because it tends to improve academic standards in Negro colleges. Yet all pointed out that there is an unfair aspect of this competition. One professor put it this way:

> The only academically sound way to select a faculty is in terms of competence. Race should play no part. There is one thing to be regretted, however, white college officials seem not to be convinced of this principle. It is not fair economically that I must compete with white professors for my position in this college, yet, no matter how incompetent a white professor might be in [————] college, I am not allowed to compete with him for his position. And so, I would say Negro colleges which employ faculty members on the basis of competence, regardless of race, are doing what is academically sound, though it is economically unfair.

The economic situation in which Negro independent professionals—lawyers, physicians, and dentists—find themselves is basically the same as that of college teachers. They must compete with white counterparts for Negro clientele, whereas laws and customs prevent them from competing with white professionals for white clientele.

Most Negro independent professionals interviewed for this study reported having rendered little more than occasional services to white people. All were aware, however, that they were in direct, often bitter competition with white professionals for the Negro clientele. For instance, a Negro physician confided that at one time several of his patients left him for a white physician who was attempting to establish a practice in the same Negro neighborhood by charging "ridiculously low fees." Furthermore, all Negro lawyers pointed out that most Negro businessmen and alleged criminals "with money" almost invariably employ white lawyers in preference to Negro lawyers because the former are believed to have greater influence with "lily white" courts and white officials. Both lawyers and physicians complain that they are handicapped because many Negroes are convinced that white professionals are better qualified than Negroes. This is the main reason why all of them have felt called upon, at one time or another, to "prove" their relative competence. Some Negro lawyers, for instance, have invited potential clients to witness their professional behavior in courts. Most accept positions as counselor to Negro uplift organizations for small or no fees. Still others have accepted so-called impossible cases (such as Negroes accused of the rape or murder of white persons) that would legitimately advertise their legal competence.

Since there are so few Negro physicians in New Orleans, as general practitioners they apparently have little difficulty in securing patients. Many Negroes retain Negro physicians, because in most instances they are subject to segregation when they visit the offices of white physicians. However, when it comes to the use of specialists, Negroes have indicated a definite preference for white physicians. This may be one important reason why a larger proportion of the young, ambitious Negro physicians and dentists migrate to other cities. There have been years during which there was not a single Negro specialist practicing in New Orleans. There were never more than one or two board-certified specialists (doctors who have qualified as specialists in some field of medicine) at any given time.

All Negro professionals in New Orleans encounter frustrating handicaps when they try to improve their competence. They are not allowed to hold active membership in professional organizations; they seldom have opportunities to "talk shop" in an informal manner with white colleagues; and they are barred, as a rule, from attending public lectures, forums, demonstrations, and informal gatherings where renowned specialists in their fields meet and exchange ideas. Furthermore, with rare exceptions, there are no formal classes open to them in the local white universities. To illustrate, Negro physicians are not allowed to practice in the local public (tax supported) hospital or otherwise benefit from its academic program, nor are they accepted as members in the New Orleans Medical Association. Likewise, Negro lawyers, as we noted earlier, are excluded from the New Orleans Bar Association and so cannot benefit from contacts with influential white lawyers. In order to minimize this handicap, Negro physicians have organized a segregated medical society, and the Negro lawyers have established an all-Negro Bar Association called the Martinet Society. All Negro leaders concerned agree that segregated societies are not very effective, because Negro professionals need to belong to associations that make it possible for them to exchange information and ideas with competent and influential white colleagues. Those involved are convinced that they cannot grow to their full professional stature until they, like other professionals, are accepted on the basis of their abilities and are not contained in the segregated Negro community.

An excellent indication of the unfair competitive advantage that white independent professionals have over Negro professionals is the fact that some successful white lawyers and doctors in New Orleans estimate 35 to 40 per cent of their patients or clients to be Negroes. No Negro lawyer ever gets more than a token number of white clients, and these usually involve simple notarial matters. Negro physicians very seldom have any white patients. One Negro doctor confided, "If any one of us had to depend upon white patients we'd starve."

There is ample evidence that Negroes in New Orleans, regardless of skill or competence, are severely restricted in their efforts to earn a living. The blue-collar workers are usually frozen on the very bottom rung of the occupational ladder. They are paid the lowest wages, and most are subject to the greatest degree of insecurity. Negroes who qualify for white-collar positions can hardly expect to secure one except in Negro-controlled enterprises. Negro professionals are also restricted to Negro institutions or must depend upon Negro patients or clients; and there are few, if any, opportunities for them to develop to the fullest extent of their abilities in their chosen professions regardless of training and skill. Laws and traditions are so designed that whites are protected to a great extent from competition with Negroes, yet Negroes on all occupational levels find themselves in direct competition with white counterparts.

BUSINESS EXCLUSION

Although there are no available data according to which Negro and white business potentials and successes can be compared, any serious observer can readily see that Negro business enterprises in New Orleans are proportionally much fewer and occupy a considerably more limited range in types than those operated by whites. Since the successful Negro businessman is still a rarity, compared with white businessmen, all Negro leaders included in this study express great concern about the relative lack of progress Negroes have made in the field of business. As a rule, they feel that Negroes have made less progress in this area than in any other. Even Negro businessmen themselves agree that this is so. Those who have succeeded usually have done so as operators of small service establishments and family-controlled insurance, undertaking, and taxi companies.

When Negro leaders were asked to give their opinion as to why Negroes have had such unimpressive success in business in New Orleans, they gave several reasons. Among the most convincing are the following:

Segregation. All interviewees were emphatic in their denunciation of racial segregation as most deleterious to the development of successful Negro businesses. Some pointed out that, unlike white businesses, which might be located in more favorable sections of the city, Negro businesses usually must locate in all-Negro or predominantly Negro neighborhoods. They cited instances in which real estate companies refused to sell or lease property to Negro businessmen in predominantly white neighborhoods or adjacent to similar white-operated enterprises.

Others called attention to another aspect of segregation in saying that it would be economically unsound to establish businesses in predominantly white neighborhoods because whites refuse to do business with Negroes. This would mean that Negro businessmen would have to outbid white businessmen for locations in which they would be disadvantaged for potential customers. Therefore, even if a Negro businessman could locate in a favorable business section (not just a Negro neighborhood) the tradition of segregation might make it economically unsound to do so. Actually, interviews with Negro businessmen located near large white neighborhoods did reveal that, insofar as potential white customers are concerned, their establishments are regarded as off-limits. Thus, Negro operators of filling stations, dry cleaners, and grocery stores near white neighborhoods, or even in racially mixed neighborhoods, report that they have no substantial white trade. Said a filling-station operator located on a busy thoroughfare, "My white customers are few and far between. Only occasionally does a white customer in this neighborhood stop for service. Even then, he has usually run out of gas and can't make it to another service station." Therefore, the unstated principle that "white people must not trade with Negroes" is so real in the minds of Negro businessmen that, with one or two notable exceptions they do not even cater to potential white customers.

Unfair competition with white businessmen. Unlike white businessmen who are protected from competition with Negro businessmen by a complex of laws and traditions, Negro businessmen have no such immunity. They encounter competition from white businessmen in every phase of their business activities. In the first place, white businessmen are not contained in the white community, as are Negroes in the Negro community. It is expected that white businessmen will locate in any section of the city calculated to be profitable. Consequently, nearly all of the most desirable business locations in the Negro community are occupied by whites. These businessmen do not encounter volunteer boycotts by Negroes, as do Negro businessmen from whites. The opposite is usually true. Thus, a Negro grocer complained that his "white competitor across the street has more customers than I do. It looks as though every time they want credit they come to me. When they have money they go across the street."

Another kind of competition Negro businessmen experience is centered around a lack of sufficient capital to compete with wealthier white businessmen. A Negro druggist found himself in competition with a chain drug store that opened only a few blocks away. His store had a more limited line of merchandise and was much less attractive than the one operated by the white owner. He lamented that "it seems that whenever I put in a 'special,' such as ice cream, to be sold at a reduced price to attract customers, [a white competitor] sells a wider variety at an even cheaper price than I can possibly afford. He gets the Negro customers. I simply cannot compete." This type of "unfair" competition with wealthier whites is experienced by all Negro businessmen, even those who operate legally segregated eating establishments. It is not uncommon for successful white restaurateurs to cater to "colored only."

One subtle method white businessmen use in competition with Negro businessmen is to cater to race pride. That is, they know full well that race-conscious Negroes prefer to trade with Negro businessmen, even though some slight financial loss might be incurred thereby. Some white businessmen counter by employing Negroes to manage their so-called "Negro enterprises." Most, however, simply employ a helper or "front man" who is well known and liked by potential Negro customers. This technique pits Negro against Negro, with the resulting profits accruing to the white-owned enterprises. In addition, it also prevents Negroes from entering certain types of businesses that would obviously be profitable. For example, practically all "for colored only" movies may be classified as "neighborhood theaters." They are usually located in the center of thickly populated Negro areas, yet all of these theaters are owned by white businessmen who employ Negroes in all positions that have contact with patrons. Therefore, even the most race-conscious Negroes, who refuse to attend any public gathering where there is racially segregated seating, seem to have little or no compunction about patronizing theaters "for colored only," so long as they get the illusion that these theaters are operated by Negroes.

The effectiveness of the "front man" or "favorite son" technique of meeting Negro business competition is brought out in a statement by a Negro leader who defended his habit of patronizing a white-owned service station in preference to one owned by a Negro. He said: "They have a very courteous, efficient Negro helper at that station. He needs a job just as much as anyone at [the Negro-owned] filling station. If my trade helps him, I don't see any logical objection to my stopping there."

Lack of business tradition. In striking contrast with the mature growth and development so characteristic of many white-owned business enterprises in New Orleans, the most notable feature of Negro-owned enterprises is the recency of their establishment. With few exceptions, they are still owned and operated by their orignial founders. The children of these founders usually attend college and prepare for professional careers. Consequently, no tradition is established. Bemoaning this situation, one of the more successful Negro businessmen confided:

> My son is to graduate from college next month. He wants to go to graduate school. He thinks he wants to be a teacher. Of course, I pay for his education, but I don't want to dictate to him. He could make three times as much money if he would come and help me carry on here. His education would be a big asset. He will not do so. I know that now. I honestly think he looks down on me because in my business I must deal with all types of people. He actually told his mother that I am a low-brow.

The lack of business tradition among Negroes serves as a multiple handicap. One, the names of their enterprises seldom come to symbolize quality and efficiency, as do the names of many of their white competitors. Two, second-generation family members, who are primarily responsible for carrying on these businesses, ordinarily regard their positions as temporary and a means to some other occupational end. Therefore, it is unlikely that the children will be motivated to put into the businesses the creative efforts necessary for continuous growth and development. Three, Negro businesses seldom have long-enough lives to become established as permanent parts of the business community. Therefore, they do not have the credit rating or the sustained contacts with other businesses that are necessary for stable and continuous development.

Exclusion from powerful business associations. Some of the most successful Negro businessmen in New Orleans feel that they are severely handicapped because, as one emphasized:

> We are isolated from the real world of business. We have no opportunities to get in on the planning and directing of the economic life of this city. When big money opportunities come along we always miss out because all deals are closed before we know about them. White businessmen overlook us until they want us to throw something their way.

What this businessman had specific reference to is the fact that there is no Negro member of the New Orleans Chamber of Commerce, the powerful Young Men's Business Club, Rotary, or any other organization where economic trends, opportunities, and planning are discussed by experts. This, coupled with the fact that the Negro Business League in New Orleans has always been anemic, means that the individual Negro businessman has few, if any, opportunities to benefit from the thinking and experience of other businessmen.

We may conclude, then, that by and large Negro businesses in New Orleans are located in predominantly Negro neighborhoods, where they must generally compete with better-established and more efficiently operated white enterprises. Most remain extremely simple and small-scale. Actually, except for a few of the larger insurance companies, Negro-owned establishments provide few jobs outside of those held by family members. Their economic status and social influence are seldom sufficient to inspire public confidence. Thus, in a corporative sense, Negro businesses, like Negro people in New Orleans generally, are ascribed second-class citizenship status.

What have Negro leaders done to equalize economic opportunities for their people?

STRATEGIES AND TECHNIQUES

All Negro leaders interviewed for this study volunteered to comment upon racial discrimination as it exists in the economic life of New Orleans. They usually described it as unjust, and expressed the opinion that it leads to a profligate use of Negro potentials. Their basic criticisms were voiced by the local Urban League executive. He said—

> A study of the occupational pattern of Negroes in New Orleans shows limited employment opportunities with concomitant low income. Such conditions produce an impaired standard of living which necessarily gives rise to many serious eco-

nomic and social conditions. . . . Negroes do not have the opportunity to special-
ize in technical and engineering courses. [Yet] the lack of educational qualifications
is not the deterring factor in most cases . . . it is company policy. . . . Negro
industrial workers who meet the best standards of qualifications often encounter
the most extreme bias in their quest for merit employment. Hundreds of Negro
college graduates are working as porters, janitors, waiters, postal employees and
in other unskilled positions because of employment limitations based on race and
color. The by-products of this are not only adversely affecting Negroes but our
community as well. We can ill afford to lose these educated citizens. The problem
of discriminatory employment is the number one problem facing New Orleans.
It gives rise to problems of health, delinquency, crime, education and housing.[2]

Race relations leaders in New Orleans have employed five distinct, though
interdiffused, strategies in attempts to obtain equal citizenship rights for Negroes. Only three of these strategies have been effectively utilized, however,
in attempts to achieve equal economic rights. These are *protest, negotiation,*
and *direct action.* Litigation and political action have not been resorted to except in rare instances. Laws, reflecting the basic ethos in our free-enterprise
system, are seldom used anywhere to force employers to hire individuals they
do not desire. Consequently, except for the litigation that led to the employment of Negroes on the police force of the city, which is under Civil Service
regulations, legal action has not been among the strategies Negro leaders
have used to gain new jobs. However, in one very important instance Negro
educators in Louisiana were able—through long, costly litigation—to equalize the salaries of Negro and white teachers.

As noted previously, the voting strength of Negroes in New Orleans has
not been sufficient to insure them political jobs. Only in a few isolated instances have Negroes received political appointments, and the positions they
have held have usually been temporary and part-time. It may be said, then,
that the Negro's fight for equal economic opportunities is hampered because
two of the most reliable strategies used elsewhere have been ineffective here.

Protest. Sixty of the 75 Negro leaders who claim to have actively participated in attempts to alleviate economic discrimination based on race acknowledged that they have limited their efforts to verbal protest. The most
frequently used techniques in this regard are public speeches, newspaper
articles, and formal arguments before committees, boards, and institutes.
Such protest is usually spontaneous, unorganized, and undirected.

Seldom does a local Negro leader end a public speech, no matter what his
central theme may be, without voicing some word of protest against economic
discrimination. Likewise, all Negro newspapers, particularly the *Louisiana
Weekly,* dedicate a large proportion of their space to stories and editorials in
which racial discrimination in employment is denounced. Typical is this editorial appearing in the *Louisiana Weekly* condemning segregated unions—

[2] J. Harvey Kerns, "Employment and Under-employment in New Orleans" (Testimony
before United States Special Senate Committee, 1960).

There are scores of qualified, licensed Negro electricians in New Orleans but not one is a member of the Brotherhood of Electrical Workers.

Pity the plight of the poor Negro plumber. He cannot be licensed in New Orleans much less join the all-white plumbers and steamfitters union.

A staff writer for that same paper protested—

Every third person in New Orleans is a Negro—though it would be difficult for a visitor to believe this if he surveyed the offices, the labs, the mechanized production lines, and the counters from behind which the goods which help make New Orleans' wealth are sold. Often porter . . . taxpayer . . . but seldom in technical or white-collar positions.[3]

Whenever Negro leaders are members of interracial committees, boards, or institutes they are expected to protest, be it ever so mild, when the opportunity arises to discuss employment policies and practices. Such opportunities often come to labor-union leaders. The Negro masses expect them to protest unfair labor practices, and in turn criticize them severely when they are believed to be lax, or Uncle Toms, in that regard.

It would be difficult to ascertain what, if any, tangible effect verbal protest has had in improving the economic status of Negroes. Apparently white men of power, who are in positions to respond meaningfully to the Negro's plea for broader economic opportunities, are either unaware of such protest or simply choose to ignore it. It seems, however, that the more or less constant verbal protest of Negro leaders has had some important psychological effects upon the Negro masses. It has at least served to inform them of the nature, extent, and negative consequences of economic discrimination. Such facts presented by Negro leaders eventually become common knowledge. Observing this phenomenon, one leader expressed confidence in verbal protest:

Put the facts of discrimination as they exist in employment before the people as strongly as possible. Let them know they deserve equal jobs with equal pay. Make them angry with those who deny them the right to earn a living. . . . When the time comes to strike hard at the roots of economic injustices they will be ready to support you. Propaganda is necessary to stir up the masses.

The psychological effectiveness of verbal protest is evidenced by the willingness of many otherwise conservative Negroes to go a step further and follow "action" leaders who employ the more drastic and dangerous techniques of protest—especially picketing and public demonstrations. These have frequently led to arrests, insults, and even violence. During 1960 and 1961 hundreds of Negroes in New Orleans joined picket lines and carried signs protesting "racial discrimination in hiring," "unfair employment practices,"

[3] April 29, 1961.

and so forth. Others have joined in marching, praying, singing, and speaking demonstrations calculated to dramatize discrimination in employment.

These techniques of action protest have been considerably more effective in eliciting responses from white men of power than verbal protest. This may be due to several things, particularly the fact that demonstrations are usually better organized, much more focused, and more news worthy than are speeches, writings, and logical arguments. "Action" leaders know the importance of publicity, and often resort to demonstrations in order to propagandize their grievances. Thus, when questioned concerning his motives for leading a walking, placard-carrying demonstration, a leader said, in effect—

> There are in this city many white people of good will. It is true that most would prefer racial segregation because they don't know any other way of life. They are good, but ignorant in the area of human relations. Demagogues have devised all kinds of barriers to prevent such people from knowing the horrible truth about discrimination. We simply must find some way to insure that such fair-minded white people get the facts about the unjust economic pressures applied to Negroes. I believe many will refuse to remain silent when they know the truth. How else can we communicate with them except by going to jail?

Publicity attendant upon mass protest demonstrations also gets some response from officials because occasionally it causes the local government considerable embarrassment. There is fear that business will be hurt and that new industries might be reluctant to locate in a community torn with racial strife. Further, there is always the very real fear that riots and ruins might stem from these demonstrations. Occasionally these fears are so obviously well founded that public officials are moved to action. First, they respond by re-interpreting old laws or passing new ones designed to prevent public protest. One leader observed:

> The threshold of democracy is very low here. [New Orleans] white officials will take away basic freedoms, such as assembly and protest, at almost any threat of disturbance.

Second, when legal measures fail to discourage action leaders, certain white men of power might accede to their long-standing demands to negotiate on some specific area of discriminatory employment.

Negotiation. Ideally, negotiation between Negro leaders and white power figures in New Orleans will be based on one of two types of encounters; race man-segregationist, which is characterized by pressure techniques, and racial diplomat-segregationist, characterized by the more refined, delicate techniques of diplomacy.

It is only recently that Negroes in New Orleans have become organized to the point where they are able to bring any meaningful pressure to bear upon white officials in attempts to achieve equal economic rights. Even now their efforts are far from being as united as would be necessary for the achievement of that goal. Nevertheless, since 1960 the newly founded Consumers' League has had some limited success in this respect. On a few occasions its program of relentless mass protests and demonstrations has led to top level negotiations.

Negotiation between Negro action leaders and white men of power are characteristically clumsy, strained, and tense. Both parties manifest deep-rooted suspicion, distrust, and even fear of one another. During such sessions action leaders first define the areas of racial discrimination and then proceed to outline their demands for fairer employment. Next, white officials counter by pointing to certain "fallacies" in the information the Negro leaders present, and attempt to convince them that their demands are exaggerated or impossible. They quote statistics and present information, much of which is naturally unavailable to anyone but the officials themselves. Negro leaders then counter by presenting information about the Negro community that would ordinarily be unavailable to the white officials. Neither side trusts the sincerity, honesty, or even the motives of the other. These sessions usually adjourn with the Negro leaders having scaled down their demands considerably, and the white officials having made some more or less cautious promise that "we will present this problem at the very next meeting of the board. We assure you that it will be given every possible consideration."

One reason why the race man-segregationist pattern of race relations is awkward and frustrating is the fact that these two parties reason from entirely different premises. On the one hand, the race man *demands* what he regards as the fulfillment of a right. His demands are in effect an accusation against the employer of being unfair and unjust. On the other hand, segregationists regard the Negro negotiators as impudent, violating "sacred southern traditions" according to which Negroes are supposed to *beg* for favors, or at least behave towards whites in a respectful, polished, gracious manner. Thus, even if segregationists regarded the Negro's demands as just, they would still resent bargaining with Negro negotiators on a basis of equality. The situation, of course, is even more complicated because segregationists tend not to see their employment policies and practices as unjust. Thus, after hearing the demands of a Negro leader a powerful white employer snapped—

> This business is run according to the very best business regulations we know. After all, we are responsible to the stockholders and to the community at large. We do what is best for the business. That is our solemn obligation. Your demands are not only untimely—they constitute bad business practices. They are out of the question.

And, as we shall see later, it is only when Negro "action" leaders use direct-action techniques such as the boycott, or the threat of it, that white officials actually attempt to meet any of their demands for equal employment opportunities.

Certainly the more conventional, and perhaps the more fruitful, form of race relations negotiation is that between the racial diplomat and influential segregationists. The best illustrations of this form in New Orleans are found in the records of the local branch of the Urban League. This organization is usually headed by well-trained, experienced executives who are highly skilled in the use of the most refined diplomatic techniques of race relations negotiation. The following is typical of the League's *modus operandi*:[4]

First, the League seeks to legitimize itself as a bona fide community organization by selecting influential white and Negro citizens from business, labor, and the professions to serve on its board of directors.

Second, it endeavors to steer clear of active involvement in mass protests and demonstrations where so-called controversial issues are dramatized. In this way it has been successful in retaining the support of some influential white persons who, according to one board member, "cannot afford to be identified with racial protest or mass action intended to eliminate traditional patterns of race relations by embarrassing local officials."

The fact that such caution is well founded was revealed during the crisis period in 1955. At that time some powerful segregationist forces branded it as "integrationist" and either Communistic or Communist-inspired. Dossiers, or "This is your Life" records, were compiled on individual board members. As a result, several influential white persons resigned from the board, and the League was eventually dropped from the ranks of the United Fund agencies.

Third, before negotiation the League conducts a survey to gather pertinent facts on the problem in question.

Fourth, a period of propaganda follows the fact-finding. After the League has gathered ample evidence to prove racial discrimination in some area of employment, it makes use of several techniques to disseminate these facts as widely as possible. Among the most effective techniques are: its public meetings where prepared reports are read and distributed, speeches by League officials, statements to the press, letters to influential white businessmen, and testimonies before agencies, committees, and individuals who have the power to assist Negroes in their bid for fair employment.

Fifth, armed with pertinent facts and figures, Urban League officials set about getting white employers to agree to negotiate on better job opportunities for Negroes in some specific area. It is usually at this point that the role of white board members becomes particularly important. It is often one of them who agrees to use his or her social, business, or professional contacts to set up conferences between League representatives and powerful white employers.

[4] Information on this point is summarized from an unpublished study by Giles A. Hubert, *The New Orleans Urban League*. This study was done in connection with this study of leadership.

Unlike meetings between race men and white officials, meetings between racial diplomats and white employers are generally conducted in an atmosphere of mutual respect, and are characterized by politeness and sympathetic communication. Throughout such discussions Negro diplomats appeal to the enlightened self-interest of the employers. They persistently attempt to rationalize their contentions for wider economic opportunities for Negroes in terms of total community welfare. Their arguments are sound, persuasive interpretations of basic Christian and democratic principles. As one Negro leader summarized—

> These conferences with business executives were truly top level. We discussed the short- and long-range effects wider employment of Negroes would have upon the economy of New Orleans and what it would do for the reputation of the city. I think they were convinced that our position is best for the general economy.

Despite years of such skilled negotiation, Hubert sees in retrospect that the League has not been able to accomplish any "real breakthrough in the employment field. . . . Even though several isolated instances of success can be pointed to, the over-all picture of discrimination in employment has hardly been changed. . . . Almost no headway has been made in the clerical or so-called white-collar area."[5]

Because Negro leaders have been unable to achieve any significant breakthrough in the discriminatory employment policies and practices in New Orleans through protest and negotiation, and since litigation and political pressure can not easily be applied, they have begun to resort to the more drastic, economically crippling techniques of direct action.

Direct action. Although it is generally acknowledged, even by public officials, that Negroes have been victims of the most flagrant economic discrimination in New Orleans, until recently Negro leaders made little more than sporadic attempts to apply any direct pressure upon employers to award them jobs that they obviously deserved. Most of these attempts were more individual than mass. That is, some individual and his friends would become impatient with white businesses located in Negro communities that depended almost exclusively upon Negro patronage and yet flatly refused to employ Negroes except in the most menial positions. They sometimes began "whispering campaigns" intended to discourage other Negroes from trading with the establishments in question. Also, occasionally, some Negro uplift organization, most often the NAACP, reported economic discrimination in the hiring practices of certain businesses receiving significant patronage from Negro people. Negroes were usually advised to initiate a program of selective buying according to which businesses having fairer racial employment practices would be supported, and those practicing the more flagrant racial discrimination would be boycotted. About the only tangible effect such sporadic, largely unorganized, efforts have had has been to inform the Negro

[5] *Op. cit.*, pp. 83-84.

masses about the nature and extent of economic discrimination. Many Negroes, of course, did actually boycott a few such business firms for a short period of time, but the movement itself had no noticeable effect upon discriminatory employment practices.

During the crisis period in race relations that came to a climax in 1961, Negroes on all socioeconomic levels developed a more determined race consciousness than they had ever had before. Consequently, efforts at boycotts proved more successful. Interestingly, the most successful boycotts were under the sponsorship of the Consumers' League, which was organized under the auspices of the diplomatically oriented Urban League. For several months the Urban League had attempted to persuade large retail merchants in a predominantly Negro section of the city to employ qualified Negroes in white-collar positions such as cashiers, salesmen, and so forth. In spite of the formidable array of facts the League presented and the skilled negotiation it conducted, the merchants in question were adamant regarding the employment of Negroes in "merit positions." Finally, the League called together a number of representative Negro leaders, presented the facts of discriminatory employment on the part of the merchants and called for action. There ensued the organization of the militant Consumers' League.

Throughout 1960 and 1961 the Consumers' League carried on boycotts in one Negro neighborhood after the other. Some of the merchants who chose to ignore this organization's demands for "merit employment" of Negroes lost practically all of their Negro trade and were eventually forced out of business. Other merchants acceded to a few demands and employed Negroes in white-collar positions. Thus, in July 1961 the Consumers' League claimed credit for having secured a total of 152 white-collar jobs for Negroes in white-owned retail establishments. In some instances this meant a significant job breakthrough, since some of these types of establishments throughout the city (such as chain stores, drug stores, department stores, and super markets) had traditionally excluded Negroes from white-collar positions.

The boycott movement received wide support from the Negro masses. For a while it developed into an almost spontaneous movement whereby unorganized Negro groups began to bring pressure to bear on white-owned establishments in their neighborhoods. Owners of these businesses were constantly in fear that such boycotts might seriously damage their businesses. Expressing this fear is a paid advertisement that appeared in the *Louisiana Weekly* which read:

NOTICE! NOTICE!

Due to the trouble the City is having with segregationists, some people are using it for personal gains.

It's the ones who know us at [————] Gro., that know we do not dislike the Negro people. Just take time out and think who gains the most from all of this.

I do not belong to any organization or support any organization against Human Rights.[6]

6 December 17, 1960.

Needless to say, the direct-action techniques employed by the Consumers' League were met with stern, sometimes violent, opposition from the white community. Old laws were re-interpreted, and new laws were passed, to curb public demonstrations, including "peaceful picketing." These laws were rigidly enforced, and on several occasions outstanding Negro leaders and their followers were arrested, jailed, and fined. The leader of this organization refers to himself as the "civil rights jailbird." Occasionally, some individual segregationist attempted to instigate violence by insulting or actually manhandling Negro picketers. Violence was kept at a minimum, however, due to the vigilance of the police department in the maintenance of law and order, and the Negroes' strict adherence to the policy of nonviolence.

Perhaps the most ambitious project proposed by the Consumers' League is the boycotting of the New Orleans Public Service Corporation, which, despite years of negotiation with Negro leaders, refuses to employ Negroes in white-collar positions. The Consumers' League proposed a boycott of city buses and limited use of power and gas. The series of negotiations that followed were extremely strained and frustrating. They ended with no definite commitment to employ Negroes being made by company officials. However, after several weeks, during which time the Consumers' League carried on almost constant mass protest and renewed threats of boycott, two Negro bus drivers were hired. This was far short of the demands of Negro leaders, yet it was a significant breakthrough because it marked the first time Negroes had ever been employed in that position.

We may conclude that, despite the fact that most leaders in New Orleans recognize that Negroes suffer from widespread economic discrimination and that this condition gives rise to many other related social ills affecting Negroes, little concerted effort has been made to alleviate this condition. A few militant race men and dedicated Negro diplomats working with a handful of white liberals have been able to get a small number of individual Negroes upgraded or employed on jobs that they did not formally hold. However, we may say that, for all practical purposes, Negroes on the whole are relatively no better off in their efforts to earn a living than they were in 1940. With this fact in mind a prominent Negro leader, in a report to a House Special Subcommittee on Labor, appealed to the federal government for assistance. According to him, there are four forces that militate against equal employment opportunities for Negroes in New Orleans:

(1) Lack of equal vocational and apprenticeship training. . . . The Orleans Area Vocational and Technical School for Negroes offers only seven courses. Delgado Trades and Technical Institute for whites, offers 47 courses. Equipment used at this school (Delgado) was valued at $1 million. This is more than twelve times the listed value of the equipment of the trade school serving Negroes of New Orleans.

(2) Discrimination by employment agencies. [Even] the United States Employment Service . . . frequently directs Negroes into only traditional and menial jobs.

(3) Discrimination by labor unions. . . . While Negro labor unions in New Orleans accepted whites in the building trades, the white unions were not so magnanimous and continue to exclude Negroes from the metal plumbing, boilermakers, pipefitters, electricians, sheet metal, welders and other trades. [Also] Negroes are victims of discrimination by unions in petroleum, chemical, aircraft and communications.

(4) Discrimination by management. Some managers simply refuse to employ Negroes.[7]

This leader recommended that the President call upon Congress to enact legislation to prohibit discrimination in employment; and that this legislation have enabling provisions to create necessary agencies for the full and expeditious implementation of fair employment practices. Most Negro leaders agree with him that only through federal action can Negro people hope to attain equal job opportunities in the nation generally, and in the South particularly.

[7] Clarence A. Laws, "The Economic Status of Negroes" (Testimony before U. S. House of Representatives Sub-Committee on Labor, January 1962).

9

EDUCATION

BECAUSE AMERICANS ATTACH great value to education, educated persons generally enjoy higher social status and more economic security than those who have not attained distinction in this wise. This is especially true among Negroes, for whom, in addition to the tangible and intangible values education symbolizes for Americans generally, a "good" education serves especially to enhance self-respect, and also to discredit the doctrine of racial inferiority which has traditionally embarrassed and penalized Negroes. Therefore, the better-educated Negroes have always been regarded by others of their race, as well as by liberal whites, as the most persuasive evidence that Negroes are mentally and morally not unlike other persons of different races, because they have "in one important respect, become equal to the better class of whites."[1] More than 50 years ago it was observed that "the eagerness of colored people for a chance to send their children to school is something astonishing and pathetic. They will submit to all sorts of inconveniences in order that their children may get an education."[2] This interest in attaining an education has not waned. Myrdal, for instance, noted that "the masses of Negroes show even today a naïve, almost religious faith in education."[3] Education has been presented to them as a kind of magic. That is, many Negro leaders endeavor to convince their followers that nearly all personal and racial problems will disappear when the educational level of Negroes increases to that of white people. This point of view was echoed by a mass-oriented minister:

I never thought of myself as a leader because I never received much formal education. There were a few schools in the community where I was reared and they closed whenever the white people needed Negroes to work in their fields. I actually never knew an educated Negro until I was grown. But, one thing my parents always said: "If you want to be respected in life, to walk tall like white

[1] Gunnar Myrdal, *op. cit.*, p. 879.
[2] Ray Stannard Baker, *Following the Color Line* (New York: Doubleday and Co., 1908) p. 53.
[3] Gunnar Myrdal, *op. cit.*, p. 884.

people, you must get something in your head." All of my life I have kept looking for knowledge. I taught myself to read and write and I've been building on that ever since. . . . I'm now pastor of one of the largest churches in the city. I preach education every Sunday. I try to get my people to see that when they get something in their heads they can get better jobs, more respect, and more dignity than they can without an education. . . . Negroes will never get the rights they seek until they become an educated people.

Negroes in New Orleans do place a very high value upon education. Many have a profound faith that it is the most estimable means whereby they can achieve first-class citizenship. Yet, despite the emphasis Negro leaders have placed upon academic attainment as the key to security, social status, and dignity, on the whole Negroes in New Orleans still lag significantly behind white people in the attainment of a good education. The proportion of Negroes with every level of schooling, from first grade through college and professional training, is substantially below that of white people. This is so in spite of the fact that during the last twenty years Negroes in New Orleans have made impressive gains in their struggle to raise their level of education. Actually, a considerable number of leaders in New Orleans feel that the gains made by Negroes in education since World War II are greater than those made by them in any other area. For example, in 1940 the average Negro adult in New Orleans had achieved only 5.7 years of schooling compared with 8.4 years for whites, a lag of 2.7 years. Twenty years later (1960) the average educational level of Negroes had increased to 7.5 years. This rate of increase is much greater than that for whites, whose average level of education was by then just ninth grade. However, the average Negro adult still had a year and a half less schooling than did the average white adult.

Perhaps a better way of pointing up the extent to which Negroes lag behind white people in their educational level is to compare the proportion of Negroes and whites with no formal education, with high-school education, and with college training, as is done in the table below.[4] In 1940, 8.8 per cent of all adult Negroes in New Orleans had received no formal education, compared with 2.9 per cent of white adults in this category. Again, only 3.2 per cent of adult Negroes had completed high school, compared with 16.4

[4] LEVEL OF EDUCATION RECEIVED BY ADULTS IN NEW ORLEANS

	1940		1960	
	Negro %	White %	Negro %	White %
No formal education	8.8	2.9	5.2	2.8
High School graduates	3.2	16.4	9.6	19.0
College graduates	1.2	6.0	2.8	7.7

SOURCE: These figures were adopted from *United States Census of Population* (1940), *General Social and Economic Characteristics of Louisiana*, and *United States Census of Population and Housing* (New Orleans, Louisiana, 1960).

per cent of the white adults. And, what is even more significant in an industrial society, with increasing need for white-collar, technical, and professional competence, is the fact that in 1940 only 1.2 per cent of the Negro adults had graduated from college, compared with 6 per cent of the white adults.

By 1960 Negroes in New Orleans had reduced their illiteracy rate to about 5.2 per cent, while whites accomplished comparably very little in this regard, although only 2.8 per cent of the white population was classified as illiterate. Also, by 1960 Negroes had increased the proportion of high-school graduates to approximately 9.6 per cent. At the same time, the proportion of white high-school graduates had increased to about 19 per cent. And, finally, according to the last census report whites in New Orleans had increased the proportion graduated from college to 7.7 per cent, while Negroes had doubled the proportion they had in 1940, but could still boast of only a relatively weak 2.8 per cent.

Negro leaders give many different reasons why their people still lag so significantly behind whites in the level of education attained. Among the most feasible reasons they offer are inadequate facilities and supplies, low economic status, limited range of occupational opportunities, and segregation.

Inadequate facilities. First, it is a long standing and well-proven contention that Negroes throughout the South—and New Orleans is no exception—have not received anything like an equal proportion of monies spent for public education. Some of the older Negro educators in New Orleans report that until quite recently (during the 1950's) practically all Negro school buildings were secondhand or "hand-me-downs." That is, when the Board of Education decided to erect new school buildings for white children their old buildings were turned over to Negroes. One of these educators expressed this resentment: "Most of the buildings set aside for Negro children should have been torn down when the white children vacated them. I suppose the board [of education] operates on the assumption that second-class citizens should be educated in second-class surroundings." Even today, despite pressure from the federal courts and national public opinion, the practice of turning over former all-white facilities for segregated Negro use is still generally practised. Consequently, not only are school buildings for Negroes often dilapidated, but other facilities and equipment are all too often lacking altogether. Thus, for years Negro educators have complained that science laboratories and equipment in Negro schools are often insufficient or antiquated, and that even the elementary science subjects could not be taught effectively. Evidently considerable improvement in this area has been made in recent years, yet Negro educators still point out gross inadequacies in science facilities and equipment.

As early as 1950 the Orleans Parish School Board inaugurated the platoon system, claiming that it was a "temporary arrangement." Yet, in 1957 there were 9,695 Negro children on platoon. And, in spite of some serious efforts on the part of the school board, there are still approximately 6,000 Negro children who go to school in shifts, one platoon coming before noon, and another in the afternoon. And even with platooning, classes for Negro children are relatively overcrowded, having from five to seven more pupils per classroom than in white schools. In other words, one survey of the New Orleans public-school system revealed that Negro school buildings are being utilized at 114 per cent of capacity, compared with only 73 per cent in white schools. Another survey by the Coordinating Council of Greater New Orleans presented the history of McDonogh 35, a New Orleans school. The school was built in 1882 for white children. In 1917, thirty-five years later, it was converted into the *first* Negro public high school in New Orleans. During the next twenty years McDonogh 35 was the only Negro public high school in New Orleans. This injustice is further aggravated by the inadequacy of its facilities. Even today, eighty years after its construction, it is being used by Negro children to 120 per cent of capacity. The school has no recreation area, and the school band is forced to practice marching on a nearby traffic island in a heavily used thoroughfare.

Physical education teachers in Negro schools continue to petition school authorities to provide at least minimum-standard playground space and athletic equipment. Most Negro public schools have no adequate fields or gyms such as are required to carry on up-to-date recreational programs. Very often it is necessary to hold football and basketball games in facilities borrowed from private schools in the area. White children in New Orleans with exceptional ability—an IQ of 120 or above—can pursue special high-standard curriculum at the Benjamin Franklin Senior High School. No such facilities are available to Negroes. And, as pointed out in the previous chapter, white youth in New Orleans can pursue technical and trade education in trade schools that are modernly equipped and have curriculums that provide adequate training for students who wish to go into well-paying, highly skilled jobs. Vocational training for Negroes is, by comparison, grossly inadequate. Furthermore, in addition to these obvious inequalities, most Negro educators are of the opinion that textbooks and other educational materials provided Negro children are in some important regards inferior to those provided white children. "One thing is certain," said a high-school principal of many years experience, "white authorities in New Orleans have given only passing lip service to the 'separate but equal' doctrine as applied to the education of Negroes. All Negro schools in some respects have been, and continue to be, disgracefully inferior."

Economic status. A second major reason cited by Negro leaders for the educational lag on the part of the Negro masses is the fact that the economic status of Negroes generally is far below that of white people. This is a logical explanation, because social scientists are in agreement that there is a direct correlation between economic status and years of schooling. Accordingly, the lower the economic status of a particular family or ethnic group the lower is likely to be its average level of academic attainment. Consequently, Negroes, who constitute the largest proportion of the economically disadvantaged in New Orleans, can be expected to have the largest proportion of illiterates and the lowest proportion of those graduating from grade school and college. All Negro educators who granted interviews for this study pointed out how seriously many of their students are handicapped by poverty. One teacher said—

> It is not just the lack of money in the home and other disadvantages related to it that trouble me, rather it is cultural poverty—the almost complete lack of books and other worthwhile reading matter in the home. But, what is even worse is the absence of the motivation to succeed.

This teacher went on to point out that most of the parents of students whom she has taught over the years had themselves attained only an elementary education or less. "They are unable to give their children any real assistance in the preparation of homework or even to offer encouragement when it is badly needed," she asserted.

Another handicap cited by teachers, and validated by several surveys of housing conditions among Negroes, is that most of the lower-income Negro families do not have sufficient space to set aside a room or some definite area in their houses for study. In many instances the houses or apartments in which they live are so overcrowded as to make any kind of study habits on the part of the children next to impossible. Small wonder then that practically all teachers of Negro children in New Orleans complain that most of them cannot be induced to do creditable homework.

A third economically related handicap frequently mentioned by public-school teachers is the high drop-out rate on the part of Negro children, particularly boys, who must assist in the support of the family. This is especially significant among some in the lowest socioeconomic class, where up to 50 per cent of the homes may be classified as matriarchates, since the husband or father is absent. Summarizing this problem, Thompson gave the following analysis of southern states, which is apropos of the New Orleans situation. He reported that—

> Negro pupils in southern states drop out of school at a rate 500 per cent higher than do white pupils. For every one Negro pupil completing high school, about 14 of his classmates drop-out along the way, whereas for every one white pupil graduating from high school only two of his classmates drop-out.
>
> As high as is the rate of drop-out for Negro students on the whole, it is considerably higher for Negro boys than for Negro girls. Negro girls remain in school longer and have, on an average, higher grades than do Negro boys. Thus, contrary to the pattern in American society generally, about two-thirds of all Negro high school and college graduates are women.
>
> The high drop-out rate of Negro boys has serious consequences also for the Negro's struggle for full citizenship. Most of the desirable jobs with high prestige and substantial salaries are classified by law or tradition as "Men Jobs." The vast majority of these jobs are monopolized by whites. If there is to be democratization of job opportunities in our society, Negro men in larger numbers must be qualified

to hold jobs which are now unavailable to them and to compete successfully with Americans of all races for other jobs requiring high technological and intellectual skills. *Therefore, the degree to which Negro men fail to measure up to high levels of technical and academic standards will be the degree to which Negroes as a race will fail to achieve the full citizenship for which they are striving so hard.*[5]

Even when Negro children from the more economically handicapped homes do manage to graduate from graded school due to compulsory school attendance, individual determination to achieve, or "social promotion," few indeed can be expected to go on to college. The vast majority simply do not have enough money to pay for a college education. Others who are financially able do not make high enough grades in high school to insure acceptance, or do not have sufficient motivation to go to college. In a word, the great majority of Negro high school graduates, especially boys, for one reason or another terminate their education and place themselves on the already overcrowded blue-collar labor market.

Limited opportunities. The third frequently cited reason for the low level of academic achievement among Negroes is the limited range of occupational opportunities available to them. This was discussed at length in the previous chapter. A 1959 survey by the New Orleans Urban League revealed that the occupational aspirations of the Negro high school seniors were "low and narrow." Few indeed aspired to prepare for professional and technical training. The investigator concluded that much of this was due to the fact that high school seniors proved to be grossly ignorant regarding the existence of most top-level, well-paying occupations in our society; those who were aware that they existed saw little if any possibility of ever achieving such a position because of their race.

According to a fruitful sociological theory, members of an ethnic group who see little possibility of their education paying off in an economic sense cannot be expected to voluntarily make the same sacrifices for an education that others would to whom a good education is a means of acquiring some estimable, lucrative job. It is not surprising, then, that practically all of the Negro youth who are willing to make unusual sacrifices to continue their education in college are those who have proclivities for teaching or the ministry, professions into which most Negro college graduates enter. Those with other aptitudes and aspirations are very likely to lose courage because of the lack of estimable symbols of success in these fields among their acquaintances. It is logical, therefore, that the narrow range of estimable job opportunities for Negro youth in New Orleans would tend to limit their motivation to achieve academic excellence.

Segregation. A fourth, and certainly the most agreed-upon, reason why Negroes in New Orleans lag so far behind white people academically is *segregation.* This point of view is basic in all of the voluntary statements by Negro leaders with whom we talked, and is indeed the central contention of

[5] Daniel C. Thompson, "Our Wasted Potential," *The Dillard Bulletin,* April 1960, p. 1.

several recent federal court decisions intended to outlaw segregation in public education. Thus the history-making *Brown* decision held that—

> Today, education is perhaps the most important function of state and local governments. Compulsory school attendance laws and the great expenditures for education both demonstrate our recognition of the importance of education to our democratic society. It is required in the performance of our most basic public responsibilities, even service in the Armed Forces. It is the very foundation of good citizenship.
>
> . . . We conclude that in the field of public education the doctrine of "separate but equal" has no place. Separate educational facilities are inherently unequal. . . . And it is doubtful that any child may reasonably be expected to succeed in life if he is denied the opportunity of an education.[6]

Negroes from all walks of life rejoiced over this decision. Some hailed it as a "second Emancipation Proclamation." It marked what they hoped to be the end of a long, costly, frustrating struggle for equal educational opportunities. Thus, sixty-four Negro leaders in the field of education at a conference in Hot Springs, Arkansas, declared that this decision was "right and moral." They said—

> We welcome the decision and look upon it as another significant milestone in the nation's quest for a democratic way of life and in the Negro's long struggle to become a first class citizen. . . . We urge that immediate steps be taken to implement the decision. . . . [It] makes possible a single school system with the opportunity for the people in the region to marshal their educational resources and develop a philosophy that brings to education generally a new perspective, and to the nation a new spirit. This cannot be done in a dual system of education. . . . We as Negro citizens stand ready to co-operate wholeheartedly in the progressive fulfillment of these democratic objectives.[7]

The optimism expressed by the educators over the implementation of the United States Supreme Court's 1954 decision was short-lived in Louisiana. Negro leaders had reasons to suspect stiff resistance on the part of local and state boards of education, but none could have predicted that the resistance to desegregation would be so punitive, violent, and total as was later revealed. The struggle between the State of Louisiana and the federal courts that ensued led to an acute and prolonged crisis in race relations in New Orleans. In order to understand the nature of this crisis it may be instructive to say some word about the strategies and techniques Negro leaders employed in their successful efforts to get the federal courts to guarantee Negroes the right to an equal, unsegregated education.

[6] *Brown* v. *Board of Education of Topeka*, 347, U. S. 483 (1954).
[7] Official Statement adopted at Conference of Southern Negro Educators in Hot Springs, Arkansas, October 26-27, 1954.

STRATEGIES AND TECHNIQUES

Protest. Except for the McDonogh Day boycott in which Negro parents heeded the advice of a council of Negro organizations, including the P.T.A., and refused to allow their children to participate in a segregated ceremony in honor of the founder of the New Orleans public-school system, Negro protest of inequal educational opportunities in New Orleans has been organized and executed largely by "class-oriented" leaders. Before and after this event there were numerous protests at mass rallies called for that purpose, public speeches at established formal gatherings, research reports, and in newspaper and magazine articles. Also several different committees were appointed to wait on public officials. All of this protest has been done according to high academic and diplomatic standards. For the most part, class-oriented protest has been calculated to initiate intervention by federal authorities.

Negro leaders characteristically employ three techniques in order to induce federal authorities to accept the primary or original jurisdiction when basic civil rights of Negroes are violated. In their efforts to achieve equal educational opportunities they have resorted, first, to propaganda. Much of this propaganda has been directed at northern liberals. The aim is to create a favorable public opinion in the North which might reflect itself in the election of liberal representatives to Congress. It is hoped that such representation might introduce and effectuate legislation designed to equalize educational opportunities for Negroes in the South.

A second technique is that of disseminating information on educational inequalities in the South in such a way that the South would be "shamed before the nation for its injustices," as a newspaper writer put it. He continued, "If we can get the great industries of this nation to know the truth about the South, many will refuse to open plants here. Maybe then, the South will wake up to the fact of what Booker Washington said, 'You can't keep your neighbor in a ditch unless you remain there with him.' " Thus, many Negro leaders regard works such as Gunnar Myrdal's *An American Dilemma* and Eli Ginzberg's *The Negro Potential* as evidence that this strategy is fruitful. These and many other works by nonsoutherners do point up the unworkability of the biracial system in the South. They call special attention to the fact that discrimination is inherent in segregation, and that if the South is to take its rightful economic place in the nation it must give all of its citizens maximum opportunity to develop their potentials.

A third function of Negro protest has been that of enlisting northern Negroes in the southern Negro's cause. This has been done in a number of ways. Among the most important, of course, is the dissemination of knowledge regarding the inequalities of educational opportunities in the South. This is intended primarily to arouse the sympathies of northern Negroes, many of whom have relatives in the South. Another is to establish psychological identity with northern Negroes. One of the most important means of doing this is to invite northern Negro leaders to speak at public gatherings in the South where racial inequalities are protested. In such a situation the invited leaders are expected to identify with their southern brethren. Northern Negroes' support of liberal political candidates and Negro uplift movements bear evidence to the effectiveness of this technique.

All in all, the southern Negro's protest movement, in which New Orleans Negroes share, has apparently accomplished two significant goals: one, it has, in fact, created a favorable northern public opinion which is sometimes reflected in the civil rights stands of northern representatives in Congress, and, two, it has succeeded in welding together northern and southern Negro leadership. This has meant that the voting strategies of northern Negroes have been calculated to give strong political backing to the southern Negro's fight for equal citizenship. Perhaps the best example of this was the deciding influence of the northern Negroes' vote in the last presidential election. The Democratic candidate, John F. Kennedy, carried the election because he was able to convince a large majority of Negroes in certain key northern cities that he could be trusted on the civil rights issue.

Though Negro protest has evidently had some tangible effect upon national public opinion and national political behavior, it has had little or no tangible effect in New Orleans, where local white officials have either ignored it or attempted to explain away its validity.

Negotiation. Where the equalization of educational opportunities is concerned, one of the strategies most frequently employed by Negro leaders has been negotiation. Negotiation between Negro leaders and white authorities on this issue has always been conducted according to strict rules of diplomacy. One might say that orthodox Urban League techniques are generally followed. That is, the problem is clearly defined; pertinent data are systematically collected; these data are disseminated widely among "men of power;" and this is followed by negotiation, during which these data are interpreted in terms of democratic principles and national well-being.

For example, beginning in the early 1940's the Urban League gathered data to show that Negroes were unable to make a maximum contribution to our national defense because of limited educational opportunities. Since then, armed with defensible data, representatives of the League have gone repeatedly before white authorities pleading for trade schools, expanded curriculums, and other educational advantages for Negroes. Several other organizations and individuals (notably the NAACP, P.T.A. and teachers' groups) have done likewise. However, so far as can be ascertained, no significant steps have been taken by the local school board or other officials to equalize educational opportunities for Negroes as a result of negotiation.

Because public school officials have persistently turned a "deaf ear" to Negro leaders' pleas for equal unsegregated educational facilities, the total desegregation pronouncement of parochial schools of the New Orleans archdiocese was all the more significant and dramatic. It had been almost a decade since Archbishop Joseph Francis Rummel had condemned racial segregation as "morally wrong and sinful." Negro leaders and white liberals became disturbed and began to complain openly because the Roman Catholic hierarchy took no definite steps to implement the ideals set forth by Archbishop Rummel. One prominent Negro Catholic layman complained: "If segregation is morally wrong as the Archbishop has said and as the Pope agrees; how long must the Church go on sinning? When will our leaders muster the moral courage to do what is morally right and proper? How long? How long?"

This question was unequivocally answered on Tuesday evening, March 27, 1962 when the Rt. Rev. Henry C. Bezou, superintendent of archdiocesan schools, announced Archbishop Joseph Francis Rummel's decision ordering that

effective at the time of registration for the 1962-63 school session, all Catholic children may apply for admission to the Catholic schools of the archdiocese, both elementary and secondary, parochial and private, according to the accepted educational standards.

Despite the fact that a few "die-hard" segregationists—three of whom were excommunicated for promoting "flagrant disobedience to the decision to open our schools to ALL our Catholic children and have even threatened and incited others to take reprisals, legal and otherwise, against our action"— bitterly oppose the Archbishop's decision parochial schools opened on a nonsegregated basis in September 1962 with little or no organized resistance.

This summary action on the part of the Roman Catholic hierarchy desegregating all of its schools stands as the most significant gain Negroes have made in their all-out bid for equal, unsegregated education. It is particularly noteworthy that this decision was reached solely as a result of diplomatic negotiation between Negro and white laymen and the Catholic hierarchy.

Political action. Political action has not been used directly by New Orleans Negroes in their fight to eliminate educational inequalities. It is true, of course, that some few politicians have lost potential Negro votes because they were reputed to be more rabid in their segregationist views than some other candidates. Yet, there has been no real opportunity for Negroes to campaign for white candidates whose views on equal educational opportunities are liberal. As a rule, there are seldom any significant differences in the racial policies advocated by candidates who run for public office. *All are avowed segregationists.* And to confuse the issue even more, some of the most avid segregationists can actually point to better records regarding "separate but equal" education than can some others who seem less bigoted. Further, the Negro community has never been sufficiently organized to have one of its own representatives become a serious contender for public office, though several Negroes have run in recent years. As one Negro leader put it, "They have been protest candidates."

Only a few Negroes have seen any hope of improving the status of Negroes through local politics. Most appeal to the President of the United States, certain national political figures, the United States Attorney General, the Civil Rights Commission, federal courts, and Congress in efforts to get federal relief from inequalities in educational opportunities.

Direct action. Negro leaders who are primarily interested in equalizing educational opportunities regard direct action as an inappropriate strategy. There have been no school boycotts to acquire equal or unsegregated facilities similar to those instigated by white students in *defense* of segregation. Thus, for example, when two formerly all-white schools in New Orleans first admitted four Negro girls (one and three respectively) thousands of white school children took a "holiday" in protest. Most students attending the two schools persisted in the boycott. (These schools were eventually declared "Negro schools.") Yet, there was never any suggestion to close segregated public schools or to boycott them by responsible Negro leaders. Neither have there been any sit-ins, or any other form of direct action protesting segregation or discrimination by Negro leaders, parents, or students.

Litigation. This strategy is discussed last as applied to education because if there is one strategy that has worked best in this area it has been litigation. Most of the progress Negroes have made toward equalization in the field of education can be attributed, directly or indirectly, to the federal government through the actions of its courts. *Insofar as the civil rights of Negroes are concerned, southern courts have served mainly as filters through which civil rights violations have been brought in "due process" to the attention of federal courts.* In a sense, then, the United States Supreme Court's 1954 decision in the *Brown* case may be regarded as symbolizing the highest achievement of Negro leadership. This is so because the primary goal of most Negro "uplift" organizations and individual Negro leaders has been to induce the federal government to actively guarantee Negroes basic civil rights.

In other words, Negro leaders have always contended that members of their race can never achieve equal protection of the law and other related rights so long as these rights are assumed to be the prerogatives of southern segregationist authorities. Thus, for instance, efforts to get federal protection against lynching, guarantee of equal justice before the courts, fair employment and universal franchise have been major issues espoused by Negro leaders. So far all of these have failed. Therefore, it was first in the *Brown* decision that Negroes have been able to receive active support from the federal government in their fight for first-class citizenship on the local level. This decision climaxed more than fifty years of constant maneuvering on the part of Negro leaders. During this period, white men of power in the South boastfully admitted that Negroes were being subjected to the most flagrant types of discrimination and injustice. Some actually used these facts to perpetuate themselves in political office. And still, despite glaring inequalities in every area of public life, federal courts repeatedly refused to rule against the obviously false and unworkable doctrine of "separate but equal." It was not until the dawn of World War II that the federal courts would even look beyond lower court rulings to verify numerous reports that segregation per se is inherently unequal.

The main question is why the United States Supreme Court refused for more than half a century to rule against the inherent inequalities in the bi-racial system presupposed by the "separate but equal" doctrine, and then completely reversed its position. This is, of course, a very complex question, and no simple answer will suffice. Among the most feasible explanations for this change in the interpretation of the spirit of constitutional law are the following:[8]

(1) In 1896 ours was a predominantly agrarian society. Approximately two-thirds of the population of the United States lived on farms or in small towns. The status of Negroes could be generally described as that of serfs. About 90 per cent of the Negro population resided in the South, with about 80 per cent living on farms. Further, all major aspects of our economic, political, and social life were built on conservative, even "folk" values.

By 1954 this picture had greatly changed. Only about 13 per cent of our population was engaged in agriculture. Negroes, particularly, had migrated in large numbers to cities. Less than two-thirds of the Negro population still remained in the South, with only about 20 per cent on farms. Thus, because of heavy population shifts, our American cities were literally bursting at the seams. Consequently, American civilization in 1954 may be described as *urban* and *industrial*.

(2) In 1896 suffrage, or "the right to vote," was considered in the South more or less as a "gentlemen's privilege." And since most Negroes resided in the South, it is not surprising that they could have no effective voice in the government under which they lived. However, by 1954 thousands of Negroes had migrated to the North and were making themselves felt at the polls. Some were even being elected to public office. Thus, as has been noted, the strong political participation in key cities outside the South has been reflected in the federal government's more realistic approach to civil rights.

(3) In 1896 the government of the United States adhered strictly to a policy of isolationism. Even as late as the 1920's isolationism was the most basic characteristic of our foreign policy. By 1940, however, it had become obvious, even to some of our most conservative statesmen, that the United States could not afford to maintain its policy of isolationism. Russia under Communism had become a world power to be reckoned with, the Fascists under Mussolini and the Nazis under Hitler had become a threat to world peace, and Japan had become an international nuisance. President Roosevelt warned that the policy of isolationism would lead the United States to be "a lone island in a world dominated by a philosophy of force," and Wendell

[8] Material in this section is taken in part from Daniel C. Thompson, "The Role of the Federal Courts in the Changing Status of Negroes Since World War II," *Journal of Negro Education*, Spring 1961, pp. 98-101.

Willkie, the standard-bearer of the Republican party, had visions of "one world."

By 1954, Communist nations were making an international football of our obviously undemocratic racial practices in a world where the vast majority is nonwhite. These nonwhite peoples had begun to express suspicion and fear of our segregated army and segregated society. Many influential Americans were insisting that if America is to maintain her position as the leader of the "free world," she must first get her own house in order "with all deliberate speed."

(4) In 1896 more than two-thirds of the jobs in the nation could be done by unskilled laborers. By the beginning of World War II the percentage had shrunk to 36 per cent, and by 1954 it was estimated that only about 19 per cent of the jobs in the United States could be performed by illiterate, unskilled workers. Consequently, the *Brown* decision emphasized the fact that segregated education not only limits the development of the individual but, because it is inherently inferior, threatens our national well-being as well.

(5) Finally, in 1896 the literacy rate in the United States was considerably lower than in 1954. At that time, only about 7 per cent of the children of high school age were actually in school. By 1954, approximately 80 per cent of all children of high school age were enrolled in school. Even children who were in school in 1896 attended only about half as many days as did those in 1954. Further, in 1896 there were only 150,000 students enrolled in all colleges in the United States. By 1954 this number had increased to close to three million.

Not only had the literacy rate among Americans on the whole increased, but the increase in the literacy rate among Negroes had been even greater. Thus, in 1896 more than half, or 57 per cent, of all Negro adults were classified as illiterates. In 1954 the proportion of Negro illiterates had decreased to only 10 per cent, and there were approximately 100,000 Negro youths registered in the colleges of the nation.

As a result of the very significant increase in the educational level of Negroes during the fifty-eight years between 1896 and 1954, the leadership potential in the Negro community was, of course, much more highly developed. And, whereas in 1896 the few competent Negro leaders in southern communities were likely to be ministers, by 1954 there were able Negro leaders in many fields of American life. Some Negroes had distinguished themselves in labor, housing, administration, government, business, literature, sports, diplomacy, scholarship, and law as well as religion. Most of these identified with, or actually took leadership positions in, "uplift" organizations. Although any basic social change, such as that heralded by the *Brown* decision, is caused by a myriad of factors, it is my contention that the most significant of these factors is the increased qualification and number of Negro leaders dedicated to the achievement of first-class citizenship for their people.

The role of leadership

It is a long and well-validated fact that leadership takes on added significance during periods of social crisis. The present stresses and strains in race relations in New Orleans began to develop in 1952 when Negro parents, in *Bush* v. *Orleans Parish School Board*, filed a suit on the grounds that segregation in public education is contrary to the Fourteenth Amendment. This suit was intended to test the legality of segregation per se, and was a class action, brought on behalf of all Negro children attending public schools in New Orleans. A federal court decision in this case was suspended until the United States Supreme Court decided the *Brown* case and companion cases. By the time the case was decided it was clear that Negro leaders had finally succeeded in getting the support of the federal courts in their fight against segregation. The struggle between white men of power on the one hand, and the Negro and the federal government on the other brought into clear focus the different types of race relations leaders.

The segregationists. In the struggle between the federal government and the State of Louisiana over school desegregation, the strategies and techniques of race relations leaders revealed the basic weaknesses of communication inherent in a biracial system. In essence, the crisis in race relations that came to a climax in 1960 and 1961 is due to a malfunctioning of communication between the races. Negroes and whites had come to see each other more as enemies than as fellow Americans. And although this struggle centered around school desegregation, it was clear to all leaders, white and Negro, that a great deal more was involved. Both sides realized that at long last the outcome of this struggle could determine whether the biracial social system in New Orleans (and throughout the South) would continue, or would be replaced by a racially unsegregated system. Specifically, the desegregation issue was interpreted by all leaders in the controversy as having decisive consequences for the total citizenship status of whites and Negroes. This is a logical result of the faith Americans place in education. Therefore, there is little doubt on the part of either segregationists or nonsegregationists that once barriers to equal educational opportunities are removed, all other barriers to equal or first-class citizenship for Negroes will soon crumble. Hence, the crisis in race relations in New Orleans, though centered around education, is actually a struggle between white men of power who would maintain and perpetuate a biracial society in which they are accorded special privileges and Negroes, allied with the federal government, whose actions would destroy this system of inequal privileges and responsibilities.

To counter this possibility segregationists resurrected all of the doubts, fears, and frustrations inherent in the superordinate-subordinate pattern of race relations in the South. These were revealed "in all their ugliness." The bitterness of this conflict between the segregationists and the federal government is indicated by the fact that between 1954 and 1961 Louisiana's state legislature enacted scores of laws and numerous resolutions intended to pre-serve the traditional rigid pattern of racial segregation in education despite federal court decisions. The rebellious nature of these acts is best seen in the Interposition Act, which held that the *Brown* case and other federal court orders pursuant thereto were null and void. This act specifically forbade any federal official from enforcing decrees or serving processes in cases based upon the *Brown* principle. It also provided criminal penalties for those in violation of the act.

Insofar as community leaders (white and Negro) are concerned, the most serious implications of these anti-federal acts were not legal but psycholog-ical and social. This is so because most of these have been declared uncon-stitutional, yet each was preceded by hours of flagrant, damaging, and de-nunciatory speeches and recriminations. Much of the anti-Negro, anti-fed-eral propaganda was disseminated by all mass media and, as a white minister said, "many fair-minded white people, adults and children, were taught to hate Negroes and distrust federalism." Again, the 1960 state legislature, which met in five Extraordinary Sessions at a cost of over a million dollars was described by a prominent white lawyer as "resembling a mob much more than it does a legislative body." During these sessions powerful indi-viduals took advantage of their legislative immunities to resurrect and make vivid outworn, discredited, and damaging Negro stereotypes and distorted memories and hates from the Civil War and Reconstruction years. Negroes were pictured as immoral, mentally inferior, and generally incapable of participating as equals in Western civilization. Federal authorities were con-stantly referred to as carpetbaggers or traitors. For example, one represent-ative with several years' teaching experience shouted angrily—

> As a teacher I would like to go on record now that I will never, never, never teach in an integrated school in this state. . . . Integration if successful will destroy Western Civilization. . . . God created the two races. You are no God Skelly Wright [the federal judge that ordered integration in New Orleans]. You are not even a competent judge Skelly Wright. You are a traitor to this state. . . . Shame on you for trying to destroy our state government. Shame on you for destroying our southern way of life.

Similar inflammatory statements were made regularly, denouncing the NAACP, the federal courts, the New Orleans School Board, and even organ-ized religion. No individual or organization working for integration, or even advocating compliance with the federal law, was exempted from constant, scathing criticism by the legislators. From time to time some even advocated open defiance of constituted law. One legislator made a speech in which he compared the situation in Louisiana to the "oppression" by kings in history, and called upon his colleagues "to make the first move for freedom." He ad-monished white people to be willing to suffer for taking a stand against the federal government. He said, "Christ followed the law of God and was crucified. . . . Christians in the catacombs dared to defy the law of the land because they believed in freedom of worship." These and many other such remarks were applauded as speaker after speaker took the rostrum in a relentless effort to prod the legislature, step by step, toward open, even armed, defiance of federal authority. The temper of the state legislature is officially recorded in its unanimous vote for Interposition.

The intemperate tirade that the state legislators directed at Negroes and the federal government has been echoed most clearly in the general community by the white Citizens' Council. In recent years this organization has spearheaded the anti-Negro, anti-federal movement in New Orleans. It is believed to have only a handful of "card-carrying" members, all of whom are extremely rabid white supremacists. The fundamental, perhaps the only, purpose of this organization is to maintain "total segregation" regardless of federal court decisions to the contrary. Although its main attention has been directed at keeping public education segregated, it has worked diligently to maintain segregation in other areas of community life when it seemed expedient to do so.

In order to propagandize despicable stereotypes of Negroes and the "illegal infringement" of the federal government in state affairs, the Citizens' Council in New Orleans holds frequent mass meetings at which nationally known white supremacists are presented. One such mass meeting triggered the mob violence in the early days of school desegregation in New Orleans. After the first day of calm (November 14, 1961), this organization held a meeting in the municipal auditorium attended by an estimated 5,000 people. Several witnesses to this meeting agreed that it reminded them of "a gathering straight out of Nazi Germany." At that time, nationally known racists ignored the facts of history as well as the principles of logic in attempts to generate mass civil disobedience. One advocated what he called a "scorched earth" policy, according to which white people would refuse to obey all laws guaranteeing Negroes equality in any area of life, and suggested that those who believe in white supremacy should use force when necessary to preserve it. Another speaker often referred to as an arch segregationist screamed, "Don't wait for your daughters to be raped by these Congolese. Do something about it now." As a result of these and other violent speeches, all given maximum publicity in the newspapers and on radio and television, thousands of white men, women and children were obviously convinced that it was their sacred duty to defend in any way they could what they had been led to believe are sacred southern traditions. They behaved as though these traditions would be totally destroyed if the four Negro first-graders were allowed to attend schools with white children. The next day mobs of white children and adults paraded through the streets chanting the illogical phrase that became a sort of theme song: "Two, four, six, eight, we don't want to integrate." Keeping this disorderly mob from destroying property and inflicting injury upon fellow citizens proved to be a Herculean task for the New Orleans police department.

The white Citizens' Council's well-organized and evidently well-financed program of propaganda laid the foundation for its ascendance to political power within a very short period of time. Inherent in its propaganda are the values, traditions, fears, and hopes of a typical southern rural culture. Therefore, since the Louisiana State Legislature is composed primarily of rural-oriented representatives, its major accomplishment during these years of crisis was the passing of numerous anti-Negro laws (as previously mentioned) to preserve what they termed "sacred southern traditions." The "strange dilemma" in which segregationists are caught in their legal defense of so-called southern traditions is pointed up in this statement—

> Although segregationists deny the propriety of the court's [1954] consideration of psychological and sociological principles when civil rights of Negroes are concerned, they quickly invoke them when their own privileges are challenged. For example, in each of the [objections to integration] except the question of "state's rights," the basic arguments against racial integration presented by the white supremacists are inherently psychological and sociological. [This dilemma] was highlighted in a statement made by Attorney Wade Heaton. In his argument begging the U. S. Fifth Circuit Court of Appeals to preserve segregation in the public schools of East Baton Rouge and St. Helena Parishes and in the six Louisiana Trade Schools, he pleaded that the court should take into consideration psychological and sociological factors.[9]

The persuasive doctrine of white supremacy propagandized by the Citizens' Council has been translated and disseminated by various organizations in the white community, including the P.T.A. Most of these organizations took little or no interest in politics or racial issues until this crisis in education arose. Since 1954, however, they have produced vocal and powerful advocates of white supremacy. In this way the Citizens' Council in New Orleans has become, within a few years, a powerful anti-Negro, anti-federal influence to be reckoned with.

The moderates. Among the racial moderates in New Orleans are persons representing all socioeconomic segments. The one thing they all have in common is the belief that law and order should be preserved by autonomous local authorities. They agree, however, that law and order are essential even if state and local governments must "bow" to certain federal court orders. Pettigrew describes the moderates as—

> Mild, not wild segregationists. . . . The gentle people of prejudice. . . . He sees himself as a realist neither demogogic nor idealistic. He abhors both violence and force. . . . [He] calls for no constructive action [regarding desegregation] until a crisis strikes the community directly, and then hurriedly arranging some type of pitifully token desegregation in order to avoid closed schools and a business decline.[10]

[9] Daniel C. Thompson, *The Case for Integration* (Atlanta: Southern Regional Council, 1961), p. 10.
[10] Thomas F. Pettigrew, "The Myth of the Moderates," *The Christian Century*, May 24, 1961.

During the public-school crisis in New Orleans those who advocated open schools, despite what they called federal court "interference," were usually thought of as moderates. And just as Pettigrew says, they pretended to deny the imminence of the public-school crisis in New Orleans until it had developed to dangerous proportions. Therefore it was not until the spring of 1960, near the deadline for the local school board to submit a plan of desegregation to the federal courts, that any influential white leader or group in New Orleans made any constructive public statement or projected any feasible plan to desegregate public schools. They preferred to ignore the fact that the *Bush* case would have to be ruled upon on the basis of the desegregation order of the *Brown* case.

Finally, after allowing segregationists to monopolize public media interpreting and criticizing the *Brown* decision for almost six years, a few white moderates began to make themselves heard. Of course, all of them made it clear in the very beginning that they were *not integrationists*. Actually, all of the moderates in public office, including those on the school board, went on record as believing that "segregated education is best for both races," though insisting, as did Save Our Schools, Inc. (SOS), that "SOS does not propose to argue the merits of segregation versus desegregation. . . . SOS invites all parents and citizens to help maintain this most basic of all rights [education]." This more or less neutral statement of racial philosophy was made in order that the few liberals who supported this organization would not find the organization obnoxious. It is interesting to note, however, that this rigid policy of racial neutrality regarding segregation was never violated by members of this organization in public utterances. Even on a two-hour or longer "Open End" television program those representing SOS were never maneuvered into approval or endorsement of the *Brown* decision, despite persistent attempts on the part of participating segregationists to force them to declare themselves in that respect. Not one time in this long program did any one of the members of SOS acknowledge the validity or even the morality of the *Brown* decision. They clung throughout to the proposition that public schools must remain open whether state officials agree with the federal courts' desegregation decision or not.

After listening to the months of debate on "open" or "closed" schools by white moderates, one Negro leader expressed what is apparently the opinion of most Negroes: "They have talked a lot but never about the real issue—segregation. They have agreed with everything the white Citizens' Council advocates except closing schools. I think they are the Negro's worst enemy." Many Negro leaders express great disappointment with the moderate position taken by white leaders whom they had previously regarded as liberals. One said accusingly, "In a way these moderates are more dangerous to democracy and freedom than the bigots; at least the bigots are honest." Another reflected philosophically, "The school issue has unveiled white leaders who have been parading in liberal clothes. We see them now as they have always been—segregationists, who want us to continue to be satisfied with the crumbs that might fall from their weighty, segregated tables."

A white scholar expressed the opinion that SOS attempts to gain support for "open" schools by recruiting members from the "power structure." The Committee on Public Education (COPE) seeks its main support from the average white parents of public-school children. Both organizations are composed of whites only and are careful to avoid the "integrationist" label. During the summer of 1960 members of these organizations became increasingly vocal. They published pamphlets, conducted public forums for white people, held press conferences, and even organized lobbies in their efforts to maintain public education "even if we must submit to token desegregation," as some of their leaders declared on several occasions.

When a moderate won an election to the school board over a staunch segregationist who was openly backed by the white Citizens' Council, those who advocated keeping the schools open "at all costs" interpreted his victory as a mandate from New Orleans's voters that "token" desegregation would be preferred to closed schools. Though still insisting that they were 100 per cent for segregation, a few more white leaders and organizations took courage from the expressed "will of the people" and declared themselves in favor of some limited system of school desegregation, "if such is absolutely necessary," to meet the letter of the law as interpreted by the courts.

For some months prior to the opening of schools in September, 1960, a prominent businessman had openly stated that "business is taking a beating." Some reported that their businesses had dropped off as much as 50 per cent. Finally, in June, after ignoring pleas from members of SOS and some New Orleans representatives in the state legislature to take a definite stand for open schools, one hundred white businessmen signed a petition that public schools must be maintained. They made it clear that they were segregationists, while expressing the belief that education is indispensable if we are to continue to develop economically. Therefore, they advocated keeping law and order and preserving the good reputation of the city. Following this announcement, several other powerful groups and individuals went on record in support of open schools despite "token" integration.

Among the groups endorsing law and order and open schools were several religious groups. A statement by ninety-four rabbis and ministers is typical of the "left-handed" way in which some segregationists take a moderate position on the school issue. They said:

> We do not believe in the wisdom of massive integration and are sincerely opposed to the amalgamation of the races. We reaffirm our conviction that the integrity of each race should be maintained on a basis of mutual esteem and free choice, rather than of force. There are some areas in which some integration in schools at this time would be possible without insurmountable difficulty, as has already been demonstrated in certain sections of the South; while there are other

areas where such integration would involve needless hardship and grave danger. We have the hope that, if our leaders will offer evidence of good faith toward providing constitutional rights for all citizens, the federal government will be willing to leave the working out of details in local hands. We believe it is possible, under the ruling of the Supreme Court, for States to take reasonable steps to comply with the law of the land and at the same time give due consideration to local situations and avoid an indiscriminate desegregation of the public schools.

During the early months of the struggle between southern state legislators and federal courts over the desegregation of public schools, the term "moderate" in race relations was ambiguous. Segregationists accused moderates of being "integrators," Negro leaders often assumed them to be gradualists, and they usually spoke of themselves as simply persons who believed in law and order as opposed to mob rule. As the school crisis lengthened, it became clear that by and large moderates are really segregationists who are unwilling to go so far as to defy federal court orders. Perhaps the most significant service they render in the area of race relations is that of keeping open some limited channels of communication between "new" Negro leaders and white "men of power."

The liberals. The souls of white liberals have been tried during the New Orleans public-school crisis. Shrewd, well-calculated, slanderous propaganda by powerful segregationists popularized the notion that a liberal is in fact a "one-worlder," an "integrator," a "left-winger," a Communist. Confronted with a relentless barrage of half-truths, innuendoes, and "investigations" by individual segregationists and the legislative-sponsored State Sovereignty Commission, "most white liberals," observed one who stood steadfast, "have run for cover." Sensing this fact, a leaflet distributed by a segregationist organization triumphantly proclaimed that "the integrators have been slowed down to a crawl."

When one looks closely at what has happened to avowed white liberals in New Orleans since 1954, he will observe that many of them have retreated to the ranks of the moderates. Whether this represents a real shift in their basic philosophy of race relations cannot be determined easily. After all, whether one is a segregationist, moderate, or liberal can only be evaluated in a relative sense. Prior to 1954, a white leader who insisted that states should provide truly equal educational facilities for Negroes was taking a liberal position. Since 1954, of course, such a statement could at best be classified as moderate. A liberal statement regarding the education of Negroes at present must necessarily be an endorsement, directly or indirectly, of equal, integrated education. The great majority of former white liberals are simply unable or unwilling to withstand the violent criticism they would have to endure if such a position is taken. They prefer instead to be identified as moderates.

Other traditional liberals have endeavored to remain neutral throughout the public-school crisis in New Orleans. Most "top" white leaders who were once regarded as liberals have elected to make no public statement regarding the public-school crisis, despite repeated pleas to do so on the part of Negro leaders and staunch white liberals. One white liberal confessed:

> I have been greatly disappointed with my friends. I have pleaded with them time and again to stand up and be counted. I know that they are fair-minded, liberal people who believe that segregation in any form, particularly in education, is morally and, now, legally wrong. Yet, they refuse to take any stand on this issue [education]. I believe if they had made themselves felt immediately after the 1954 decision school desegregation would now be an accomplished fact, and New Orleans would be a good place for all of its citizens.

The retreat of the liberals means much more than the fact that certain democratic-spirited individuals are refusing to speak out on a fundamental community issue. It means also that certain influential organizations in the field of race relations, such as the Louisiana Council on Human Relations, collapse because those who have come to be known as the "liberal white element" in New Orleans have withdrawn their support.

Regardless of criticism, character-assassination, and harassment, a few white individuals in New Orleans still espouse a liberal philosophy of race relations. Some of these have deliberately identified with the Negro's cause at great personal and family sacrifice. When one such liberal was asked why she and her husband took a firm position for integrated public-school education, she said—

> We don't think of ourselves as doing anything special. We are doing simply what we regard as right. And it may be that if others had done the right thing [insisting that public schools should be integrated], it is likely that we would have kept our peace. Since practically all other whites are segregationists, or allowing the segregationists to have their way, we are doing what somebody has to do. If we don't, democracy will become a mockery. We don't think we deserve any medals for doing what any good American knows in his heart he ought to do.

Such persons as quoted above often regard themselves as ambassadors among their white associates. In private conversations and even in public meetings, they defend the principles of equality and democracy in race relations whenever the opportunity presents itself. One woman told an interviewer, "Whenever my friends see me coming, they say 'here comes the integrationist. Tell us some other good things about Negroes.' I have talked so much to them about integration that sometimes I actually think I am doing some good. At least they don't boast about being segregationists any more," she laughed.

Perhaps the most characteristic thing to be said of white liberals in New Orleans in recent years is that they are becoming more and more organized on an informal basis. Our interviewers were often surprised to learn how closely the staunch liberals identified with one another. They reminded one interviewer of the "psychic unity one would expect to find among members of an underground movement, such as was true among the French loyalists during the Nazi occupation." What he was referring to is the fact that avowed white liberals in New Orleans are acutely conscious of being a minority among a hostile segregationist majority. Like any minority, they would win converts from among the majority, yet they go about it in an over-cautious, timid, apologetic manner. An illustration of this is a series of meetings of "interested liberals," most of whom later proved to be moderates. They met in order to find some way of getting powerful white business and professional men to endorse a policy of open schools, despite "token integration." After several hours of trying to find some delicate, yet effective means by which they could approach such individuals without being mistaken for "do-gooders," or "nigger-lovers," as one feared, they finally called off the discussions without any definite steps being planned. One member of the group, who represents a powerful financial enterprise, brought the group to accept the suggestion that "the mayor should be apprised of our deep concern in this matter. He will know what to do." One of the more dedicated of the liberals summarized the group's action, or rather nonaction, in this way:

> What we have witnessed here is a meeting of intelligent, economically secure white people. We apparently want to see New Orleans adjust to a revolutionary change without really changing itself. We have demonstrated at least one thing: As a group we are unwilling to take the bull by the horns. We prefer instead to let things drift, hoping and even praying that somehow things will be all right. I guess you could best describe us as "Pollyannas."

These meetings of "interested liberals" and one Negro leader, served to delineate some of the major weaknesses of the so-called liberal element in New Orleans. Many express naïve confidence in powerful local officials to guarantee Negroes civil rights, despite their publicly pronounced allegiance to the doctrine of white supremacy. Others are afraid of political or economic retaliation. Some underestimate their social effectiveness. Thus, a university professor insisted, "No one wants to hear what an egghead has to say about such an explosive political issue as desegregation." More than anything else, white liberals seem to fear social ostracism for themselves or members of their families. This fact was projected in several statements made by those attending the aforementioned series of meetings. For example, frequently some suspected liberal was excused for not having endorsed "open" schools because, so to speak, "he is a good man and can be trusted to do the right thing in this school situation, yet I'd hate to ask him to take any public stand because I hardly think his . . . family . . . friends . . . business associates would understand." Therefore, for one reason or another most liberals in New Orleans have preferred to steer clear of the public school controversy.[11]

In sharp contrast with the hands-off policy generally adhered to in the public school controversy is the forthright effort of a few dedicated liberals to break down racial barriers in the admissions policies of Tulane University. Realizing that Tulane lagged behind most southern universities in this respect they sponsored the applications of two young Negro women college graduates who had been denied admission to the graduate school solely because they are Negro. They raised sufficient funds to employ two white attorneys highly skilled in Constitutional law. These attorneys filed the complaint of Barbara Marie Guillory and Pearlie Hardin Elloie, who claimed that their civil rights under the 14th amendment had been abridged. This case was heard by Federal Judge J. Skelly Wright on March 28, 1962. At the close of the hearing it was Judge Wright's official opinion that Tulane University must admit the plaintiffs. He said:

> The bitter fruit of the board's segregation policy of the past should not be visited on the young men and women of the future, of all races seeking admission to the University.

Judge Wright raised the question

> whether any school or college can be so "private" as to escape the reach of the Fourteenth Amendment.

Quoting Thomas Jefferson, he said:

> In a country dedicated to the creed that education is the only "sure foundation . . . of freedom, without which no republic can maintain itself in strength," institutions of learning are not things of purely private concern.

> The Supreme Court of the United States has noted that in these days, "it is doubtful that any child may reasonably be expected to succeed in life if he is denied the opportunity of an education."

This decision was reviewed by the Fifth Circuit Court of Appeals and no definite decision has yet been rendered.

The most significant thing about the suit against Tulane University is the fact that it marked the first time white citizens in New Orleans (and perhaps in any other southern community) assumed the total responsibility of seeing that federal courts uphold the right of qualified Negroes to receive equal, unsegregated education.

Negro leaders. As we have noticed throughout this study, Negro leaders

[11] See also Daniel C. Thompson's report to the Civil Rights Commission, "The Role of Leadership," in *The New Orleans School Crisis*, 1961, pp. 38ff.

are often divided on many social issues and in regard to the efficacy of certain leadership strategies and techniques. Nevertheless, where the desegregation of education is concerned they present a united front. All segments of the Negro leadership class have made it known through resolutions, fund raising, and public statements that they are anxious to see segregation in education eliminated as soon as possible. Some are outspokenly optimistic, others are quite pessimistic about when desegregation will be an accomplished fact. All to whom we talked expressed impatience with what they described as the "snail's pace" with which the local school board is moving to obey the 1954 Supreme Court's decision. However, all top Negro leaders in New Orleans have publicly expressed faith in the legal maneuvers of the NAACP and have made no other effort to accomplish school desegregation except through the courts. They regard this as a legal and constitutional struggle and feel confident that sooner or later the local school board will in fact comply with federal court rulings.

10

CONCLUSION

THIS STUDY OF leadership confirms the conclusion about New Orleans that Floyd Hunter reached after his study of Atlanta: The status of Negroes in New Orleans is nowhere near the top power group. "None of the leaders in the Negro community may operate in the same echelons of power as the top leaders in the total community."[1] *No Negro in New Orleans holds membership or participates in powerful decision-making organizations.* Thus, insofar as the formulation or execution of policies and practices governing the civic, political, economic, educational, professional, and cultural life of the community is concerned, Negroes are powerless. We come back, then, to our original question: Since there are no Negroes operating in the top echelons of power in New Orleans, *how do they get things done?*

The answer to this question takes on added significance because, as the study establishes, whites who occupy top power positions in New Orleans are pledged, or assumed to be pledged, to the preservation of a biracial social system that, according to its inherent nature, relegates all Negroes to an inferior social status. This means that Negroes who seek to achieve racial equality are automatically resisted by white men of power. Therefore we approached the answer to the cardinal question by analyzing the structure and function of the Negro leadership class.

THE NEGRO LEADERSHIP CLASS

The Negro leadership class in New Orleans is characteristically a loosely organized social category representing every significant segment in the Negro community. Those who identify with this class have been perennially at odds regarding the most effective strategies and techniques to be applied in the achievement of racial equality. In effect this has lead to the formation of three typical patterns of race relations leadership: segregationist—Uncle Tom, moderate—racial diplomat, and liberal—race man.[2]

---

[1] Floyd Hunter, *ibid.* pp. 138-139.
[2] On the basis of a careful examination of leadership roles as played by the 75 top

Segregationist—Uncle Tom. The oldest pattern of race relations leadership (dating back to the antibellum period) in the South is composed of the segregationist and the Uncle Tom. The segregationist's avowed racial philosophy is that a biracial social system is morally and legally right and socially expedient. He insists that all loyal southerners, Negro and white, have a "sacred" duty to preserve and defend the biracial social system. The Uncle Tom not only accedes to the power of the segregationist, but, what is perhaps more significant, he acknowledges the legitimacy of his authority. Thus, in a functional sense, the Uncle Tom is primarily an ally of the segregationist, a preserver of the status quo.

Negro leaders who operate in this parasitic-paternalistic pattern of race relations must necessarily *beg* for "favors," rather than demand in terms of inherent civil rights. As a rule the Uncle Tom type of leader employs only one basic strategy—protest. To be sure, this protest is mild, moralistic, and humble, yet it is made. It has a two-fold objective: first, Negroes are reminded of what they should expect from white men of power. In this way the leader prepares the stage, so to speak, for the recognition and respect he hopes to receive from his grateful followers as he acts in their behalf. Second, he uses this strategy to establish himself in the total community as the spokesman for the Negro masses.

In attempts to persuade white officials to grant some favor to Negroes, the Uncle Tom generally relies on two traditional techniques: one, challenging highly respected, influential whites to qualify for the charitable status of "friend of the Negro" as long as he "keeps in his place." Some white people seem to attach great value to this status. As a carryover from antebellum society it was supposed to indicate something of the "gentlemanly qualities" expected of the slaveholding aristocracy. And two, a direct or indirect pledge to assist in the preservation of the biracial social system.

Throughout the history of New Orleans trusted Uncle Toms, skilled in the art of race relations, have had some nominal success in getting white men of power to grant Negroes limited gains. It was often due to their leadership that local white officials were induced to insure Negroes the segregated use of certain public facilities, improved housing, more police protection, better working conditions, and increased educational opportunities. However, as an ally of segregationists, the Uncle Tom naturally cannot press for equal citizenship privileges for Negro people.

Roughly since World War II and definitely since the May 17, 1954, Supreme Court decision outlawing the "separate but equal" doctrine of race relations, the Uncle Tom leader has lost face among Negroes, and his influence among white men of power has diminished proportionally. That is, since the Negro masses no longer trust his sincerity and refuse to submit to his leadership, segregationists can hardly depend upon the Uncle Tom

---

Negro leaders constituting the basic sample for this study, we may conclude that at present approximately 5 per cent of the Negro leaders in New Orleans characteristically operate as Uncle Toms, 25 per cent as racial diplomats, and 70 per cent as race men.

as an effective ally in their efforts to maintain the biracial status quo. Therefore, the Uncle Tom has had little success in getting things done for Negroes in New Orleans in recent years.

Some of the older informants interviewed for this study estimate that a generation ago the majority of Negro leaders in New Orleans operated as Uncle Toms. Today the small number (about 5 per cent) who continue to play this role are usually representatives of some special political, labor, school, or neighborhood group and are seldom chosen as representatives of the Negro masses.

The more or less abrupt departure of the Uncle Tom from the leadership scene has left top white officials with almost no reliable line of communication with Negro leaders. This situation developed because segregationists, who nearly monopolize decision-making in Louisiana, generally refuse to accept any but the Uncle Tom as a legitimate representative of Negroes. The almost total lack of honest communication between bona fide Negro leaders and powerful segregationists is perhaps a primary reason why the crisis in race relations in New Orleans has persisted since the early 1950's.

Moderate—racial diplomat. White moderates and Negro racial diplomats have two basic characteristics in common: a strong sense of community pride, and a willingness to compromise on social issues if such is deemed necessary for the welfare of the total community. Thus, throughout the history of race relations in New Orleans these two types of leaders have worked effectively together in terms of mutual respect, despite their very unequal social power.

Though refusing to sponsor any Negro for a position of community-wide authority, moderates in power have customarily sought the advice of racial diplomats on problems of general community concern as well as on strictly racial matters. And occasionally some racial diplomats are officially appointed to serve on "citizens' advisory committees" where special problems such as housing, welfare, and delinquency are discussed. Also certain moderates serve as directors or trustees of Negro institutions and of local chapters of the Urban League.

Negro leaders operating within this pattern of race relations leadership have achieved some notable changes in the status of Negroes in New Orleans. They have been able to get white officials to improve housing, health facilities, educational opportunities, and, to a more limited degree, employment opportunities for Negroes. In these efforts they have relied primarily upon the strategy of negotiation. However, they have been known to make effective use of the fact that some other Negro leaders were apt to resort to litigation, political pressure, and direct action if negotiation failed.

Moderates and racial diplomats seem to have maintained a fruitful, harmonious relationship as long as both types recognized the legitimacy of the "separate but equal" doctrine of race relations. Nevertheless, as early as 1950 there was some obvious strain in their relationship. Racial diplomats increasingly voiced impatience with the slow progress being made in achieving civil rights for Negroes within the biracial social system. Some of them began to insist upon a frontal attack upon segregation per se. This tended to make the moderates uneasy and some of the most influential among them resigned from race relations organizations and refrained from any public race relations activities.

By 1958, as New Orleans approached its great crisis in race relations, moderates and racial diplomats had very few remaining functional ties. A small contingent of Negro and white ministers continued to meet occasionally, and a few moderates remained on certain Negro boards, but for all practical purposes they steered clear of the main civil rights issues—the desegregation of schools and public facilities. The disassociation of the moderates and the racial diplomats was generally recognized in 1960, at the height of the public school desegregation controversy. It was then that the active moderates (with some liberals) organized the "Save our Schools" movement and deliberately excluded Negroes from membership, and vowed to take no position on the merits of desegregation as opposed to segregation.

Racial diplomats responded to this break by becoming more and more allied with the more militant race men who were quick to recognize that their diplomatic skills would be valuable in situations where white men of power are pressured into negotiation.

Liberal—race man. Leaders constituting this pattern have two basic characteristics in common: a strong feeling of loyalty to the federal government, and a firm conviction that the primary purpose of any government is to guarantee the equal rights of all its citizens.

According to the most reliable information available (printed materials, reports of race relations organizations, and interviews with knowledgeable informants) the number of liberals in New Orleans always has been small, seldom more than 25 being active in race relations at any given time. Though few in number, liberals were accorded respect by city officials until they joined forces with race men in attempts to break down barriers to equal, nonsegregated citizenship participation.

It is not easy to assess the contributions this pattern of race relations leadership has made to the advancement of Negroes in New Orleans. Very often such leaders are idealists unwilling to compromise on what they believe to be fundamental principles of the American Creed: individual freedom, equality, and inherent human dignity. Such principles are not readily understood by the average practical politician, "hard-headed" businessman, or opinionated segregationist. Therefore there is a tendency for most avowed liberals and race men to think of themselves as ambassadors of the American Creed. This role involves two inherent obligations: one, educating the masses, or certainly those with whom they have sustained social relations, concerning the nature and primacy of the democratic commitments that constitute the foundation upon which the American Republic is founded. And two, applying these principles to specific race relations situations. Consequently, since nearly all men of power in New Orleans have been segregationists or cautious moderates, liberals and race men can point to only a few tangible achievements they themselves have made in race relations in New Orleans. As a rule they have been, in a sense, architects of the civil rights movement. They are the ones who set the goals to be attained, devised strategies and techniques to be employed, and manifested a willingness to sacrifice for the attainment of the ideals they espouse.

However, some leaders in this category are realists, in the sense that they rely mainly upon rational social action to achieve equal citizenship status for Negroes. They have been in the vanguard of action programs intended to force white men of power to accord Negroes equal citizenship. Some have worked with such militant uplift organizations as the National Association for the Advancement of Colored People, the Southern Christian Leadership Conference, the Congress of Racial Equality, and so forth, while others have concentrated upon voter registration drives, drives to expand employment opportunities for Negroes, and on other specialized efforts to raise the status of Negroes.

Perhaps the chief characteristic of liberals and race men is their willingness to employ all legal strategies to achieve democratic ends. They have protested, negotiated, resorted to litigation, political pressure, and direct action (sit-ins, boycotts, and mass demonstrations) in order to desegregate public facilities. In recent years their efforts have met with considerable success. They have been able to get a few new jobs for Negroes; at least token school desegregation; and the desegregation of public parks, transportation, and some lunch counters.

All efforts to accomplish desegregation in New Orleans have been strongly and bitterly resisted by powerful segregationists. So vicious has been the attack on liberals that most have retired from active race relations activities. Those who have stood by their principles during the years of crisis in New Orleans receive sincere adulation from Negro leaders. They are often presented plaques, awards, and citations. Typical of the tributes paid liberals is one made to a distinguished, and highly respected, New Orleans woman. This citation was presented by William O. Walker, publisher of the *Cleveland and Call-Post*. It said:

Mrs. Charles Keller of New Orleans, La. is Southern in every sense of the word . . . yet she is one of the most liberal of Southern whites, and a real crusader for human rights. . . .

Despite all the taunts she has had to take, she has been one of the consistent and determined fighters for justice in the city of New Orleans. . . .

I couldn't help but think about the price this modest white woman of the deep South has paid and is paying for her beliefs in the rights of Negroes. . . .

Being willing to sacrifice for a cause and a principle is the ultimate of one's dedication.

If we had more Negroes who believed in their own cause with the zeal and sacrifice of Mrs. Keller, our progress up freedom's road would be much more rapid.

This tribute to a white liberal has been widely echoed by Negro leaders in New Orleans. Some leaders are convinced that racial desegregation in that city depends heavily upon the extent to which all types of Negro leaders and white liberals find common grounds for cooperation.

Until 1954 the various segments of the Negro leadership class were unable to find a single set of issues through which they could achieve harmonious, functional unity. In retrospect, however, a fruitful set of conditions for unity was spontaneously revealed on May 14, 1954 (just three days before the *Brown* decision). Negro parents, public-school teachers, and most Negro leaders in New Orleans publicly expressed resentment that Negro children were discriminated against in the celebration of the birthday of John McDonogh, the founder of the New Orleans public-school system. The boycott of this occasion by Negro teachers and their pupils, with the support of the parents was a clear indication that the segregation of children is an issue of such great concern that all segments of the Negro community can be brought together in efforts to abolish it. Therefore it is not surprising that the public-school crisis in New Orleans has had at least one important effect upon the Negro leadership class: *it has tended to bring about greater unity than has been experienced at any previous time.*

Perhaps the best indication of growing unity and strength among Negro leaders is the organization, during the darkest days of the school desegregation crisis (December 1960), of approximately one hundred Negro leaders, representing about as many different organizations, into the Coordinating Council of Greater New Orleans. The expressed purpose of this organization is to coordinate the resources and talents of the various types of Negro leaders in the solution of common problems. That this could be done was unequivocally demonstrated in a short voter-registration drive just prior to the 1962 mayoralty election. This effort was based upon what amounts to a new approach to political behavior. Thus, whereas political parties are active locally in terms of geographic areas, wards, and precincts, the Council conducted its voter-registration drive upon the assumption that concentrating on organizations would be more effective than concentration on the traditional neighborhood. Each member organization, therefore, was asked to assume responsibility for seeing to it that *every one of its own members* become registered voters. The basic strategy was to get as many groups as possible participating under the general direction of the Council, which handled their publicity and helped them to set up voter-registration schools. Within an eight-week period more than a hundred organizations responded. They generously contributed money, time, facilities, and equipment in order that the Council might have permanent headquarters and fulltime personnel for the execution of this program.

Groups cooperating in the Council represent all segments of Negro life.

According to an official report of the Council, all major religious denominations, civic organizations, political factions, professional societies, educational agencies, and social clubs in the Negro community are represented. These organizations apparently forget their differences in planning, propagandizing, and executing its program. Thus, in an evaluation of the accomplishments and promises of the Coordinating Council the editor of the *Louisiana Weekly* wrote:

> Unprecedented unity among Negroes—that is, the amalgamation of more than one hundred political, social, religious, fraternal, labor, and civic groups into one massive nonpartisan organization marching toward one particular goal—was achieved in New Orleans during the past year through the diligent efforts of the Coordinating Council of Greater New Orleans.

> . . . it must not be overlooked nor forgotten that the Coordinating Council has given a lasting example of the power which can be generated when Negroes are united in a determination to press forward against all odds. . . .

> A most encouraging sign was the whole-hearted cooperation of the miscellaneous organizations and splinter groups in this Herculean effort to secure the ballot for the thousands who had been denied or rejected, misled, or discouraged in numerous previous attempts to register. The willingness of these groups to unite and follow under the banner of the Coordinating Council indeed commands a greater respect for all Negroes of New Orleans as well as a better understanding of their particular problems and the injustices which are heaped upon them.

> More than that, the Coordinating Council has exemplified representative and substantial Negro leadership in the community by the simple but democratic device of counseling with the heads of all progressive organizations, deciding on a plan of action, and following the prescribed course with unwavering determination and with unfaltering courage.

> True leadership—the sterling quality so aptly displayed by the Coordinating Council—calls for unselfishness, intelligence, courage, prudence, and determination.

> It is indeed fitting to salute the Coordinating Council for a job well done!

Finally, if the first few months of this organization's program can be taken as a valid indication of Negro leaders' willingness to cooperate under a single banner, we can expect that the increased unity among them will be manifested in more significant "strides toward freedom" and first class citizenship than has been possible in the past.

INDEX

* Also available in limited clothbound edition.

* Also available in limited clothbound edition.

Twentieth Century Views

* Also available in limited clothbound edition.